I0800132

IMAGES
of America

NORTH CHARLESTON

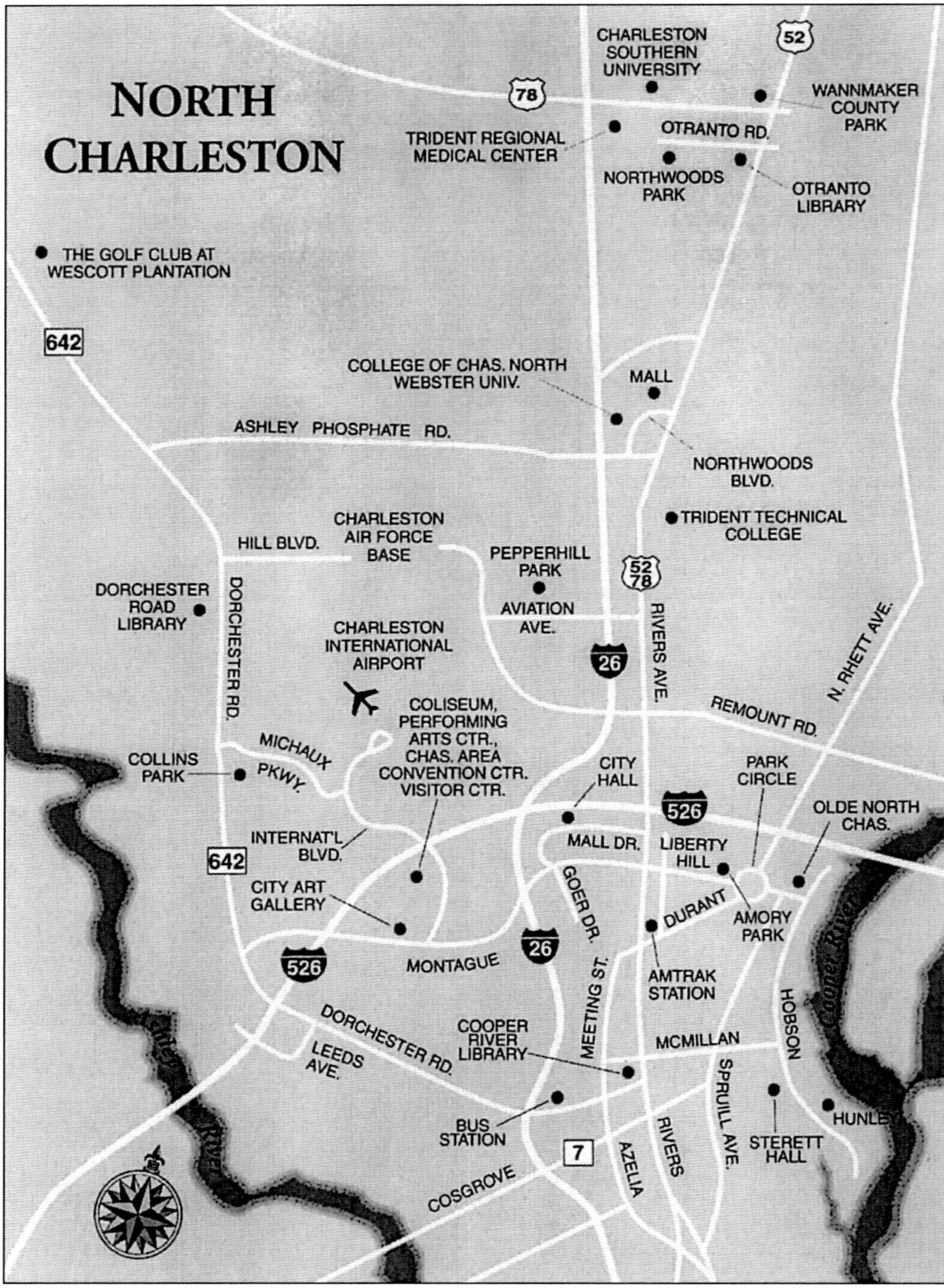

This recent map shows the locations of some of North Charleston's key points.

IMAGES
of America

NORTH CHARLESTON

North Charleston Heritage Corridor
with
Donald Wilkinson
Project Coordinator

ARCADIA
PUBLISHING

ISBN 978-0-7385-1390-4

Published by Arcadia Publishing
Charleston, South Carolina

Printed in the United States of America

Library of Congress Catalog Card Number: 2001095917

For all general information contact Arcadia Publishing at:
Telephone 843-853-2070
Fax 843-853-0044
E-Mail sales@arcadiapublishing.com
For customer service and orders:
Toll-Free 1-888-313-2665

Visit us on the Internet at www.arcadiapublishing.com

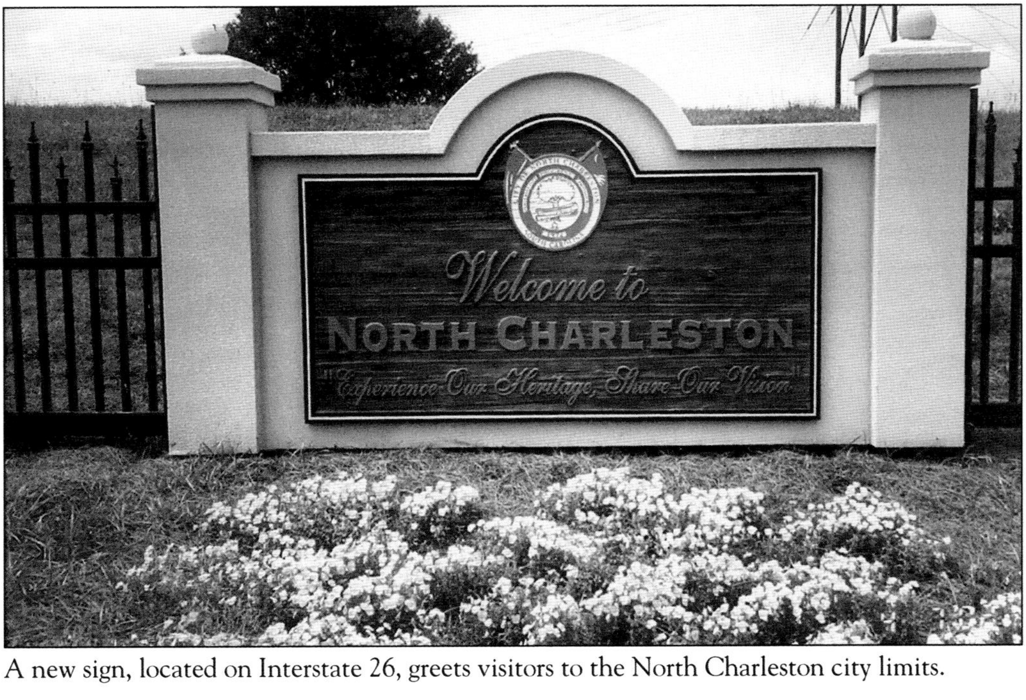

A new sign, located on Interstate 26, greets visitors to the North Charleston city limits.

Contents

Acknowledgments

The North Charleston Heritage Corridor consists of the following members: Eyda Arroyave, Eleanor Attaway Fuller, Marty Besancon, Becky Beaman, Joe Byas, Annie W. Boyce, Anice Carr, Caroline Collins, Betty Corner, Henry Darby, Ramona Eade, Lala Fyall, Benjamin Grant, June Griggs, Dawn Henry, Sandra Hubbert, Becky Lee, Alta Mae Marvin, Jack Martin, Bonnie McMakin, Sheri Pearson, Marian Rossilo, Ed Riggs, T.M. Rhodes Sr., Sharry Schenk, Mr. and Mrs. Fred Skipper, Hallie Q. Smith, Suzanne Thigpen, Lawrence Walker, Creola Washington, and Cori Ziegler.

We would like to thank the following for their time and cooperation with the production of this book: Avery Research Center for African American History and Culture, Edwin Barfield, Helen Blanton, Q.P. Brooks, Vicki Chamberlain, The City of North Charleston, Ruth Cupp, The Elms Plantation Homeowners Association, Eleanor Attaway Fuller, Priscela Grimsley, Bob Henderson, Ellen Lewin, Dr. Thomas Martin, Mr. and Mrs. William Mazyck, Shontel Middleton, Miss South Carolina USA Inc., Rosemary Moore, Mt. Moriah Baptist Church, The Noisette Group, North Charleston City Council, The North Charleston Coliseum, North Charleston Recreation Department, Palmer Olliff, Edith Painter, Sherri Pearson, Ruby Preacher, Marion Rosillo, Keith Summey, Sue Thigpen, Launa Thompson, Jesse Tolbert, Martha Wilkinson, Kenny Wilkinson, and Don Wilkinson.

Introduction

Although North Charleston did not officially become a city of its own until the 1970s, the area boasts a rich history that extends into the early years of our nation's settlement. Even the name of the city has been around since the early part of the 20th century, which is surely a logical extension due to its location from the city down the river. Many people are familiar with the history of Charleston, and the north area has been used for many of the same purposes as the land on the lower peninsula.

Prior to the 1600s, Tidewater Indians, including the Kiawah, Stono, Wando, and Etiwan tribes, inhabited the land along the various rivers flowing in and around the greater Charleston area. Later, during the American Revolution, British troops employed the Quarter House Inn, as a garrison. Only a marker remains today. Later, beautiful plantations so readily identified with the South dominated the region with names such as Ingleside, The Elms, and Marshlands. During World War II, the Charleston Naval Base, built on the site of the Marshlands Plantation, played a vital role in the defense of the United States, and its presence brought dramatic and rapid change to the area.

In 1972, North Charleston was incorporated and became a city of its own. Since that time, just thirty short years, North Charleston has become one of the fastest growing cities in South Carolina, attracting millions of visitors annually. Today the city faces a new dimension in quality living while enjoying an atmosphere of prosperity and continued growth; yet, its citizens possess a deep and abiding interest in keeping the city's heritage intact for the enjoyment of future generations.

Much has occurred in North Charleston since the first settlers arrived, and the purpose of this book is to capture through the eye of the camera the essence of the city's rich history and to invite everyone to "Experience our past and share our vision" for the future.

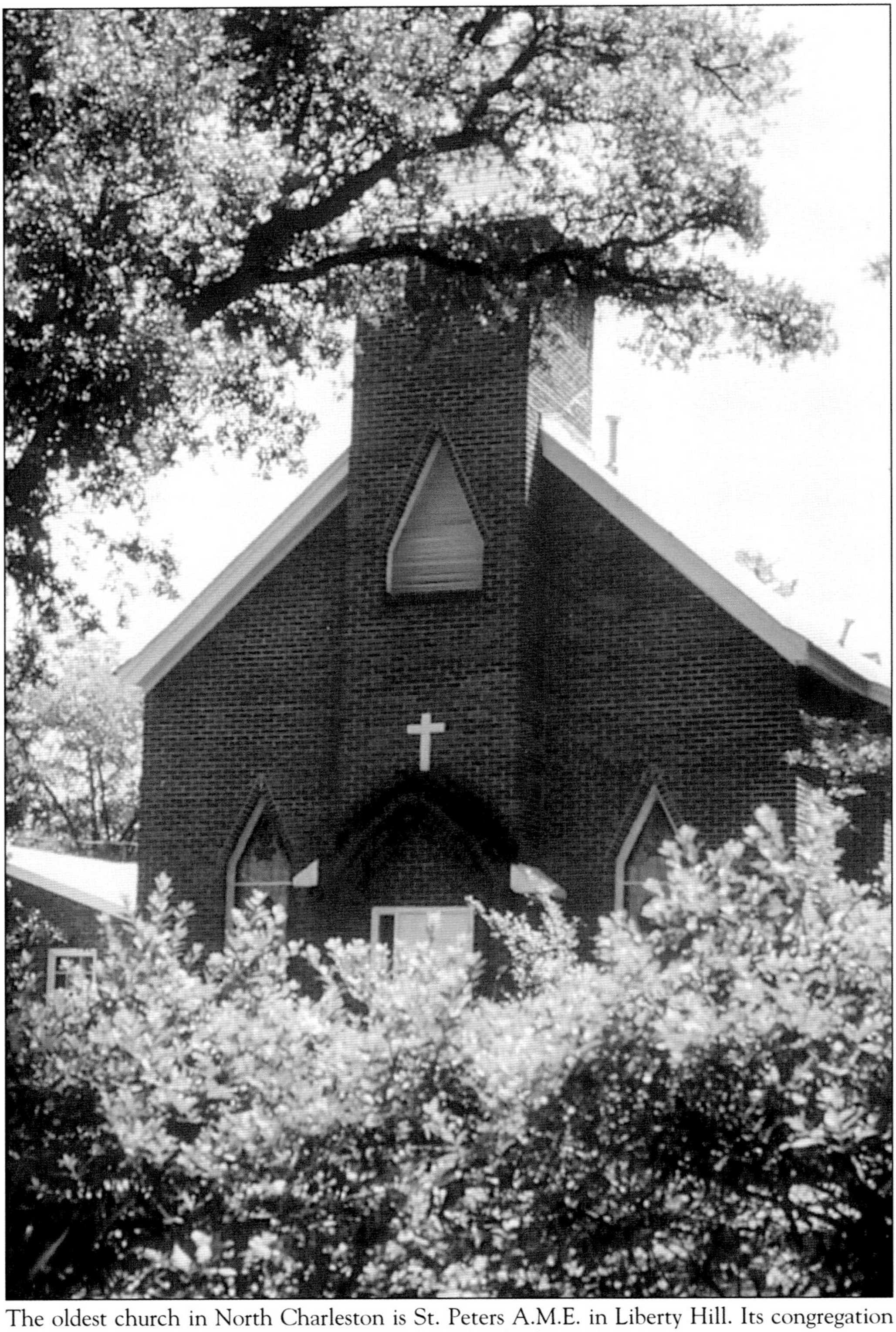

The oldest church in North Charleston is St. Peters A.M.E. in Liberty Hill. Its congregation first assembled in 1860. (Courtesy of City of North Charleston.)

One

In the Beginning

With the Cooper River on one side and the Ashley on the other, the area now known to us as North Charleston was once a wilderness with abundant flora and fauna that suited the Tidewater Indians who inhabited both banks. Many of these tribes proved helpful to the white colonist as they made their way through the area in search of a place to settle. By the mid-1600s homesteads and plantations sprang up throughout the area. In the 1700s Eliza Lucas Pinkney was experimenting with growing silk by planting trees and importing silk worm eggs. Pinkney perfected a method of dying material with indigo. Andre Michaux, the father of American Horticulture, established a botanic garden and introduced new plants, such as camellias and mimosas, to the area; Phillippe Noisette, another famous botanist, experimented with roses and developed a rose that is now internationally famous. During the American Revolution a local tavern served as a British garrison and the Native American trail later known as the "Broad Path" became the main road to Charleston. The coming of the railroad was one of the most important events of the time, having the ability to connect people to towns far from their homes. After the Civil War, many of the local plantations were divided into smaller farms. The first freedman community was established in this area at Liberty Hill, and phosphate mining on the Ashley River became the way of life.

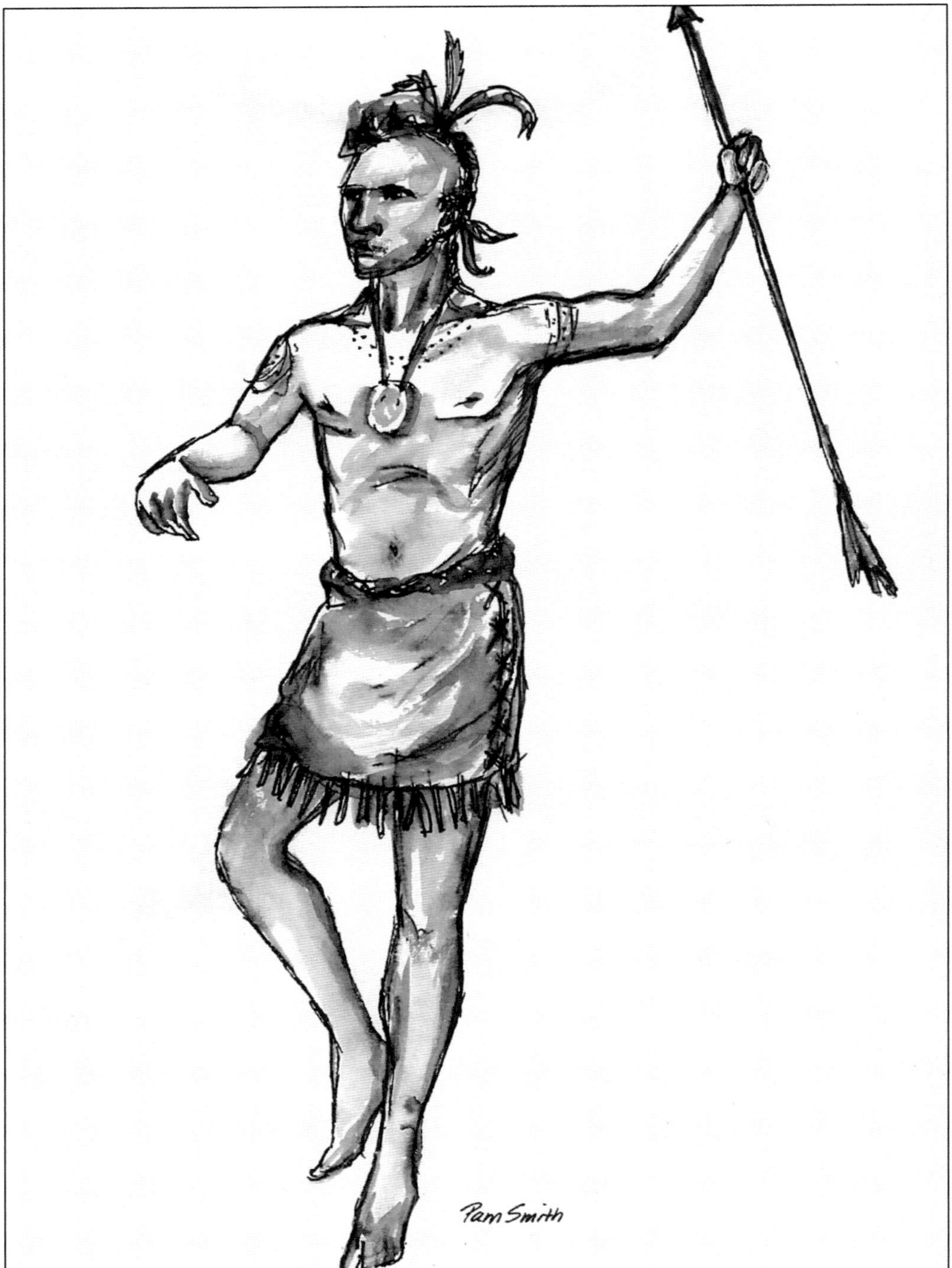

This drawing depicts the a typical Tidewater Indian, a member of one of various tribes who inhabited the banks of the local rivers. The Wando, Etiwan, Kiawah, and Sewee were helpful to the English and supported them against Spanish raids. Some tribes, like the Stono and Kussoe, were less than friendly to the white colonists; however, the threat of attack receded with the expansion of the frontier. As white settlements grew to the north and west, Native Americans were less of a threat in the area. (Drawing courtesy of Pam Linder Smith.)

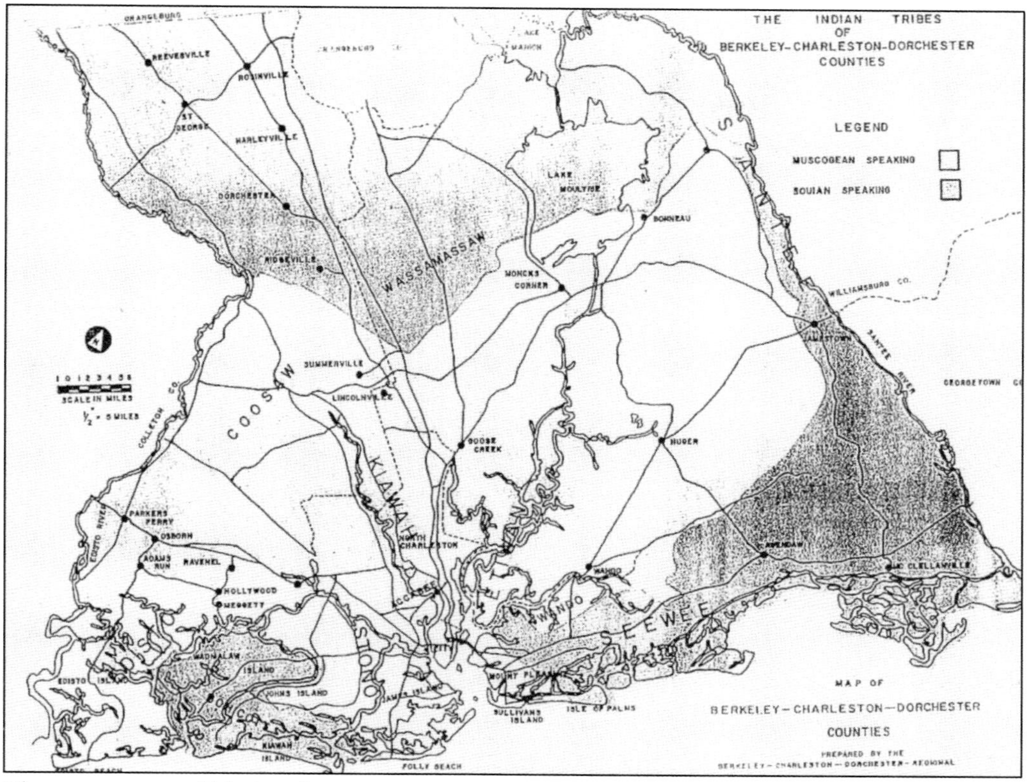

There were several Native American tribes in the North Charleston area. While no above-ground sites in North Charleston associated with Native Americans exist today, several historic place names originated with the Native Americans. Such names include Accabee, Woosah (an early name for Filbin Creek), and Etiwan (an early name for Cooper River.) (Courtesy of the City of North Charleston.)

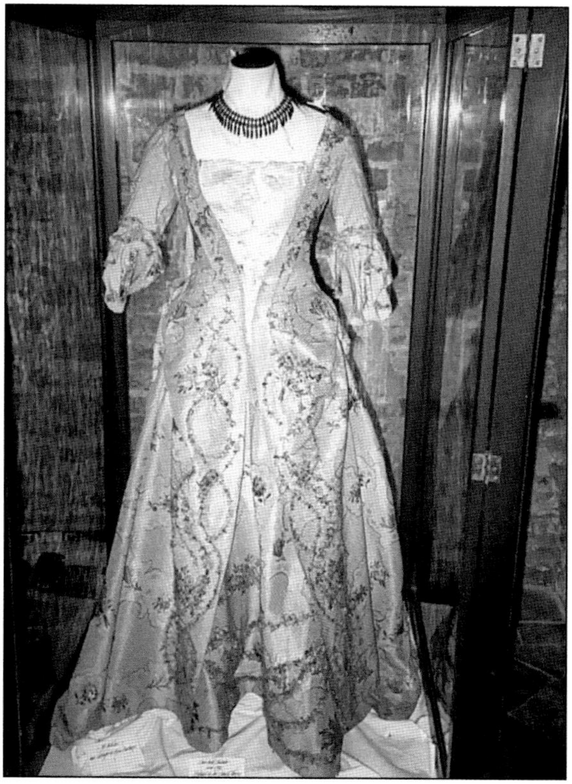

Eliza Lucas Pinckney and her husband, Chief Justice Charles Pinckney Lucas, owned Belmont Plantation in 1744, located on what is now Old Meeting Street Road. Eliza experimented with growing silk by planting mulberry trees and importing silk worm eggs. Pictured is one of three gowns made from silk produced on her plantation. She also perfected a method of making blocks of indigo cakes and turning them into dye. The technique was used in military uniforms and dress coats of the day. (Courtesy of Ruth Cupp.)

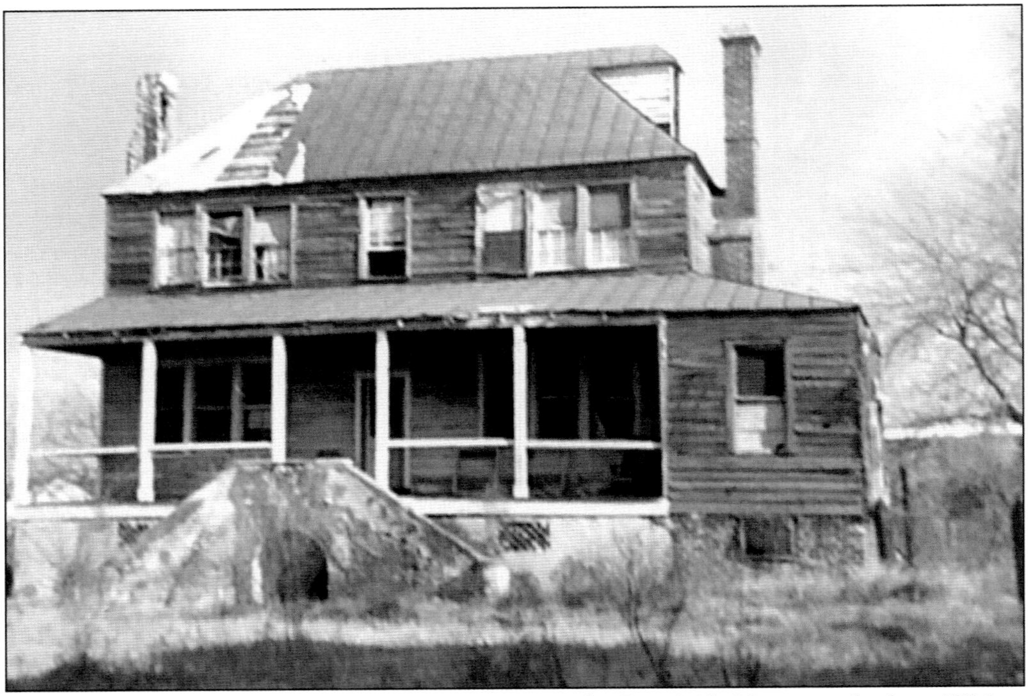

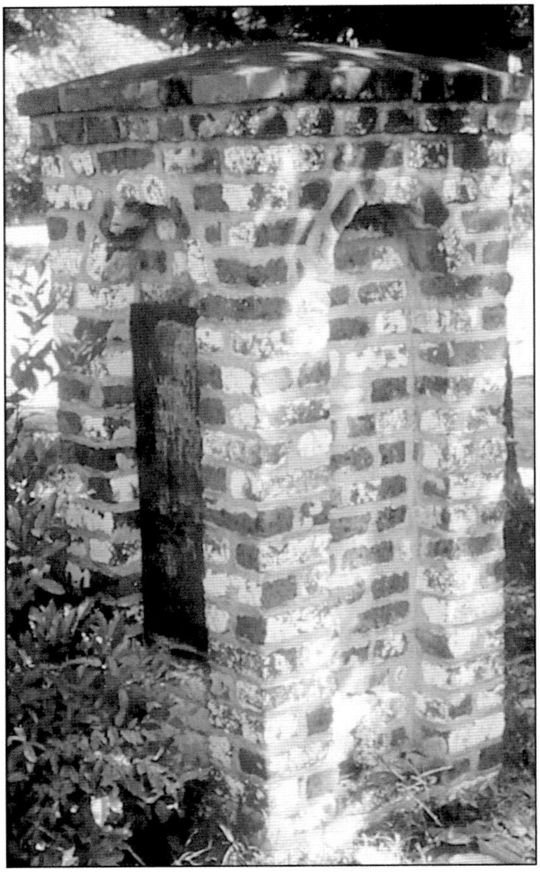

The Four-Mile House was built in 1786 and used as a tavern to accommodate overnight travelers. The house is remembered today for its murderous history. In 1819, Lavinia and John Fisher were arrested for murder and highway robbery. An area beneath the dining room revealed human bones, while a trap door was reportedly found beneath the dining table. Both husband and wife were executed on February 19, 1820. (Courtesy of Ruth Cupp.)

The Quarter House Marker is all that is left of the inn that was built in 1720 near the crossroads of Old Meeting Street Road and Success Street. The first public racetrack was built on the site in 1734 and was called The York Course. The tavern served as a British Garrison during the American Revolution. German Hessian soldiers sent to march down the neck area camped near the Quarter House. The original tavern burned shortly after the American Revolution. (Courtesy of the City of North Charleston.)

The north area was home to many prominent plantations, including Marshlands, Yeamans Hall, and Pettigrew. The map to the right shows plantations along the Cooper River as they were in 1842. (Courtesy of the City of North Charleston.)

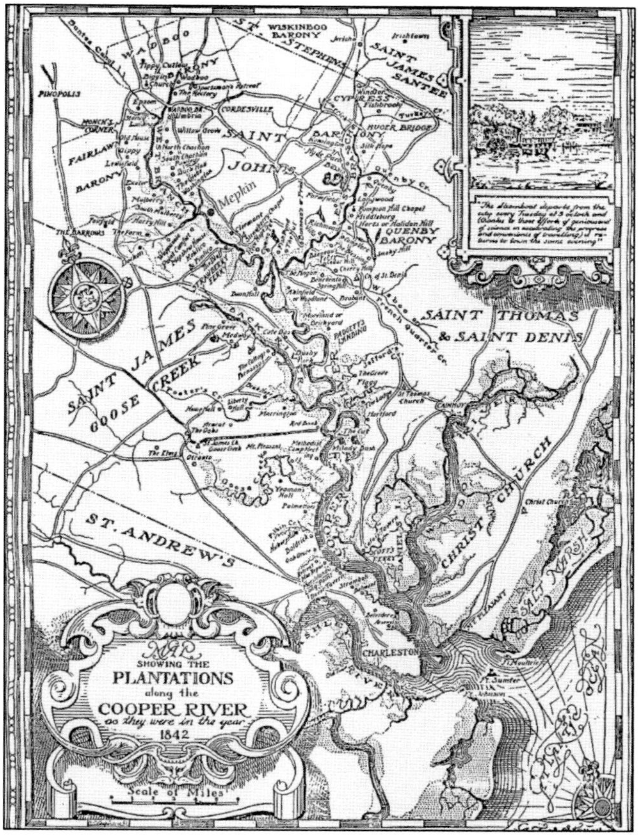

English colonists bought land grants and developed large plantations along both the Ashley and Cooper Rivers. At the time of the Revolution, over 60 plantations were active in the North Charleston area. The locations of plantations and settlements within today's North Charleston are shown in the map below. (Courtesy of the City of North Charleston.)

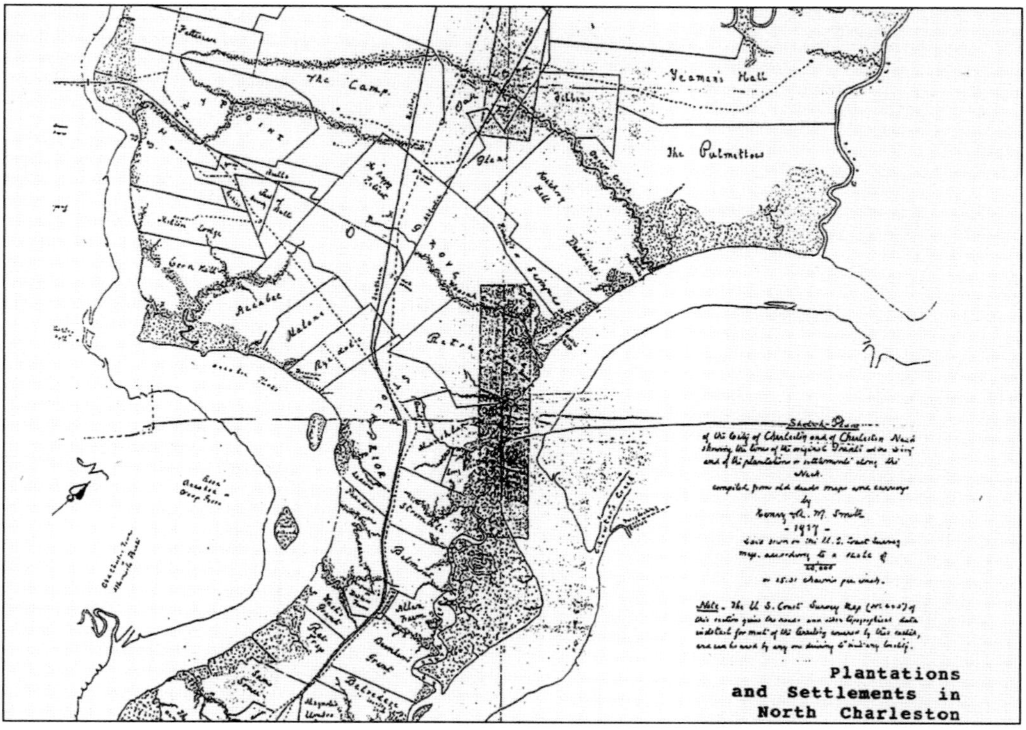

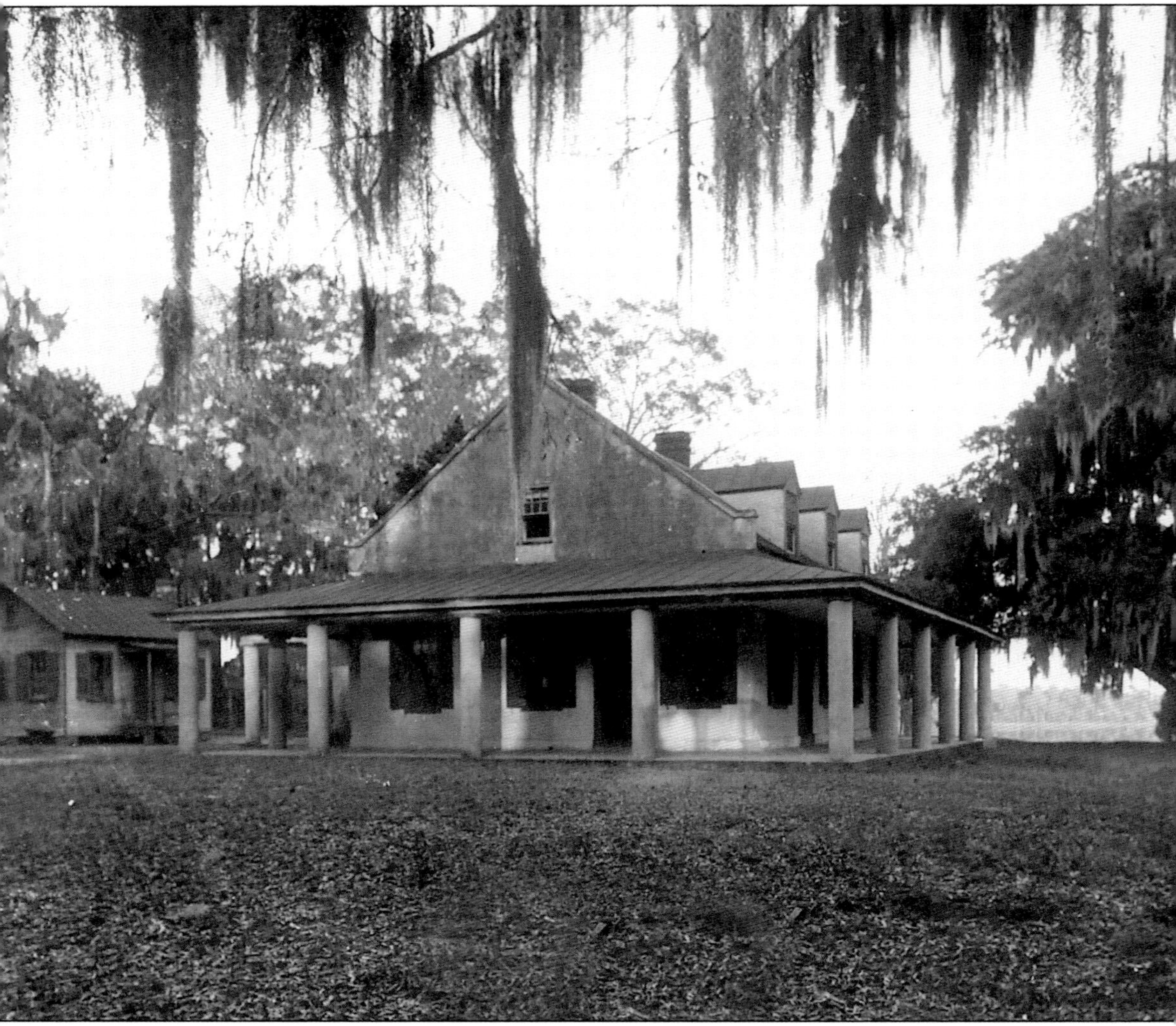

The Otranto Plantation House was constructed around 1790 and still stands in the north area in Hanahan. The photograph shown above shows the house and grounds as it looked in 1920. (Courtesy of Dr. Thomas Martin.)

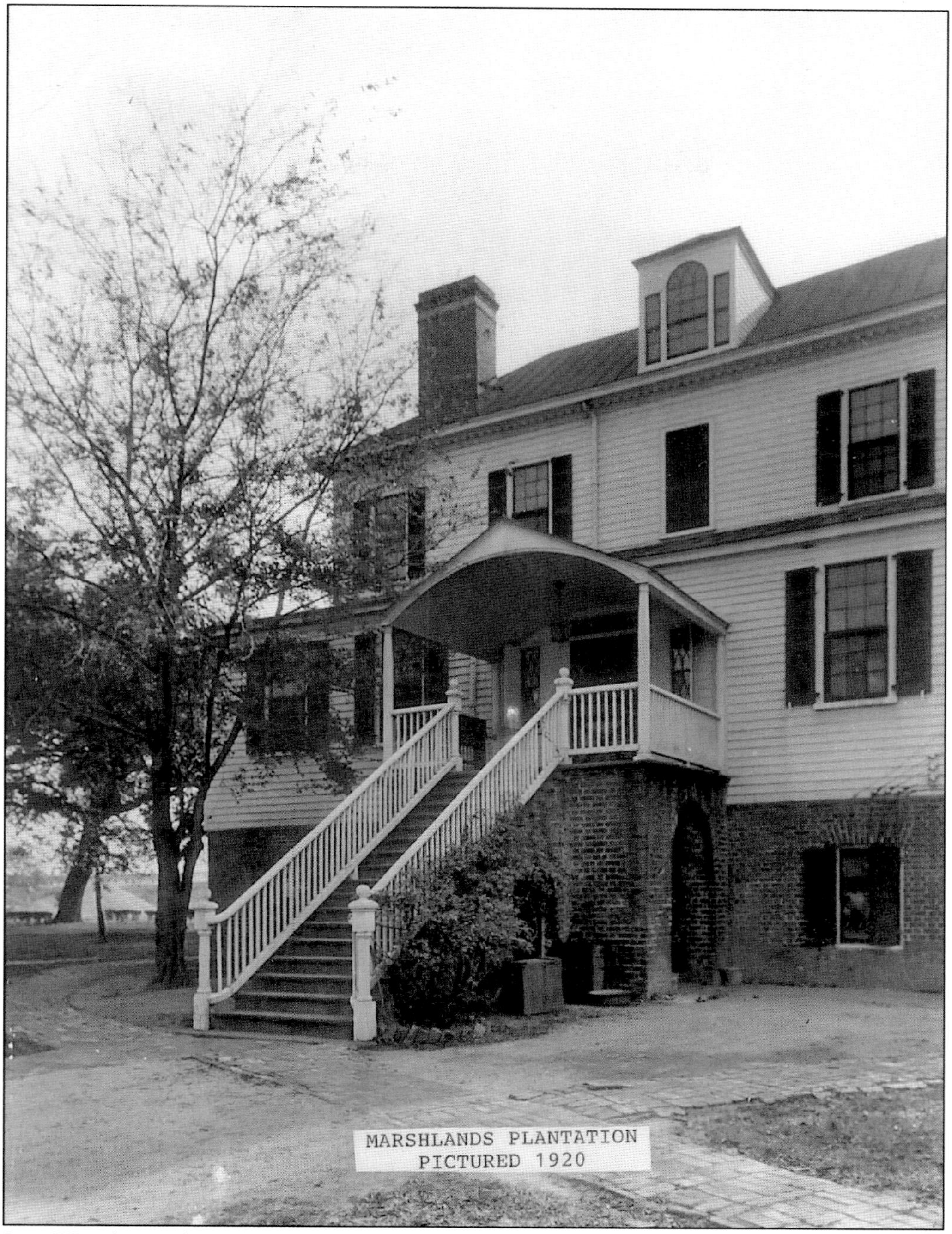

In 1677, Christopher Edwards received a land grant for 270 acres. Named Marshlands for the great marsh on the Cooper River, the plantation later became the Navy Yard and Chicora Place. The plantation house was converted into an officer's club and later moved to James Island by barge. It currently houses the South Carolina Wildlife and Natural Resources Department. This photograph was also taken in 1920. (Courtesy of Dr. Thomas Martin.)

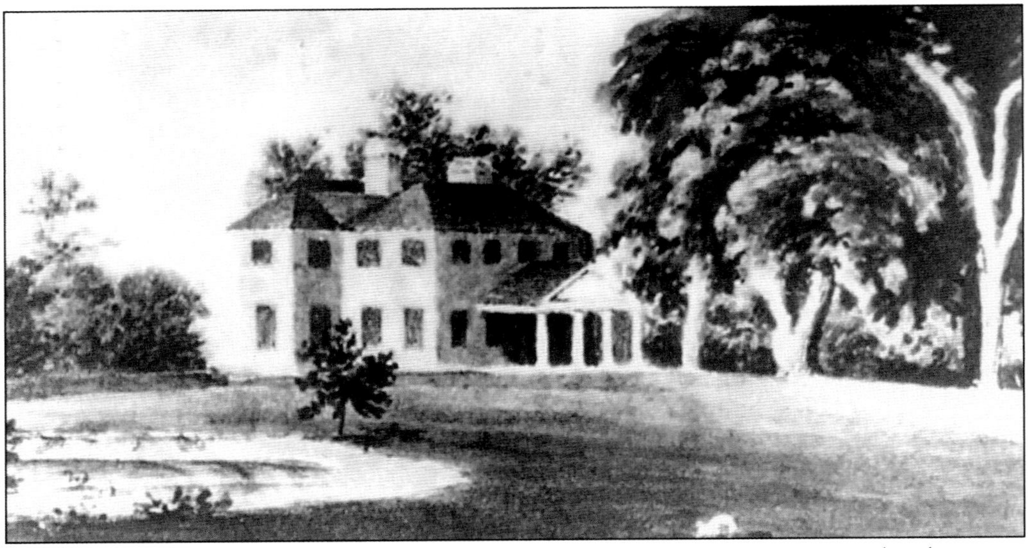

In the late 1700s, Ralph Izard acquired what was to become The Elms Plantation. The plantation house, shown above in an artist's rendering, was located on land that today is Charleston Southern University. (Courtesy of The Elms Homeowner's Association.)

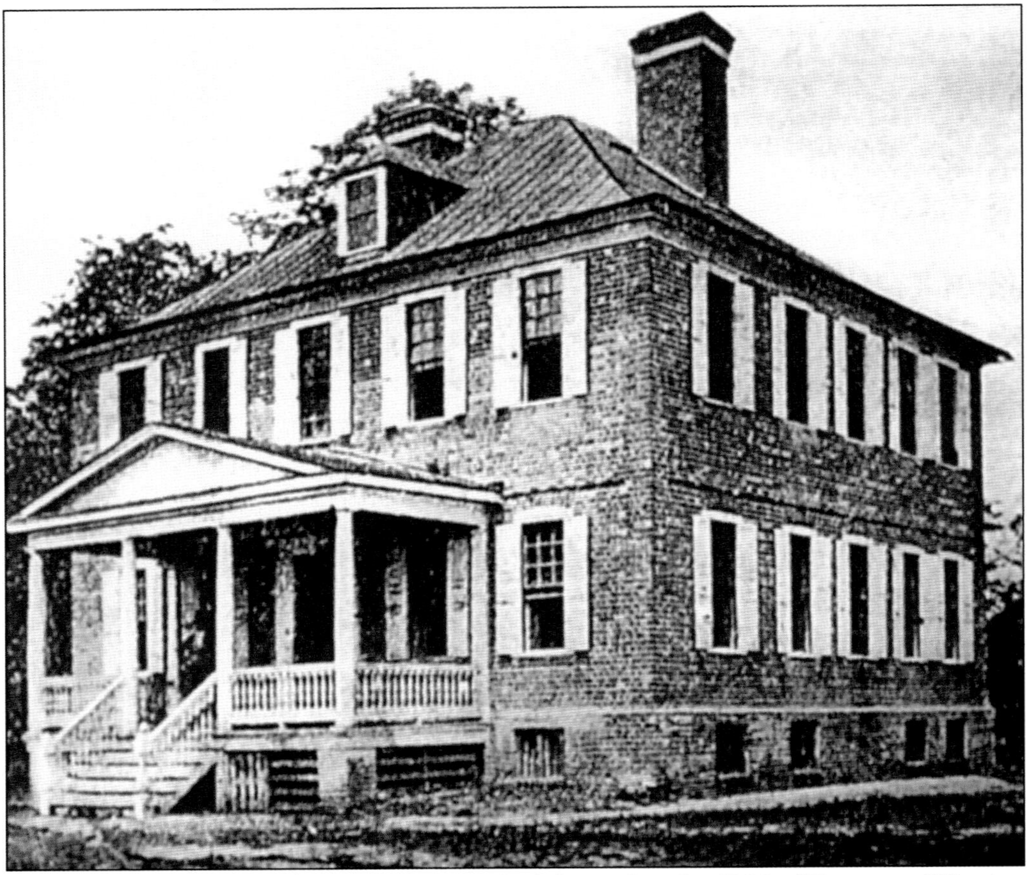

Pictured is the Ingleside Plantation House, which burned in the 1920s. (Courtesy of Harriett Kershaw Leiding, Historic Houses of South Carolina.)

These headstones are located in Riverview Cemetery, which is located on the former Accabee Plantation. (Courtesy of the City of North Charleston.)

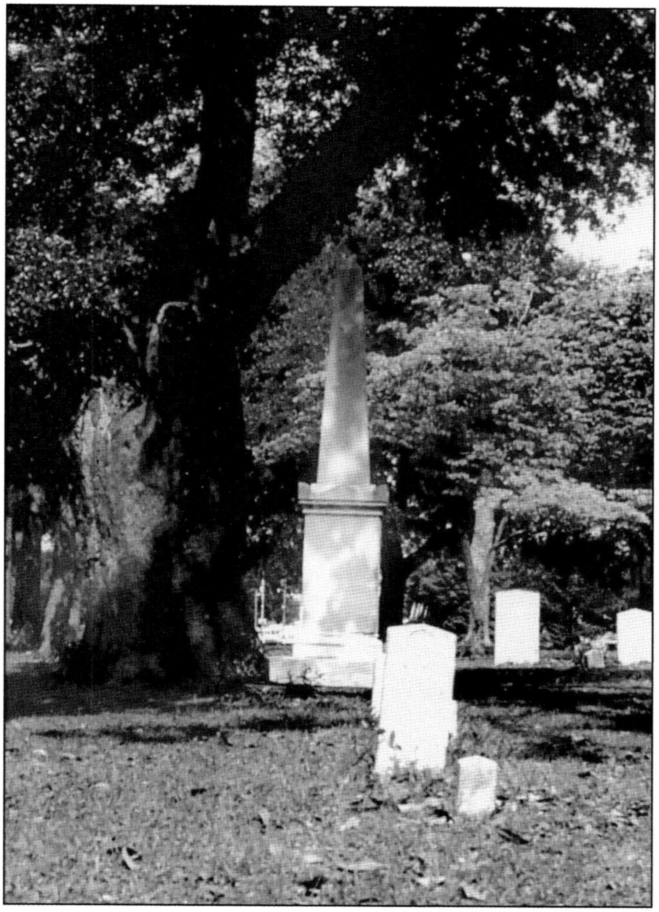

The *c.* 1800 painting below shows Wigton Plantation, which was located near today's Goose Creek. (Courtesy of *A Charleston Sketchbook, 1790–1806* by Charles Fraser—Charleston rep. 1959.)

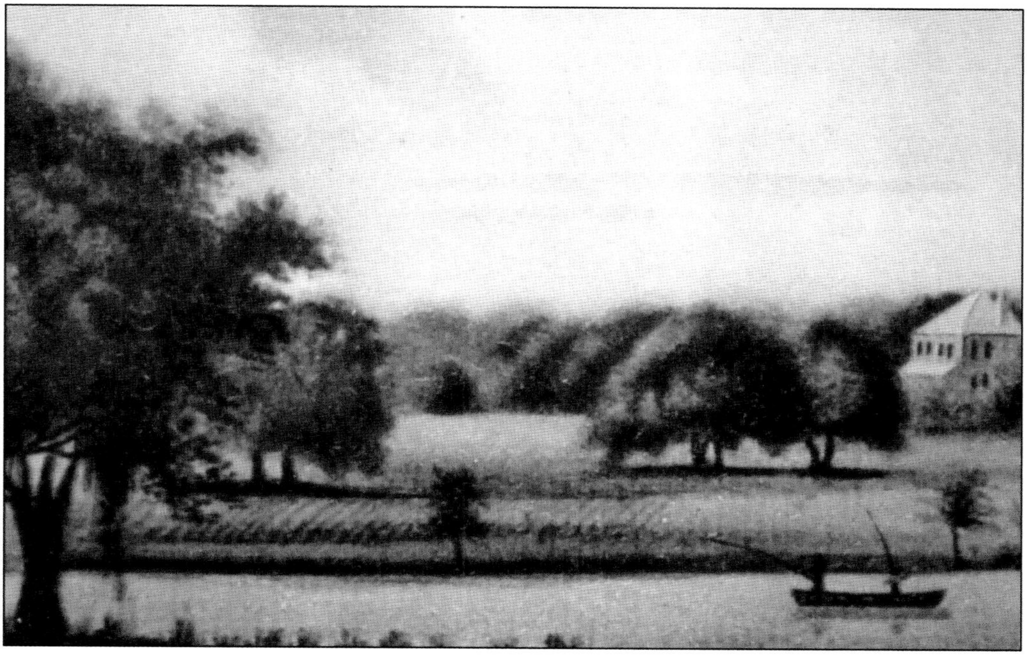

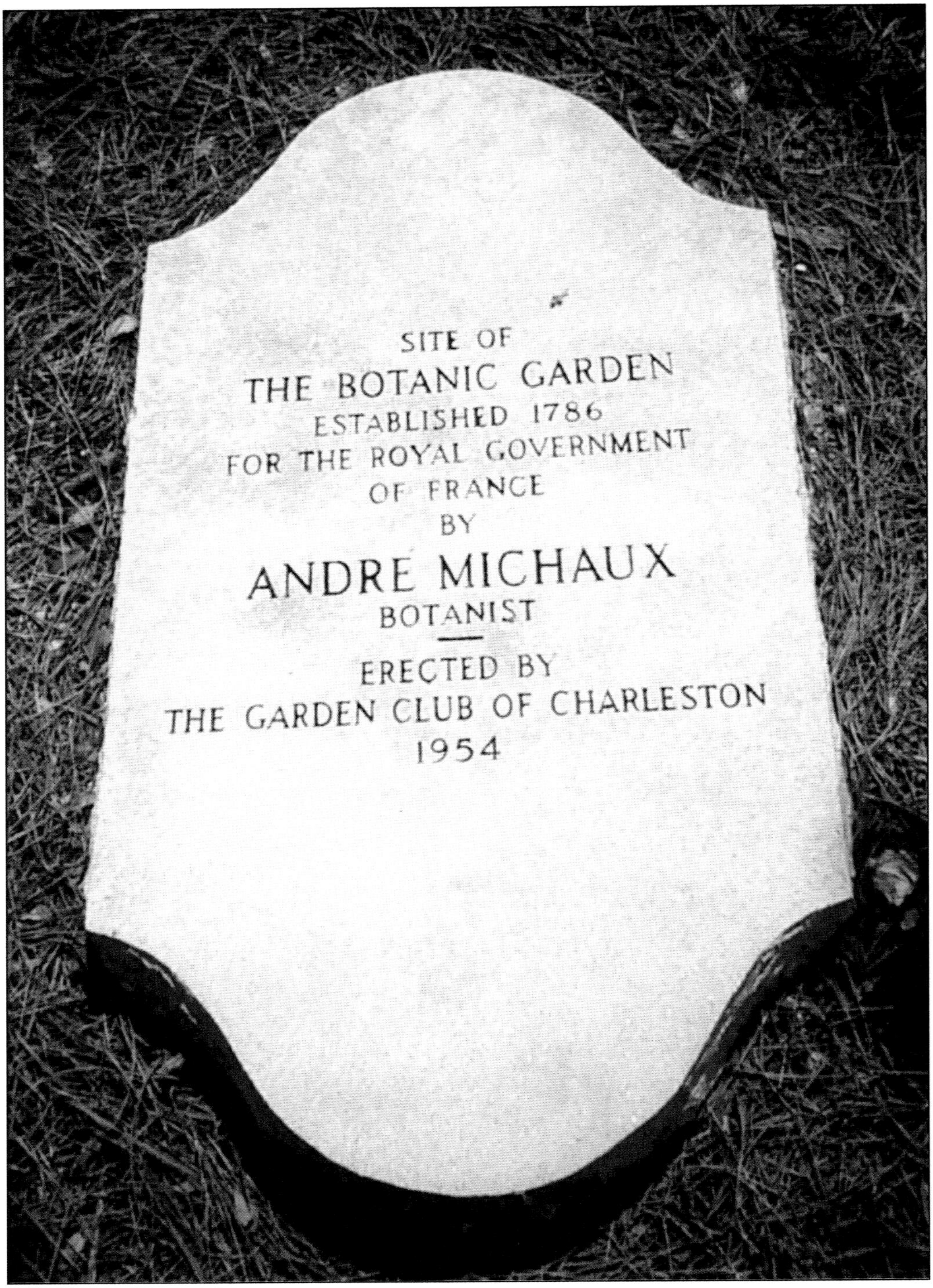

A marker was erected in 1954 by the Garden Club of Charleston at the site of The Botanic Gardens established by Andre Michaux in 1786 for the Royal Government of France. The site is located near the end of West Aviation Avenue and Michaux Parkway. Michaux introduced many new species of plants and shrubs to the South, including the camellia, japonica, mimosa, and ginkgo tree. (Photo courtesy of Don Wilkinson.)

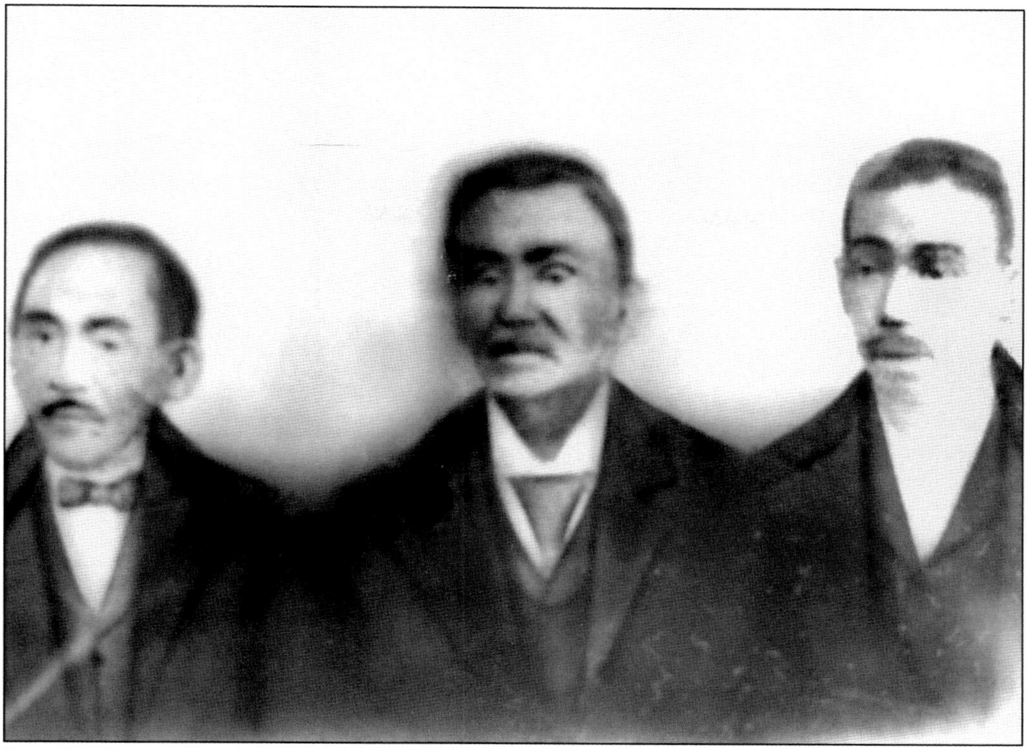

Four freedmen, Ismael Grant, Aaron Middleton, Pastor William Lecque, and Plenty Lecque purchased 110 acres of land for $900 in 1871. They called this land "Liberty Hill." Pictured above, from left to right, are Pastor Lecque, Plenty Lecque, and Elijah Lecque. (Courtesy of Mrs. Ruth Cupp.)

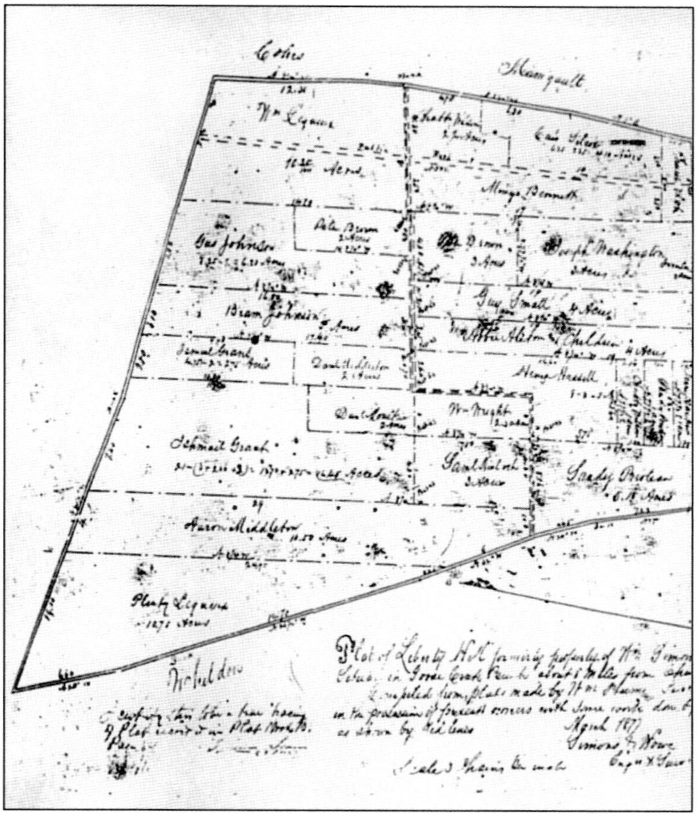

This 1871 plat is of Liberty Hill, which may be the oldest neighborhood in North Charleston. Liberty Hill was established in 1864, before the Civil War ended. As the plat shows, lots were several acres in size to allow for houses and small farms. (Courtesy of the Charleston County Register of Mesne Conveyance.)

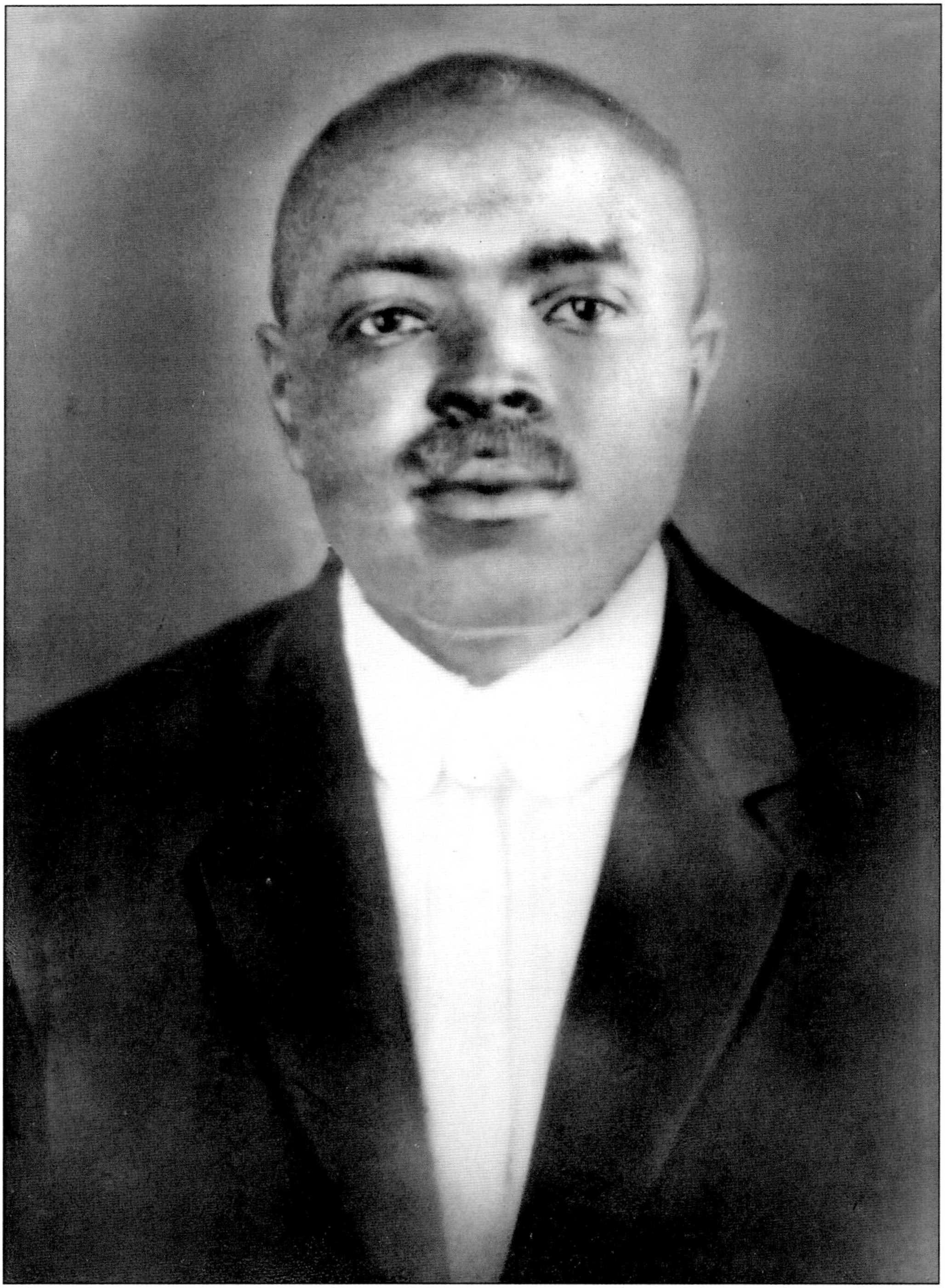

Felix Pinckney, a son of Mr. and Mrs. Thomas Pinckney and the husband of Isabella Black Pinckney, was an important civic leader in Liberty Hill, having served as a Master Mason and as a trustee for St. Peters A.M.E. Church, the oldest church in North Charleston. The Felix Pinckney Community Center was named in his honor because of his contributions and dedication to community. He lived from August 17, 1880, until December 20, 1948.

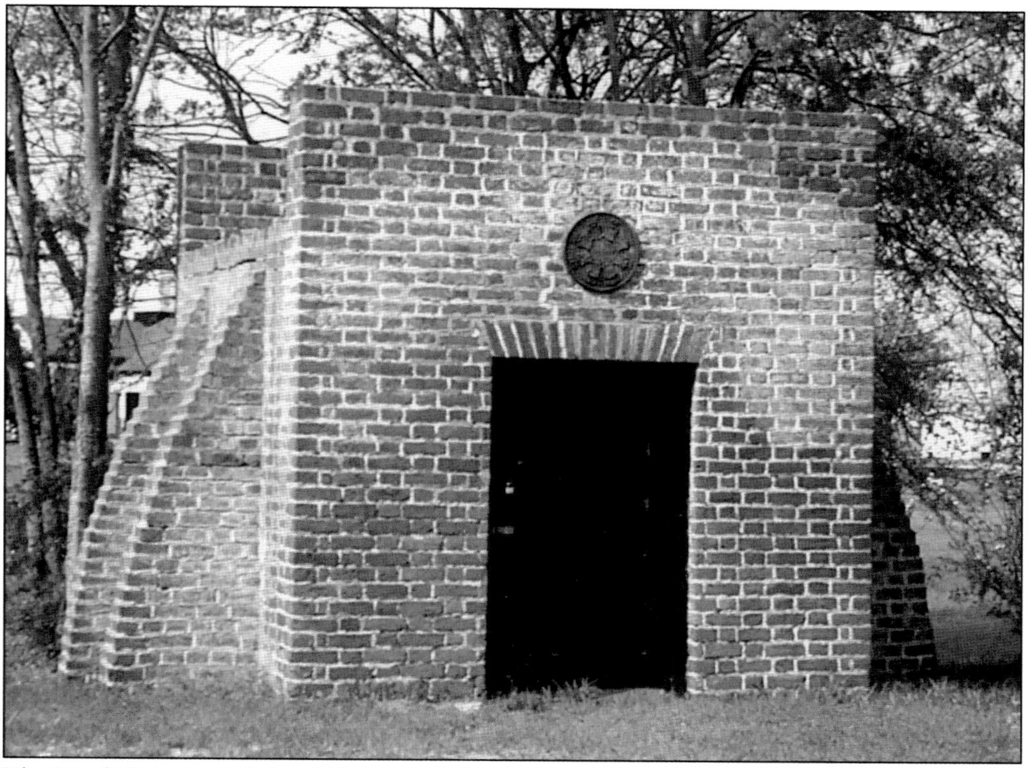

The Dead House, which is still located on the old Naval Base, was used during colonial times to house the deceased until burial. The seal of the Lord Proprietor is the official signet above the doorway. (Courtesy of the City of North Charleston.)

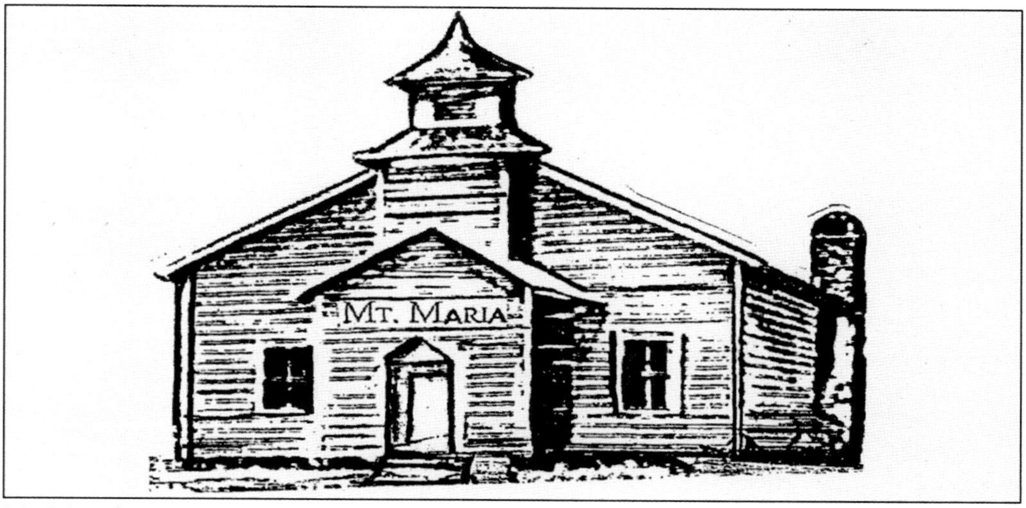

Mt. Moriah Missionary Church was founded in 1898 by Rev. Stephany Milligan the church's first pastor and pastor of Union Baptist Church. Built on a parcel of land belonging to J.P. Clark, the log structure was situated near a pond, just off the main road between what is now Northwoods Mall and Ashley Phosphate Road. It was built with the lumber gathered from clearing the land. Pictured is an artist's rendering of Mt. Maria, which was pronounced "Mor-i-ah." The spelling was later changed to reflect the pronunciation. (Courtesy of Mt. Moriah Missionary Baptist Church.

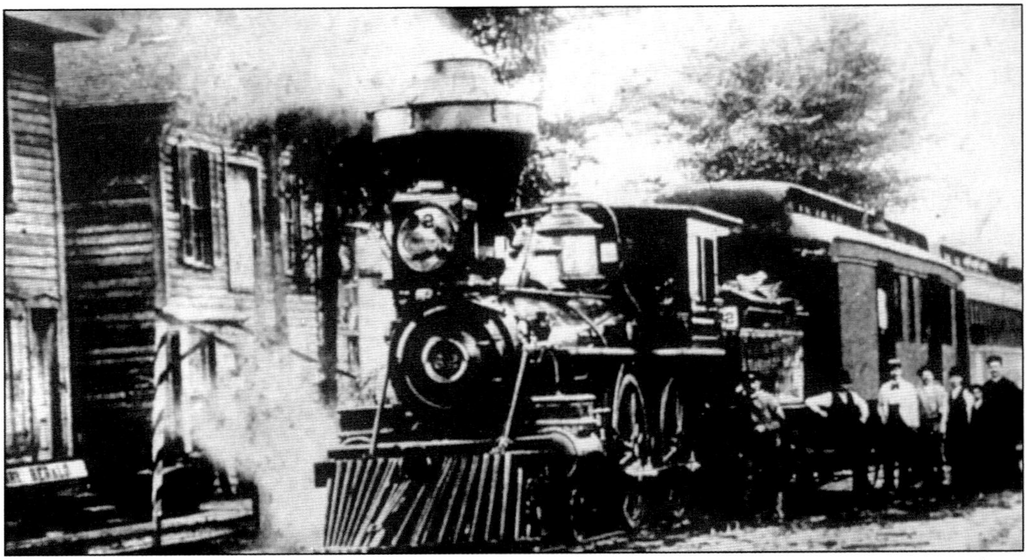

Railroad tracks criss-cross North Charleston and represent several rail companies. The earliest track, laid in 1830, was completed near today's Beach and Beach Insurance Company on Rivers Avenue. In 1865, thousands fled Charleston by rail and crossed North Charleston on their way northwest after Union troops occupied the city. (Courtesy of the City of North Charleston.)

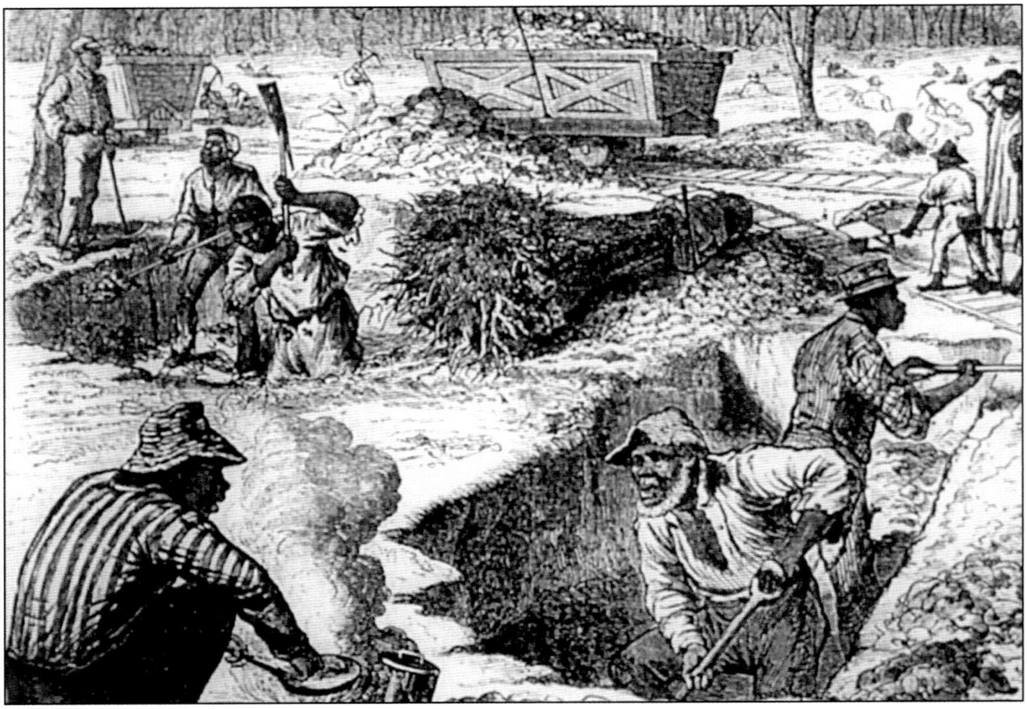

In 1867, the mining of phosphate rock created a boom in the economy that lasted nearly 40 years. It was a major factor in the Lowcountry's recovery from the Civil War and in the establishment of a wage-labor class of freedmen. Ashley Phosphate Road and neighborhoods along Dorchester Road such as Wando Woods, Evanston Estates, Lambs, and Hunley Park still show evidence of the parallel pits and mounds that resulted from the excavation of phosphate. (Courtesy of the Carolina Library, University of South Carolina.)

Two

A City at the End of the Line

In the 1900s, the presence of the E.P. Burton Lumber Company and the US Naval Yard attracted many new residents to the area, and the need for housing became apparent. A group of Charleston businessmen constructed a city designed by W.B. Marquis that was very modern for that time. The goal was for residents to be able to work in the surrounding factories and return to homes just a short distance away. The Park Circle area, with its radiating streets heading outward, provided the location for industrial, commercial, and residential use. Because Marquis was instrumental in the design of garden cities in England during that time, North Charleston's scheme models those of the overseas cities. General Asbestos and Rubber Company (GARCO) arrived in the area and bolstered the city's economy. Houses and mill villages sprouted throughout the area as the population grew, and areas developed further out. Schools were built for the children of the new residents so that they could obtain quality education. Streetcars traveled all the way from Charleston to what was being called North Charleston or "the end of the line." The east end of Montague Avenue became the business district and in 1935 the North Charleston Public Service District was established, bringing fire protection, garbage disposal, water, and sewerage for the residents.

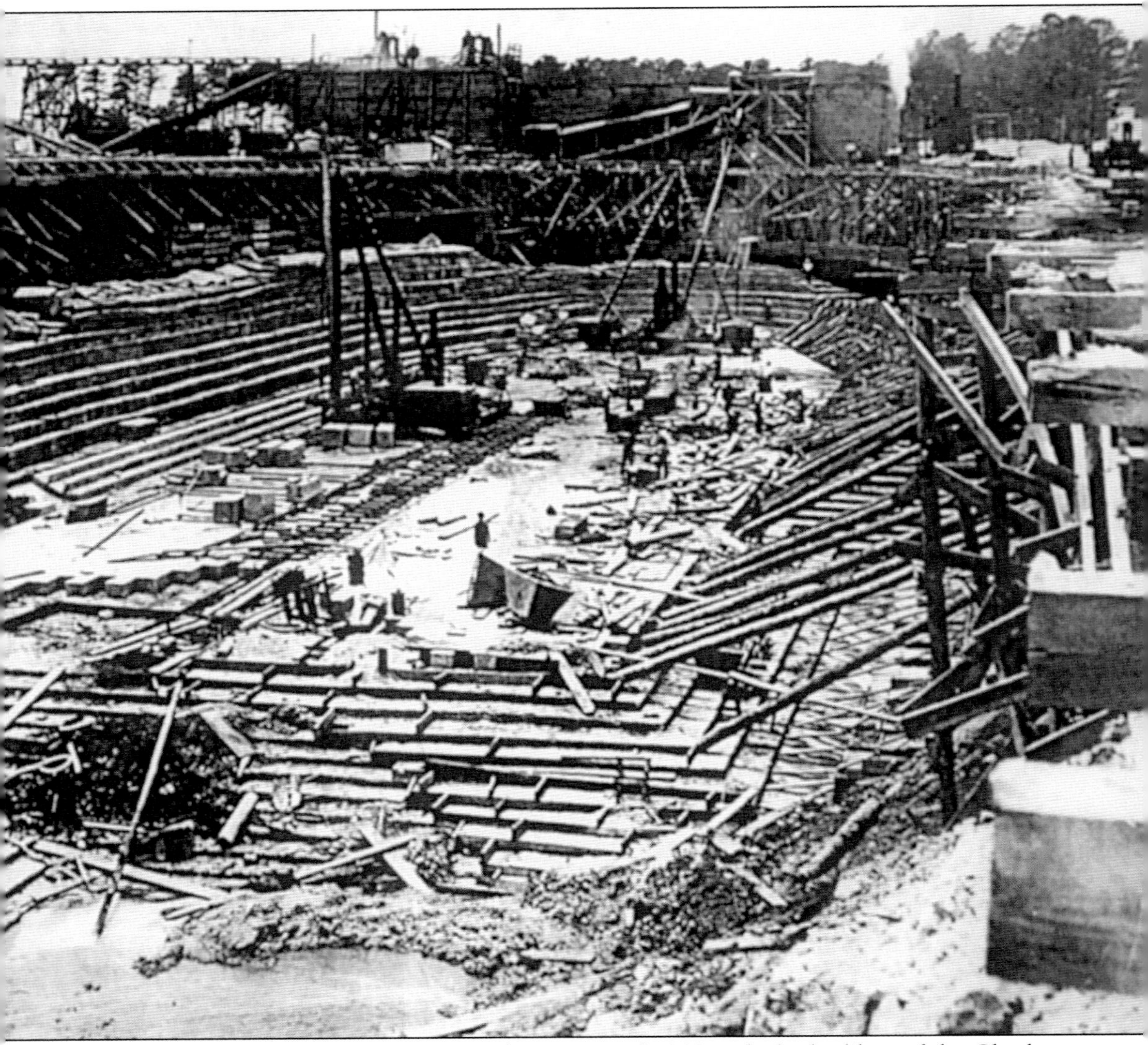

The modern era in North Charleston began around 1900 with the building of the Charleston Naval Base on the side of Chicora Park. Pictured is the construction of one of the first dry docks on the base. (Courtesy of the City of North Charleston.)

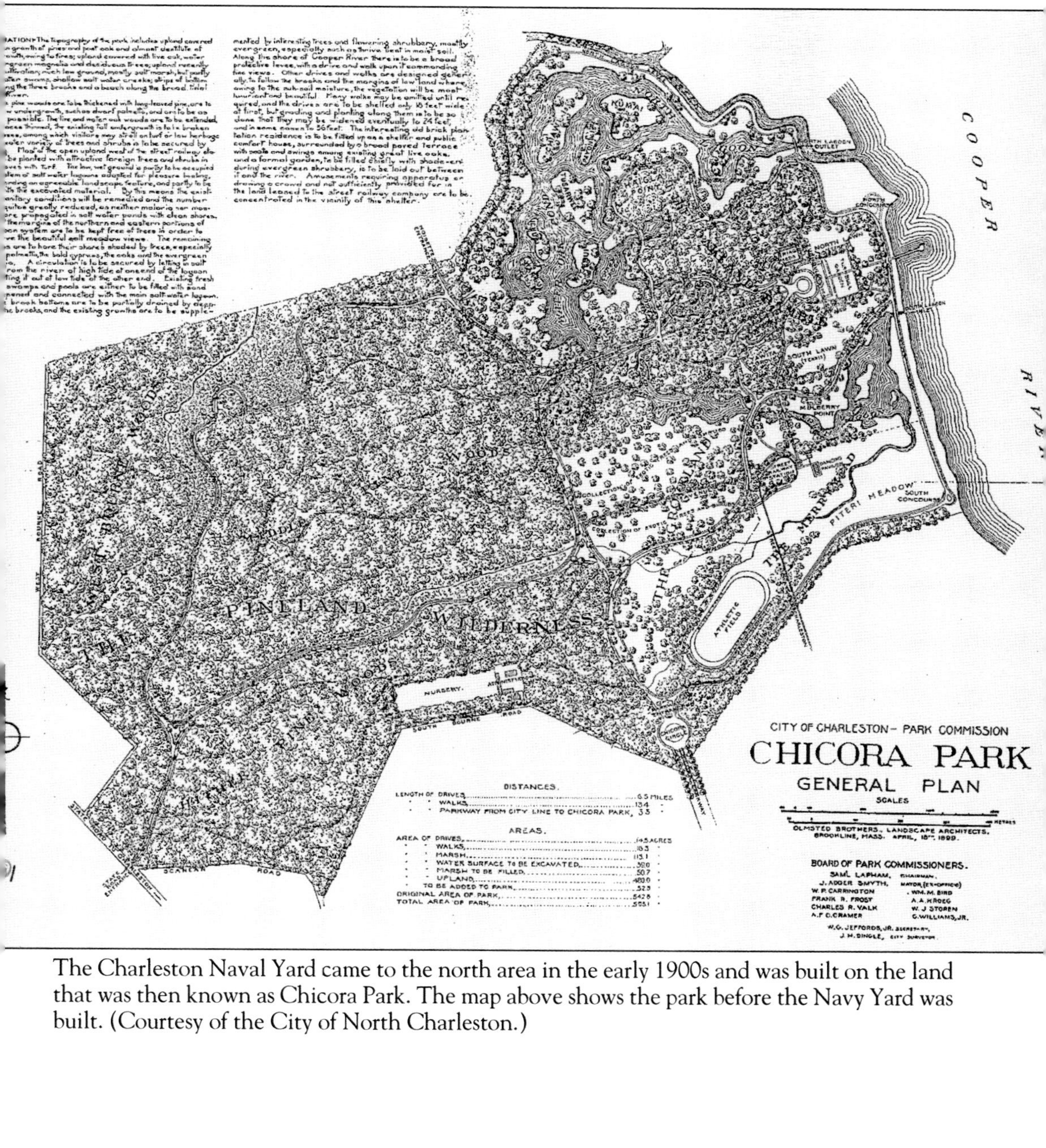

The Charleston Naval Yard came to the north area in the early 1900s and was built on the land that was then known as Chicora Park. The map above shows the park before the Navy Yard was built. (Courtesy of the City of North Charleston.)

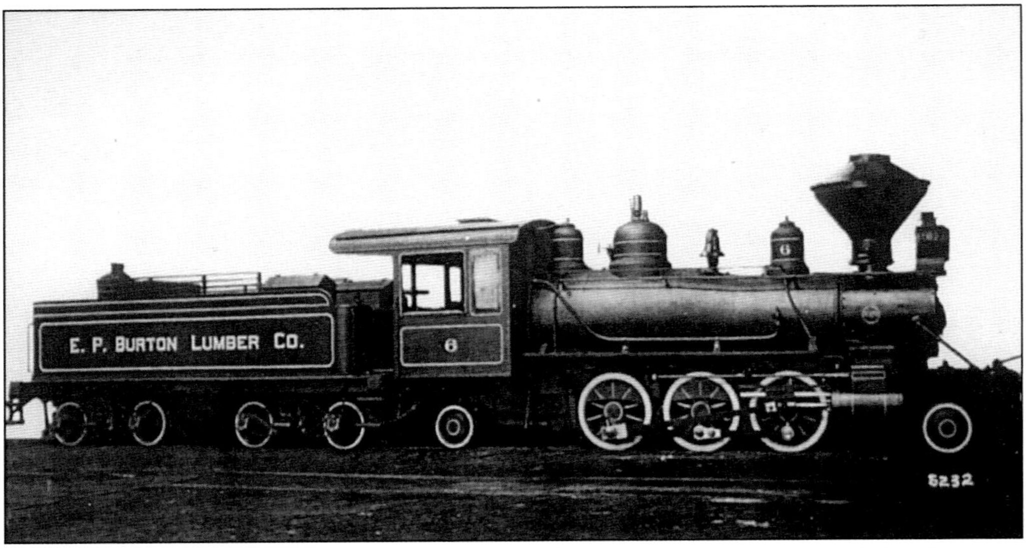

Burton Lumber Co. was located north of Noisette Creek on the Cooper River. (Most longtime residents called the creek Burton's Creek). The lumber mill opened in the early 1900s; the docks on the Cooper River provided a place where lumber could be loaded onto vessels and shipped to more northern ports. A company store that also provided housing for some of the mill personnel was adjacent to the mill, and the Hammerton Masonic Lodge was first located above it. The mill was destroyed by fire in 1923 and never rebuilt. The site of the old Burton Lumber Co. is now part of the former Naval Shipyard. Pictured above is a train that transported lumber from the Burton Lumber Co. (Courtesy of the City of North Charleston.)

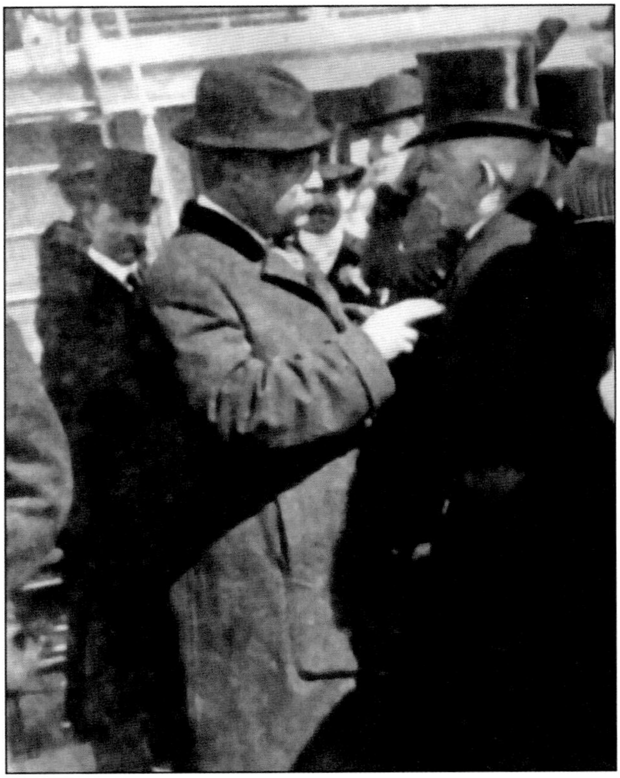

President Theodore Roosevelt gestures to Charleston Mayor J. Adger Smythe before taking a tour of the site of the new navy yard in 1902. (Courtesy of Palmer Olliff.)

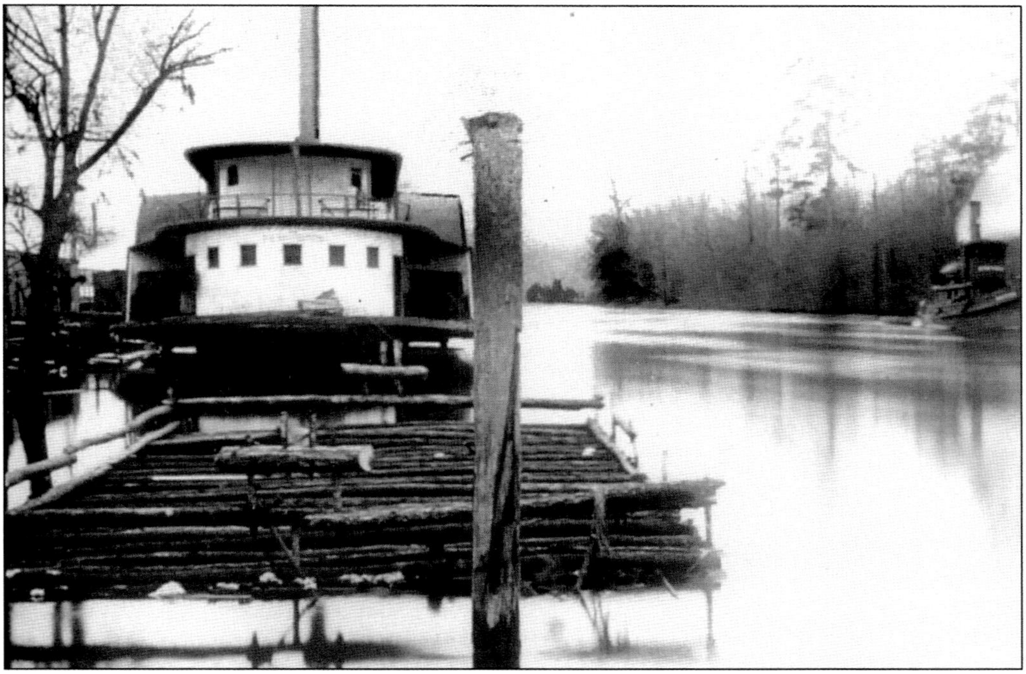

Lumber boats like this one transported timber up and down the Cooper River from Burton Lumber Co. (Courtesy of the City of North Charleston.)

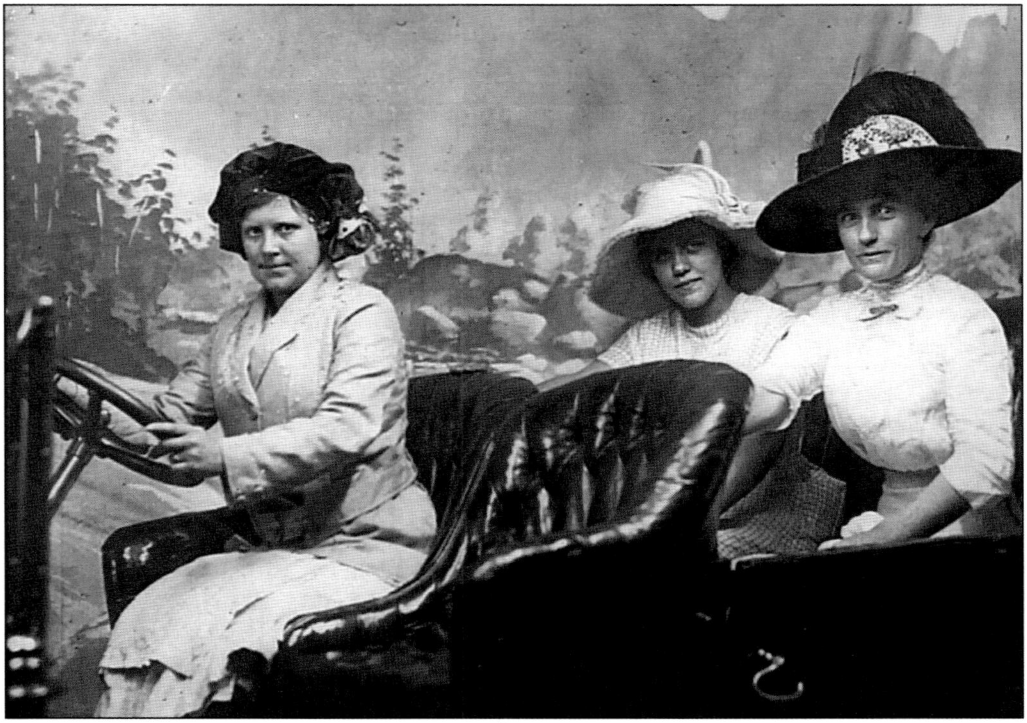

These Mazyck family members pose for a picture in a new 1913 Cadillac in North Charleston. (Courtesy of Bill Mazyck.)

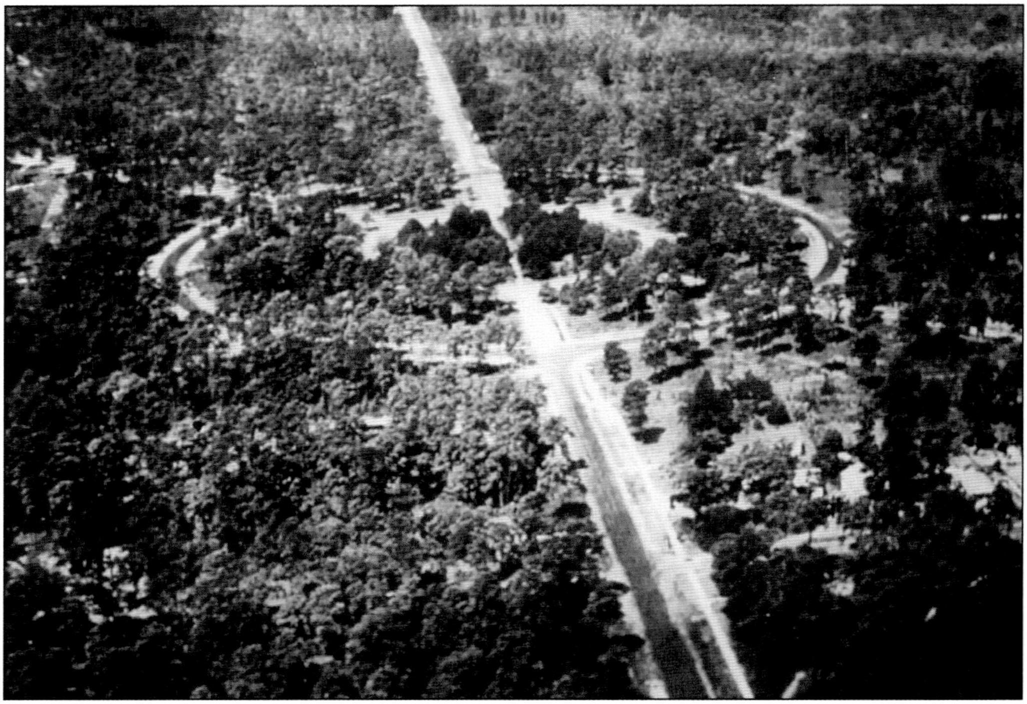

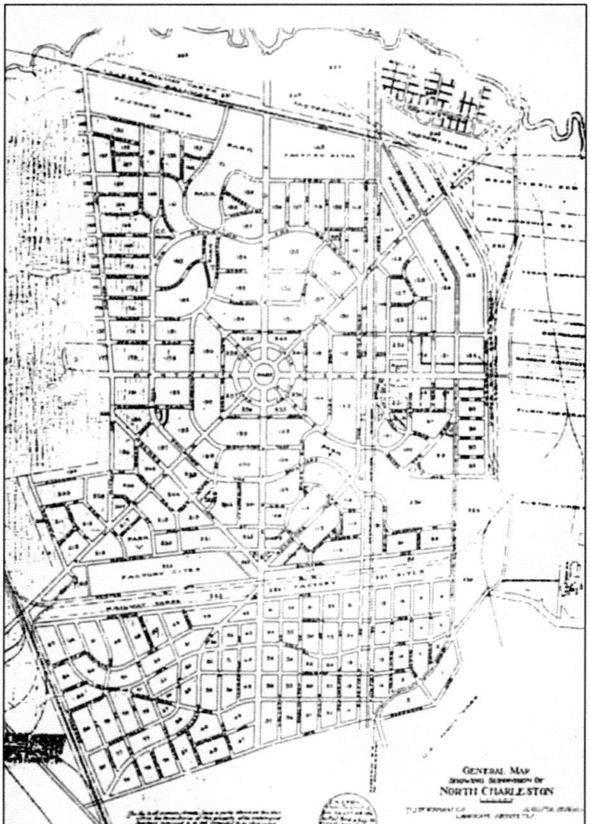

Old North Charleston's city plan was very modern with national trends in its landscape design. William Bell Marquis drew the original design of the city. Around this time there was a movement in England to establish garden cities, which were independent areas meant to stand alone with their own industries, parks, and farms. The scheme of Letchworth, England, is very similar to the design used for old North Charleston. The goal was for people to be able to work in factories just a short distance from their homes or farmsteads. Pictured above is Park Circle and its streets radiating out from a central point that are named for some of the early developers including Rhett, Buist, Durant, O'Hear, Hyde, and Montague. (Courtesy of the City of North Charleston.)

Pictured at left is a 1913 plot of North Charleston drawn by W.B. Marquis of Olmstead Brothers Engineers of New York. (Courtesy of the City of North Charleston.)

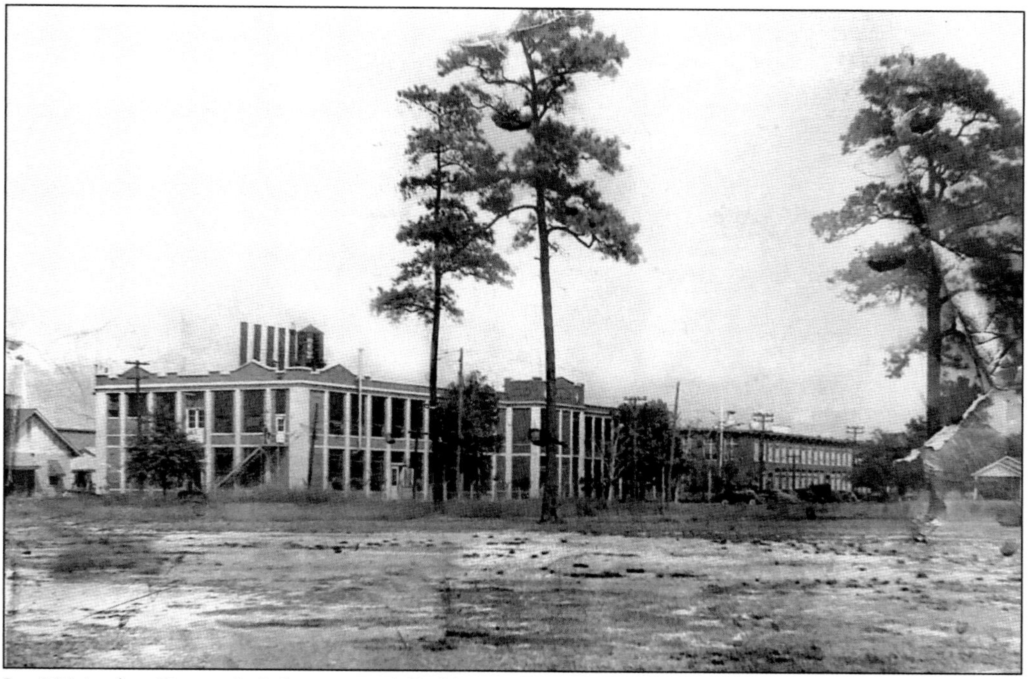

In 1914, the General Asbestos and Rubber Company (GARCO) was established in North Charleston. Pictured is the facility on O'Hear and GARCO Streets.

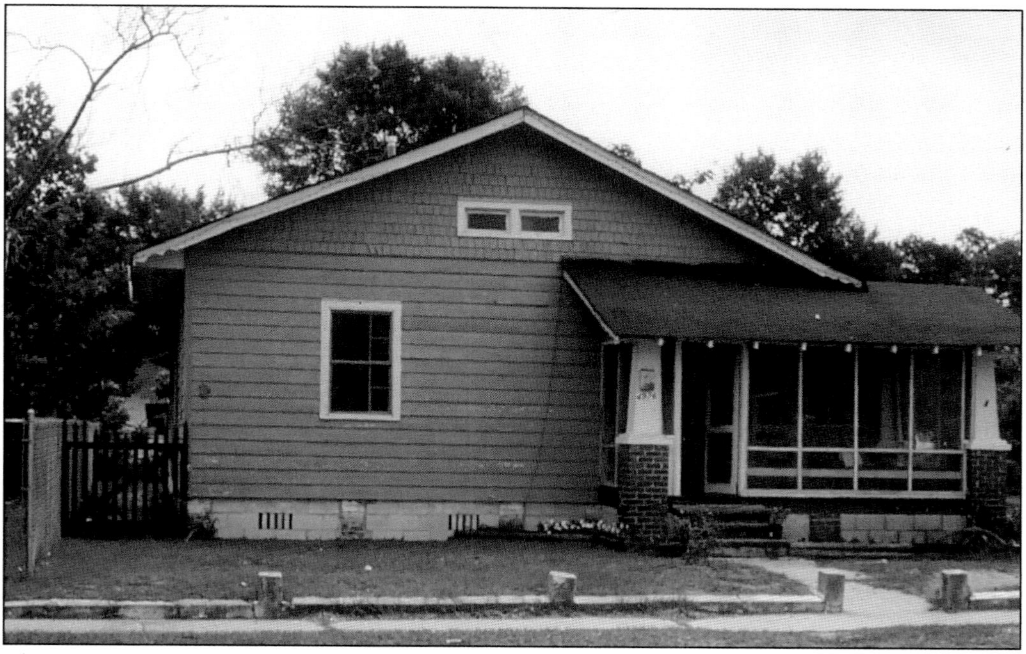

The concept of a mill village had been imported from England and began with the construction of 75 houses designed by Fred J. Orr of Athens, Georgia. The houses at the GARCO Mill Village had five or six rooms and screened porches. Rent was approximately a dollar per room. Maintenance, fire protection, and garbage pick-up was provided by the company. Pictured is a typical GARCO village house built around 1919 and still in use today. (Courtesy of City of North Charleston.)

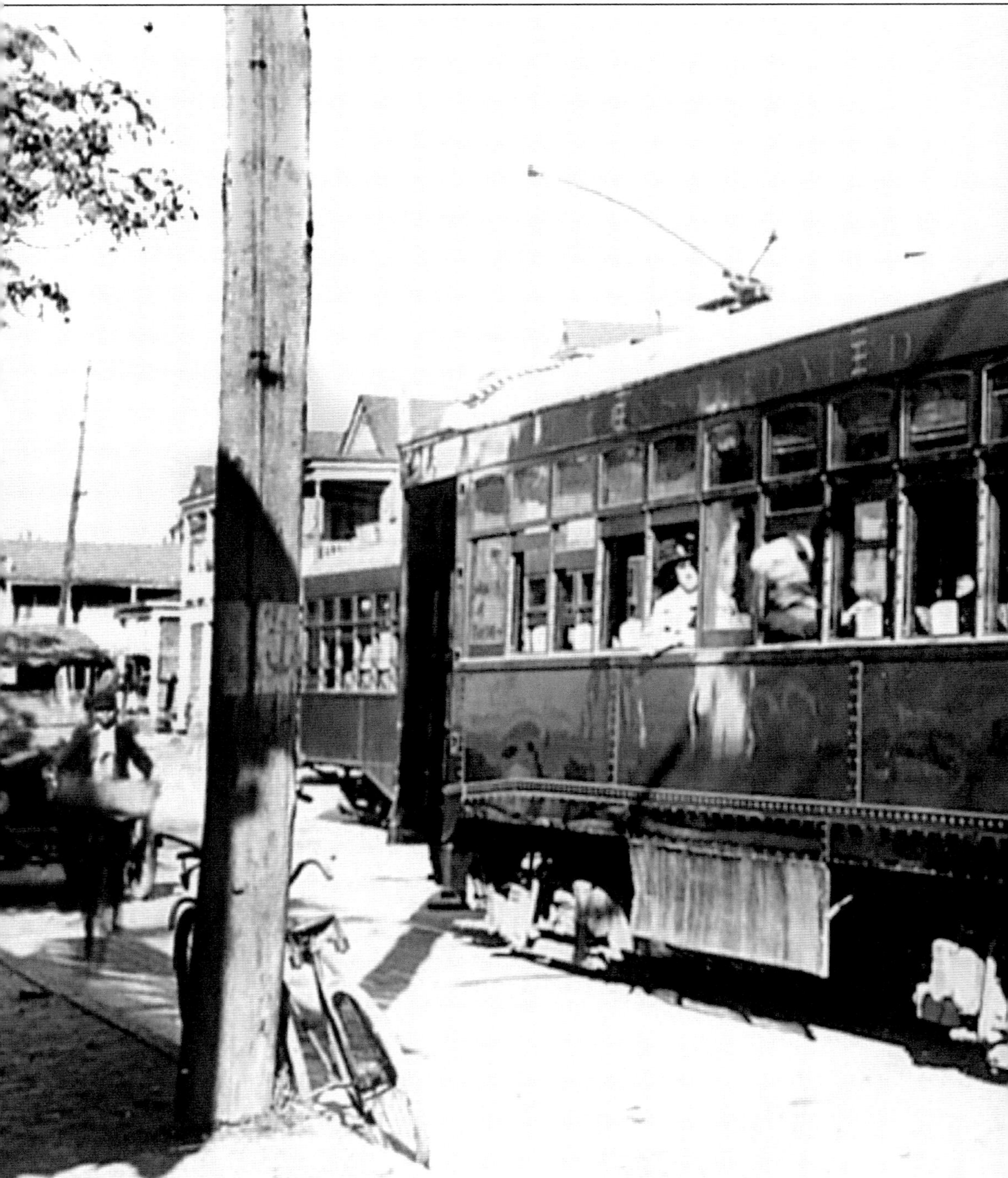

In 1915, streetcars traveled from Charleston to what was known as the end of the line at O'Hear and Montague Avenues. People living on O'Hear Avenue were known as "car line people." The car was double-ended like a ferry boat. When the car reached the end of its route, the front became the rear and the rear became the front. Before the return trip, the motor man would lower the power line trolley at one end of the car and raise the trolley at the other end.

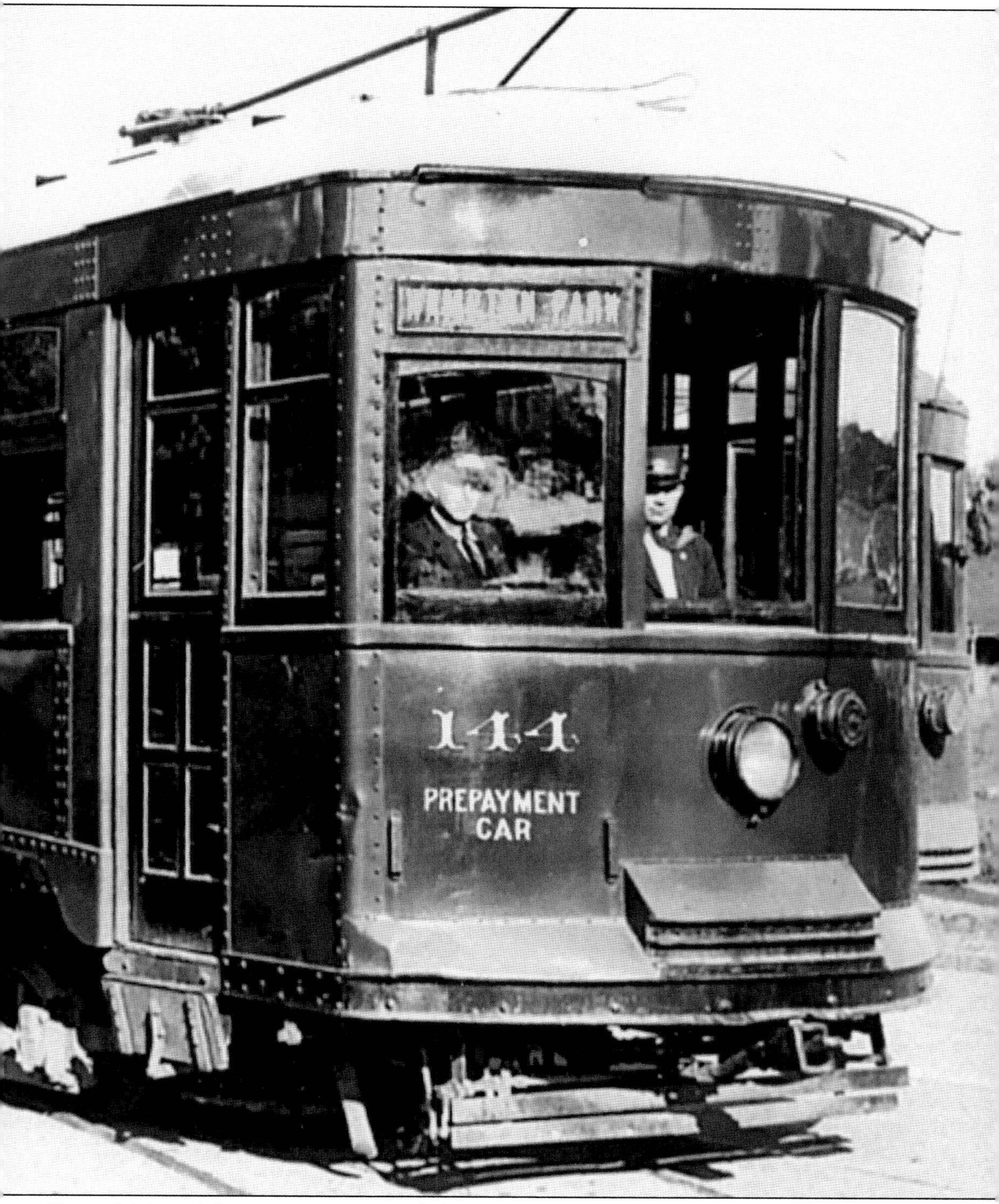

He would then shift the operating controls from one end to the other and reverse the seat backs to the new travel direction. Before returning to Charleston the motorman would take a short break and go to Colie's Store for a Coke. By 1932 the use of private cars began to take revenue from the street cars. In 1934, the last trolley made its run down the neck to the north area. (Courtesy of Sue Thigpen.)

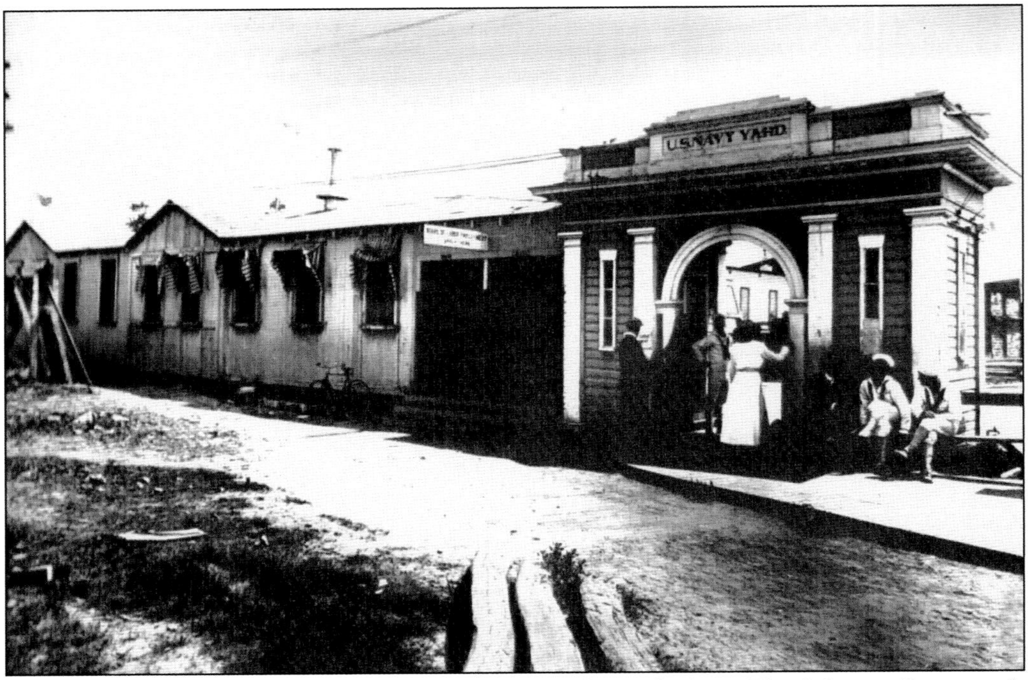

Around 1916 the main gate of the Navy Yard was located where Third Street Gate stands today. Pictured are people entering and leaving the Naval Base. (Courtesy of Palmer Olliff.)

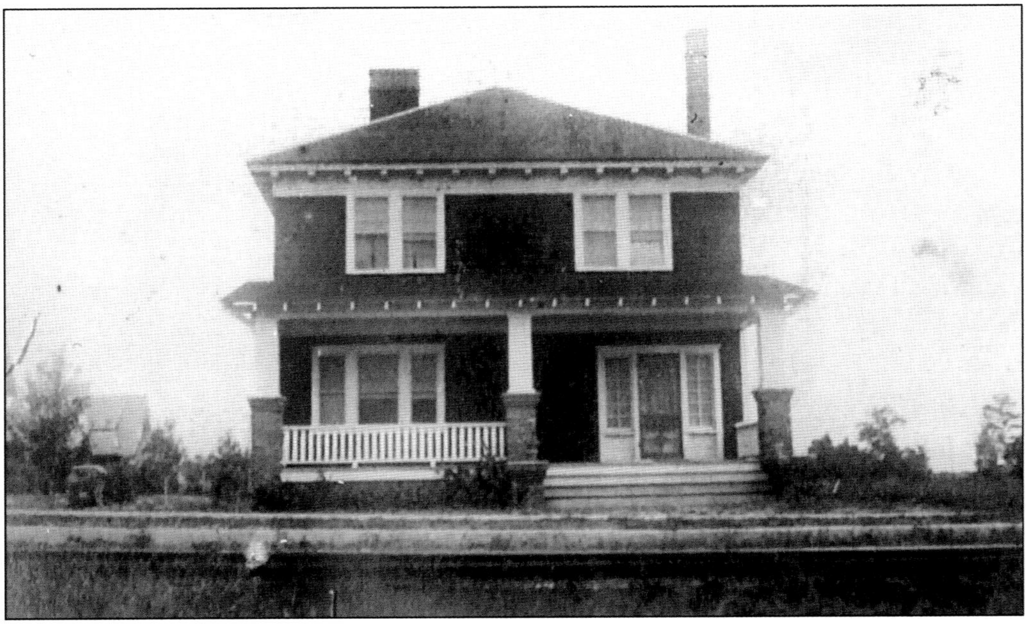

Q.P. Brooks owned this house, one of the first homes to be built in North Charleston and located on O'Hear Avenue. Note the streetcar tracks at the bottom of the picture. (Courtesy of Q. P. Brooks Jr.)

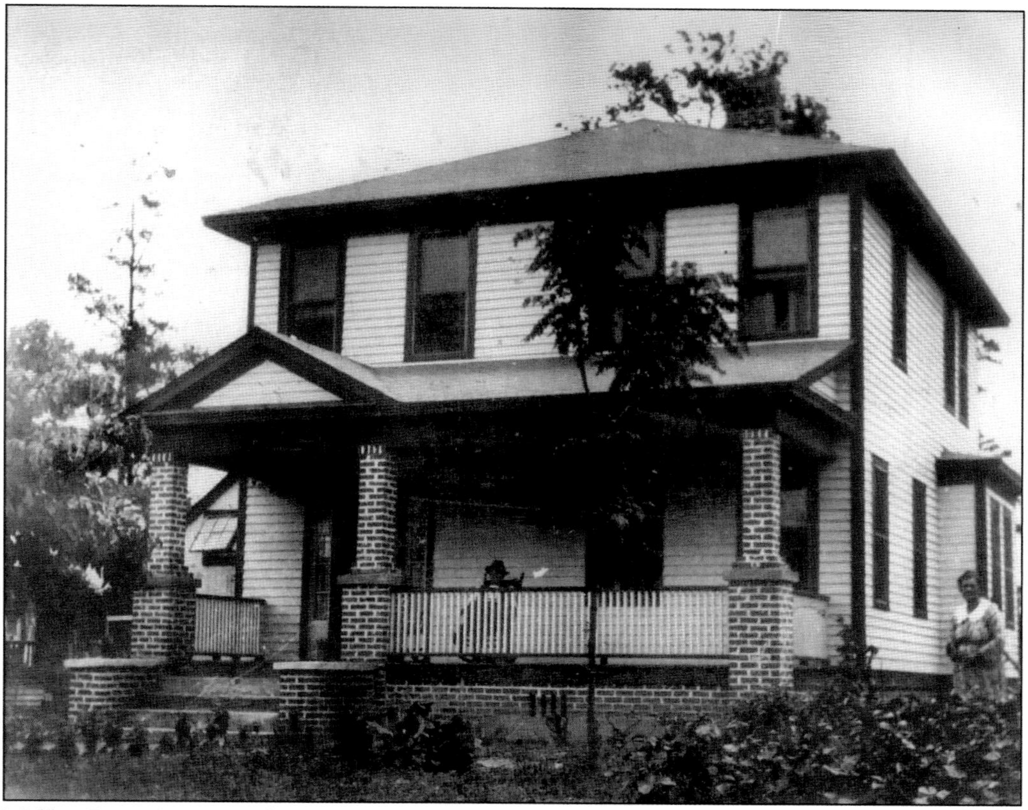

Mifflin Burris Morse and Annie Lewie Morse built this house in 1922 at 105 Cherry Avenue with lumber purchased at Burton Lumber Mill. (Courtesy of Launa Thompson.)

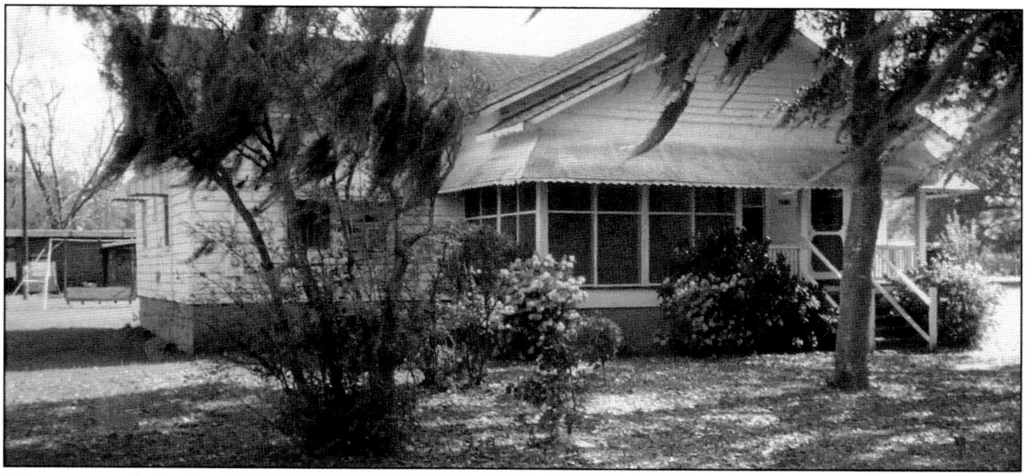

Herman and Catherine Fuller built this house on Midland Park Road in 1916 on five acres of land surrounded by oak, pecan, peach, and pear trees. It was the first in the area to have electricity that was provided by a 1923 Kohler diesel generator. It also featured indoor plumbing and a telephone. Mr. Fuller sold water in five-gallon glass jugs at 50¢ each to customers in the lower peninsula in today's downtown area of Charleston. The water was drawn from a 15-foot artesian well that still exists on the property. (Courtesy of Eleanor Attaway Fuller.)

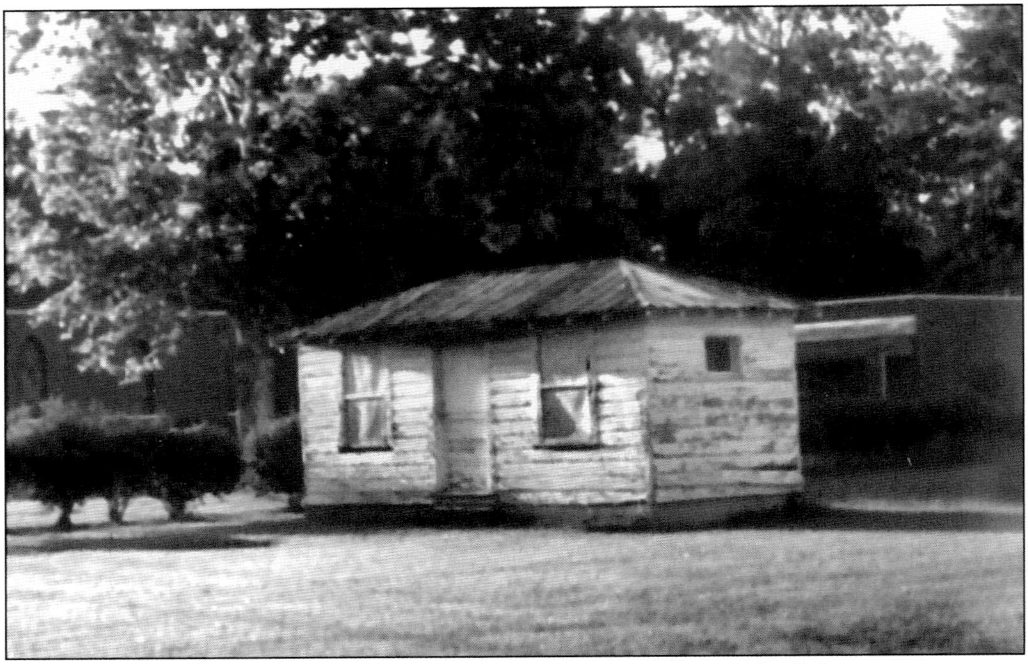

This small building located on the Fuller property was used to store and sell their artesian water. (Courtesy of Eleanor Attaway Fuller.)

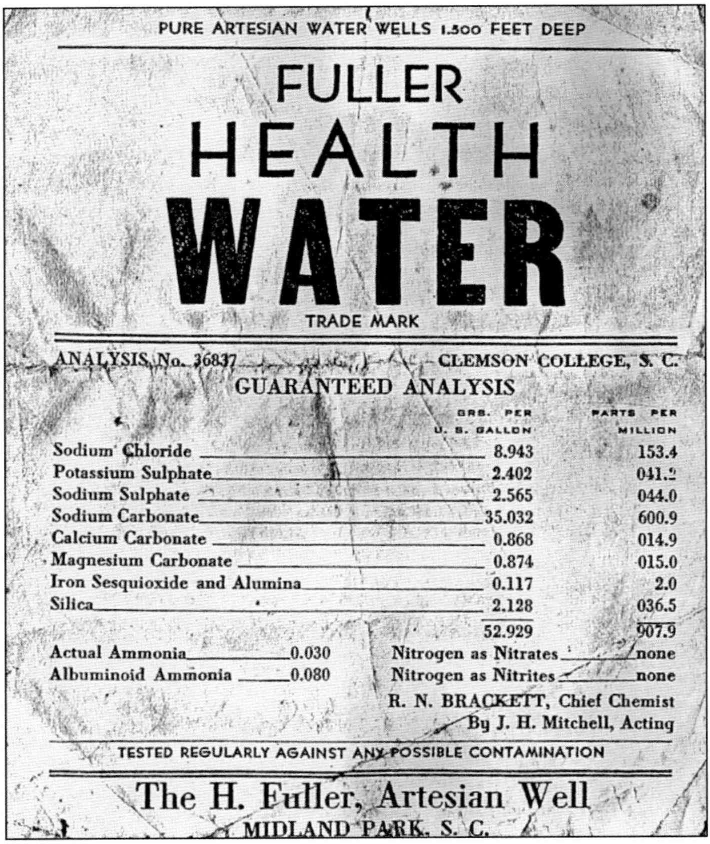

A flier advertises Fuller Health Water from the H. Fuller Artesian Well in Midland Park. (Courtesy of Eleanor Attaway Fuller.)

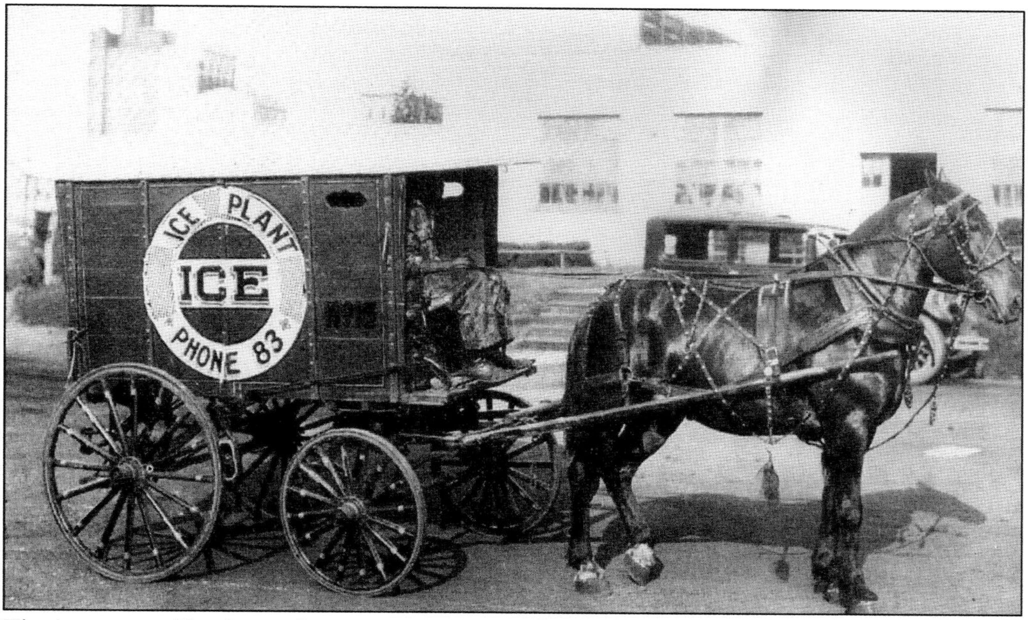

The iceman and his horse-drawn wagon was a welcomed sight for many people in 1929 North Charleston. (Courtesy of the City of North Charleston.)

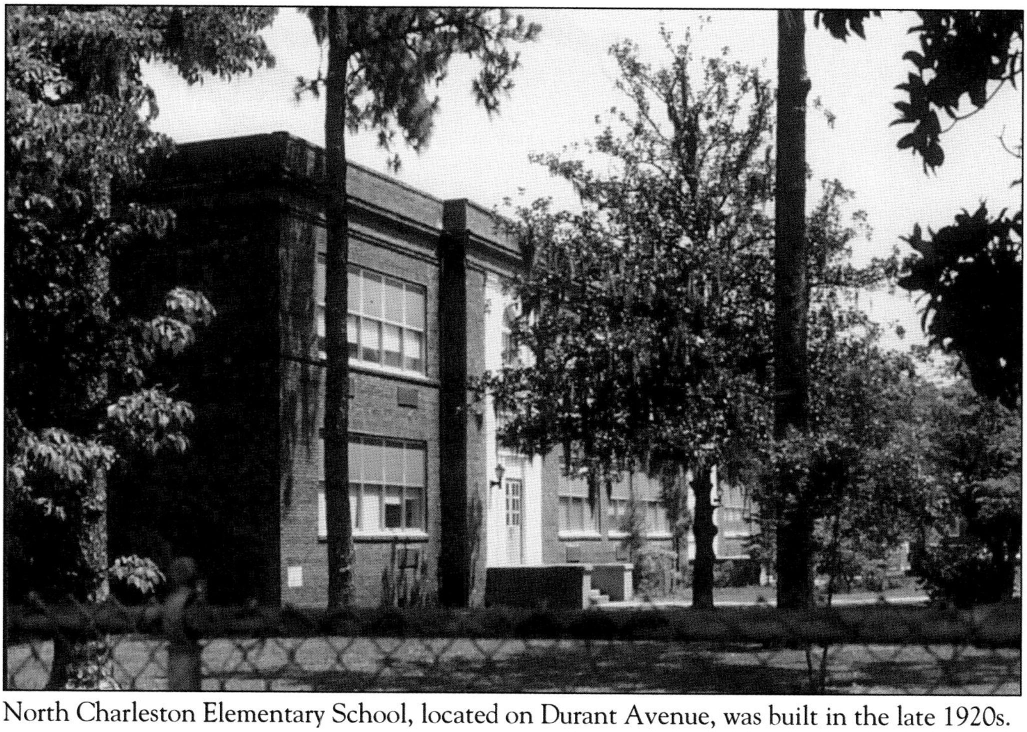

North Charleston Elementary School, located on Durant Avenue, was built in the late 1920s.

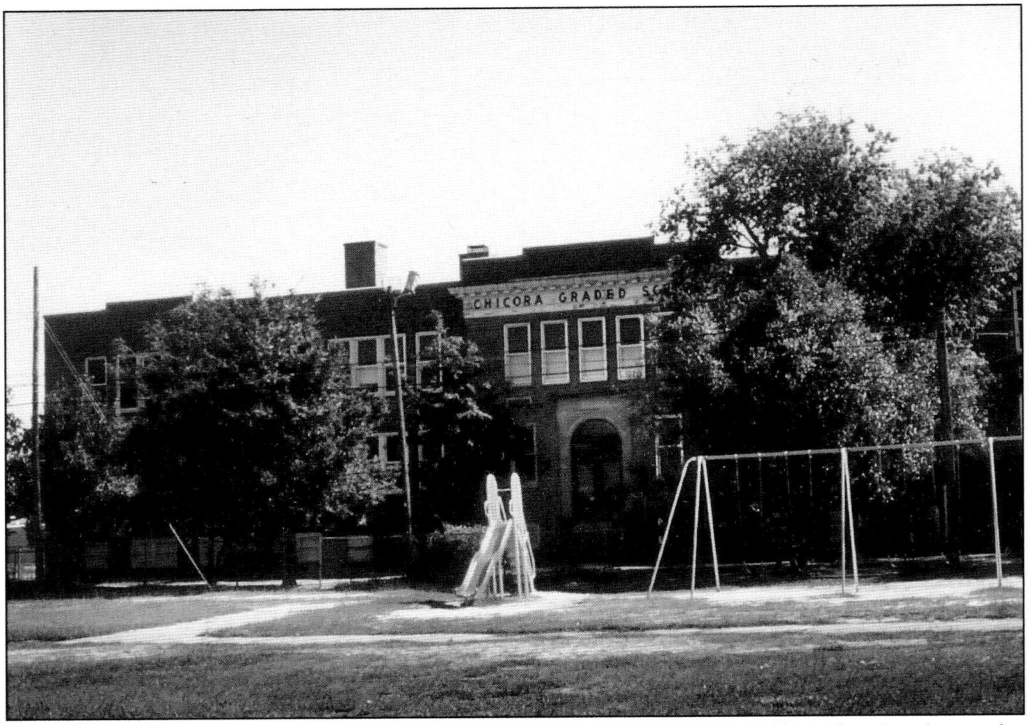

Chicora Elementary School, which was built in the early 1930s, is still used today for grades kindergarten through fifth grade

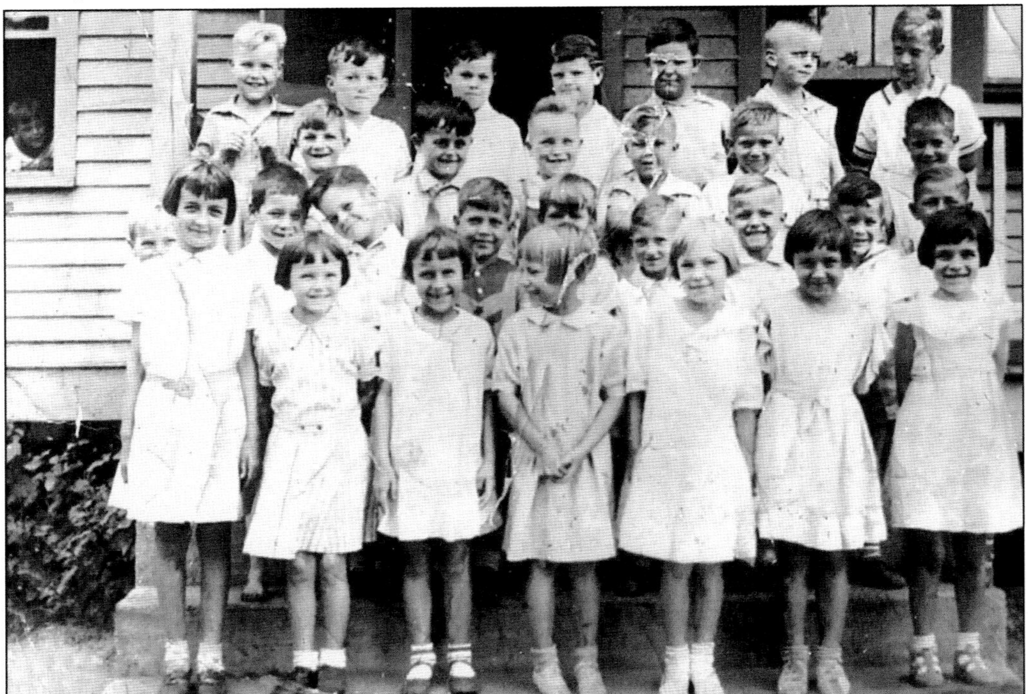

The class picture above was taken at Chicora Graded School in the early 1930s. (Courtesy of Ruth Cupp.)

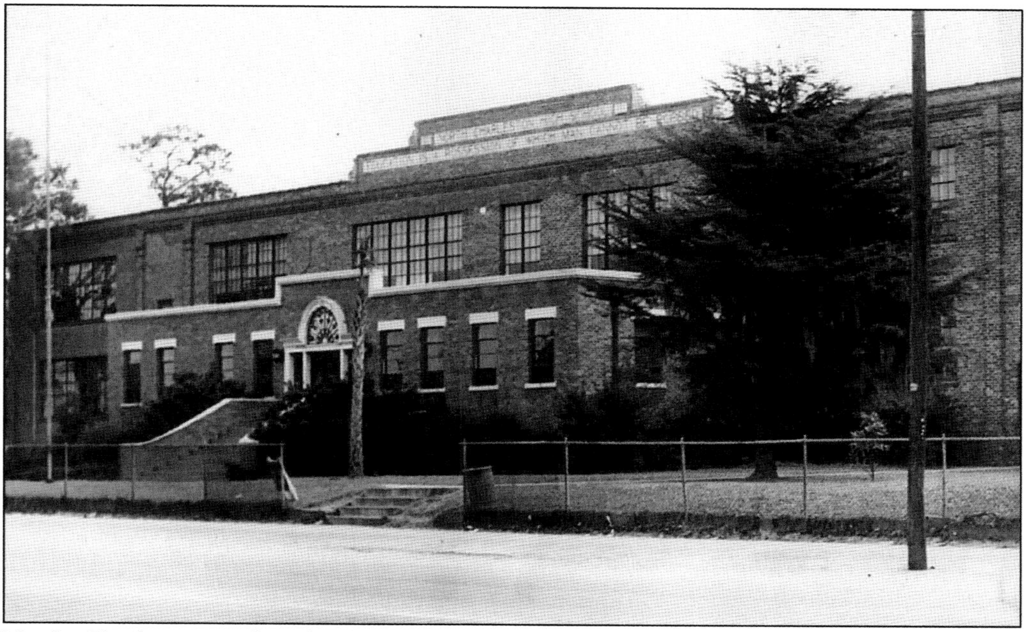

North Charleston High School was built in 1922 and William Thayre served as the first principal. The original wooden building burned in 1925, and a new brick school was built in 1926. (Courtesy of Ruth Cupp.)

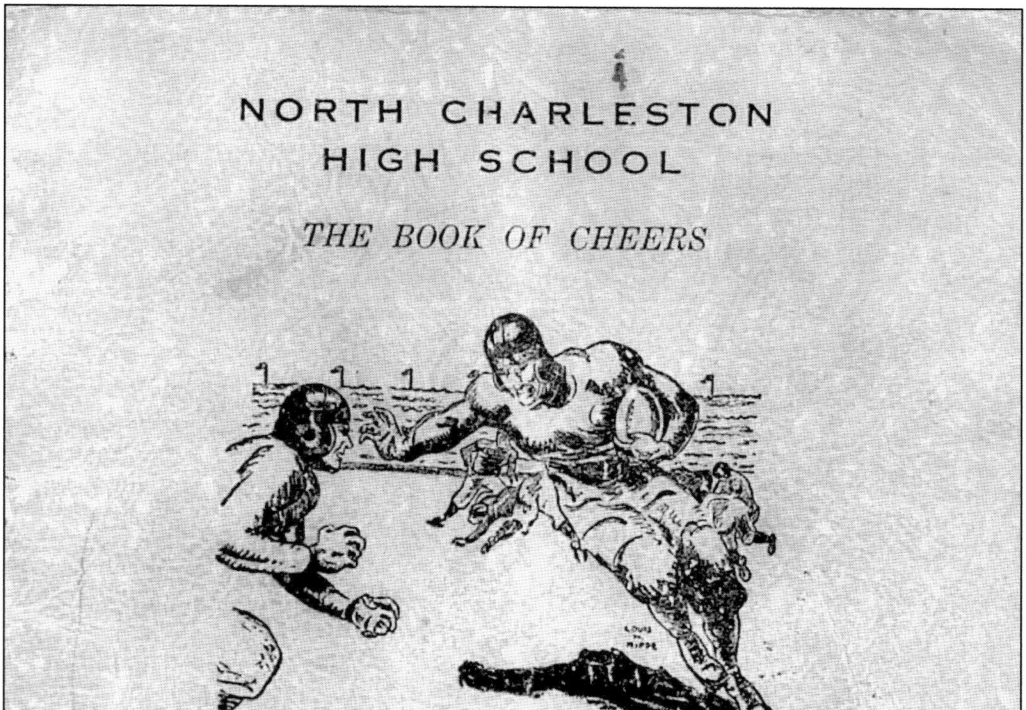

"Coca Cola, Cherry Cola, Ginger Ale, Pop! North Charleston Blue Devils always on top." This cheer is just one of many featured in the North Charleston High School "Book of Cheers" for the 1936–1937 school year. (Courtesy of Launa Thompson.)

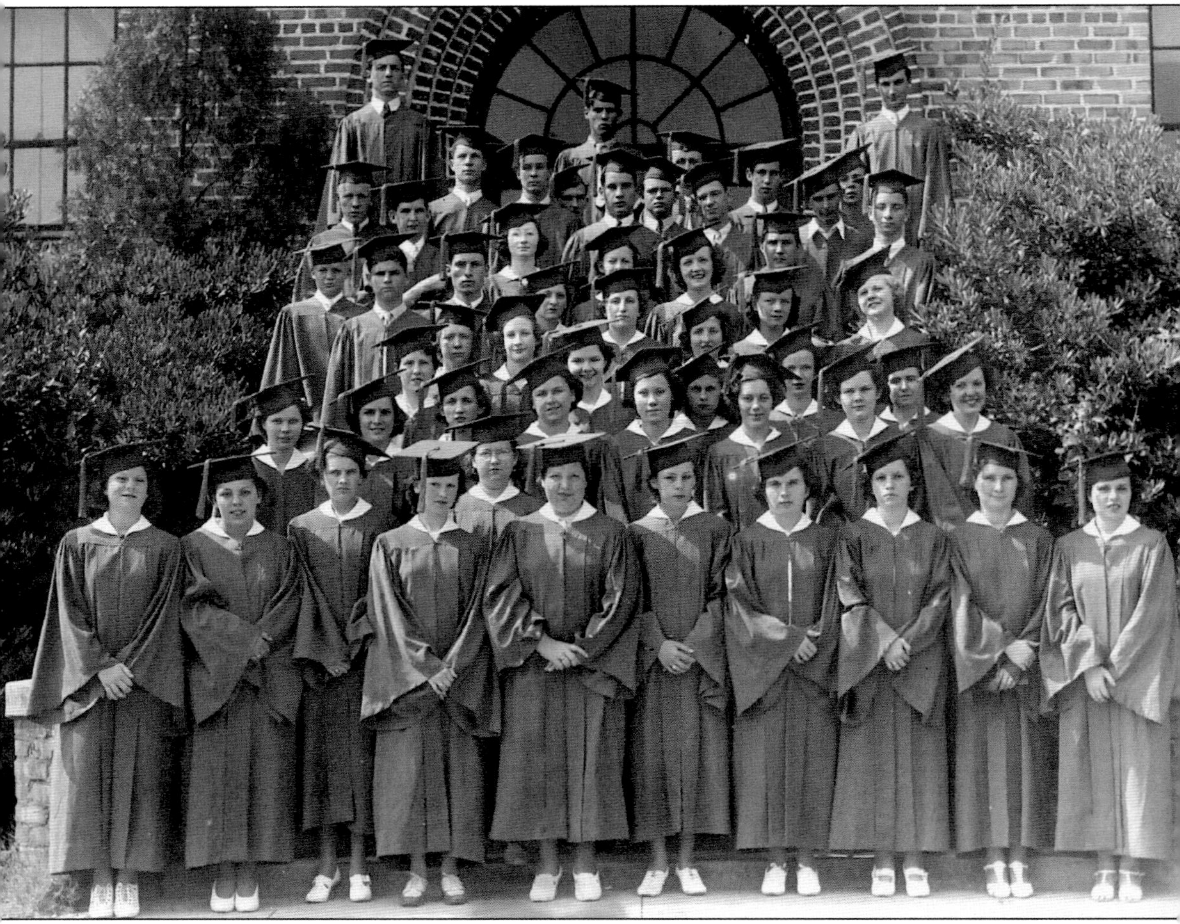

The North Charleston High School Class of 1937 pose for a graduation photo. From left to right are the following: (first row) Myrtle Ganey, Annie Williamson, Lila Sparkman, Nelma Pigott, Helen Carson, Anna Warren, Louise Reeves, Martha Streets, Clara Jordan, Emma Johnson, and Louise Martin; (second row) Louise Thornal, Evelyn Montenese, Ruth Williams, Maxine Baylor, Vera Cumbee, Lucille Sap, Alice Timmerman, and Bernice Woods; (third row) Emma Cooper, Elizabeth Timmerman, Nelle Park, Margaret Poplin, and Ruby Gantt; (fourth row) Agnes Gruber, Georgianna deMore, Maree Estridge, Jean Hadley, Anne Rouston, and Lucille Biezunski; (fifth row) Jack Payne, Margaret Knight, and Charlotte Berry; (sixth row) Hiram Lane, C.R. Floyd, Annette Walters, Adele Dantzler, Wilson Farr, and Herbert Holzberg; (seventh row) George Holtz, Laurence Flynn, Louie Vallenga, Joe Borwick, and Jimmy Voight; (eighth row) Louis Ridgeway, Bailey Gary, Henry Legrea, John Hunt, Q. P. Brooks, and Thomas McMillan; (ninth row) Jack Miller, Clifford Songer, Hugh Johnson, and Louis Flynn.

The city of North Charleston got its first post office in 1831 at Sineath's Railroad Station located near what is now Trident Technical College. Pictured to the right is the post office that was located on the northeast corner of Montague Avenue and Virginia Avenue, which was at one point known as Cosgrove Avenue. The dark-brown building was one-story and made of wood. Mr. Henderson was the postmaster and the building belonged to the Henderson family. The North Charleston Post Office was in the Henderson Family for more than 50 years, passing through the hands of Mrs. Henderson and her daughter Oleda Garrett, wife of Gordon Garrett. Mrs. Garrett, who served as postmistress until 1953, built a new post office building on the corner of Chateau and Montague Avenues. Today, the post office in the Olde Village Area is located at Aunt Bea's Restaurant. (Courtesy of Launa Thompson.)

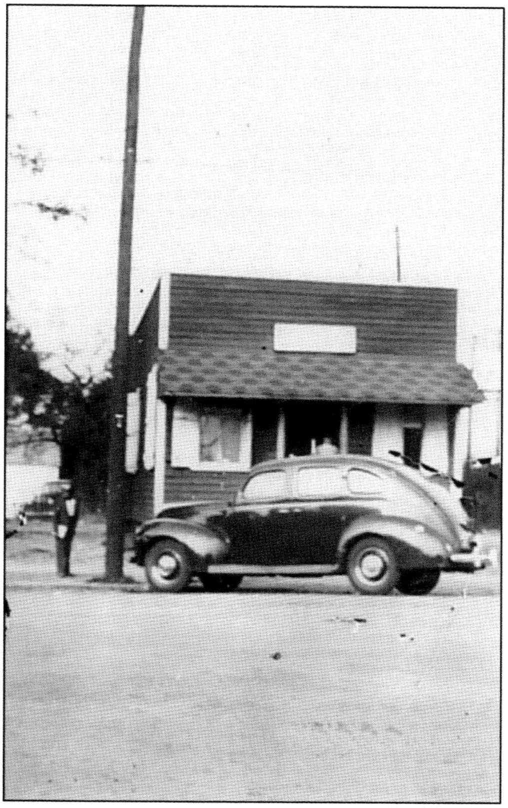

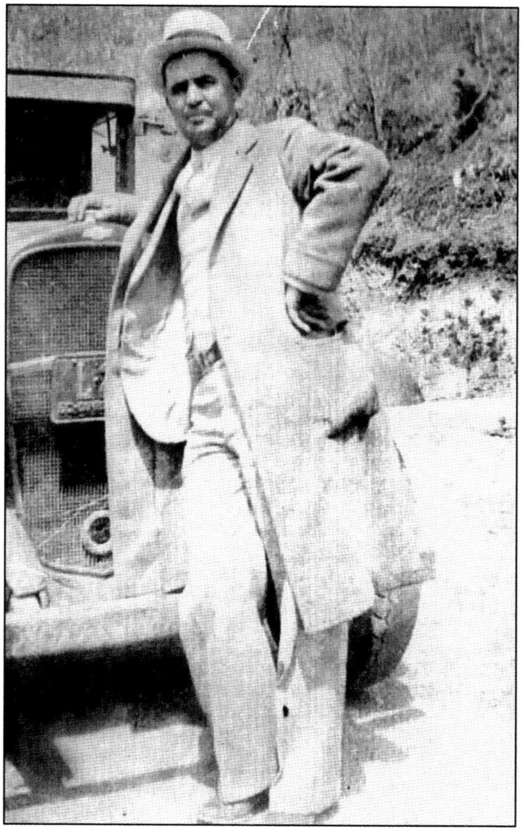

Often considered the "unofficial mayor" of North Charleston, Colie Morse ran a cluttered sign store on East Montague at the end of the car line. A friend to all, his business phone became the community phone, and the store was the meeting place for many politicians of this time. Here Colie is pictured around 1930. (Courtesy of Jesse Tolbert.)

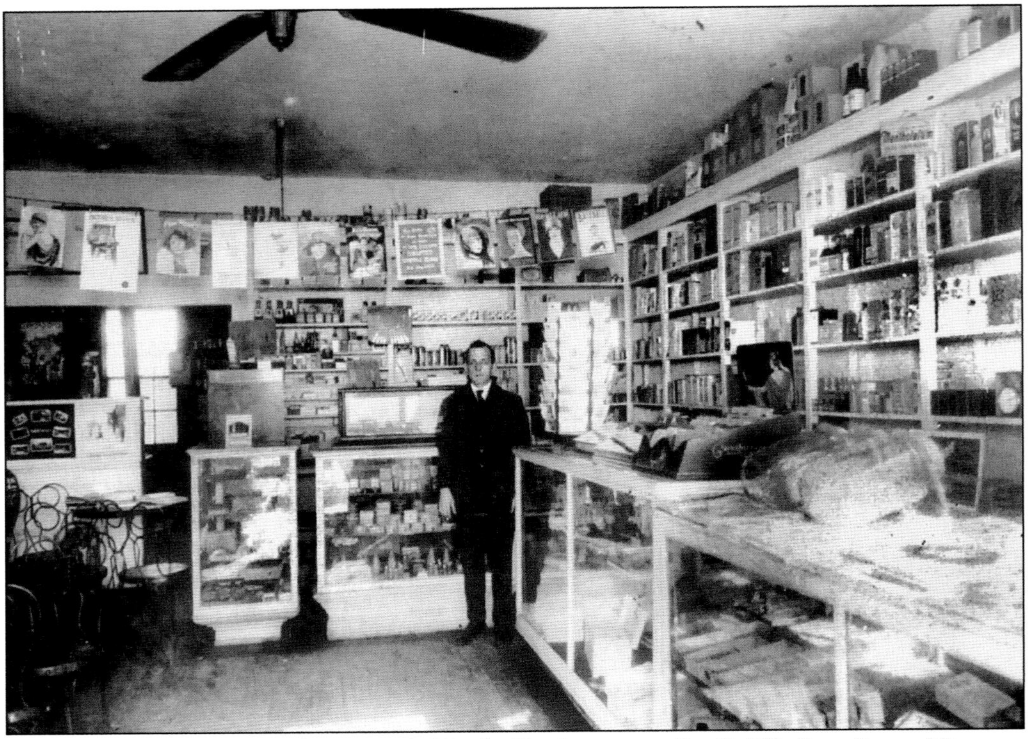

Another popular meeting place in early North Charleston was Dr. Califf's Drug Store. His was a one-story frame building, raised off the ground. The first thing customers noticed upon entering was the marble soda fountain. Califf was proud of the drinks and banana splits he served, and he kept bottled Cokes on crushed ice do that they would be ice cold. Rumor has it that one day when he ran out of cold Cokes and a customer asked him to pour a warm one into a cup of ice, he refused to do so, saying that the Coke would be watered down and flat. Pictured is L.G. Holroyd at Califf's Drug Store. (Courtesy of Jesse Tolbert.)

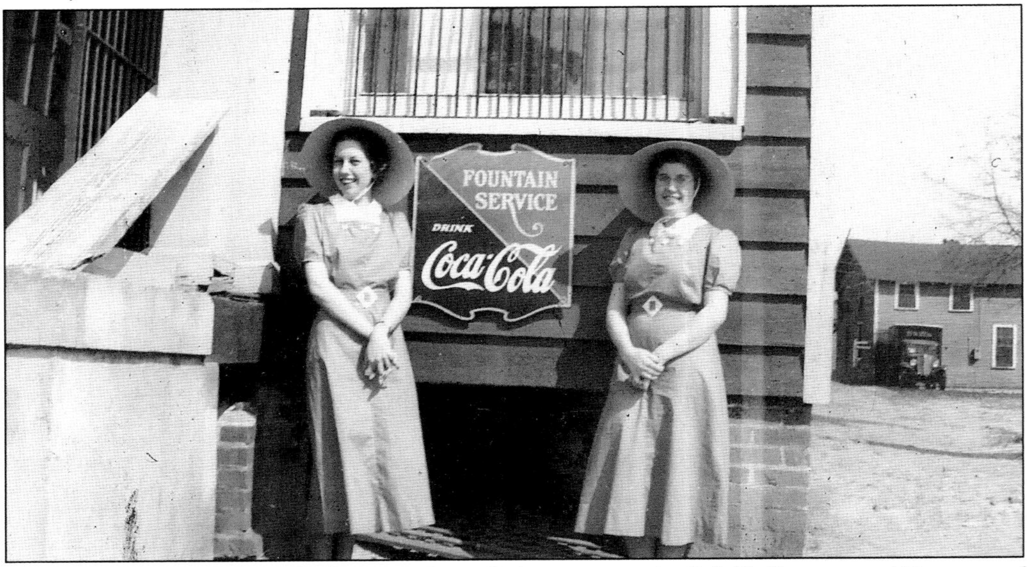

Two lovely ladies pose with the new Coca-Cola sign outside Califf's Drugstore. (Courtesy of Ruby Preacher.)

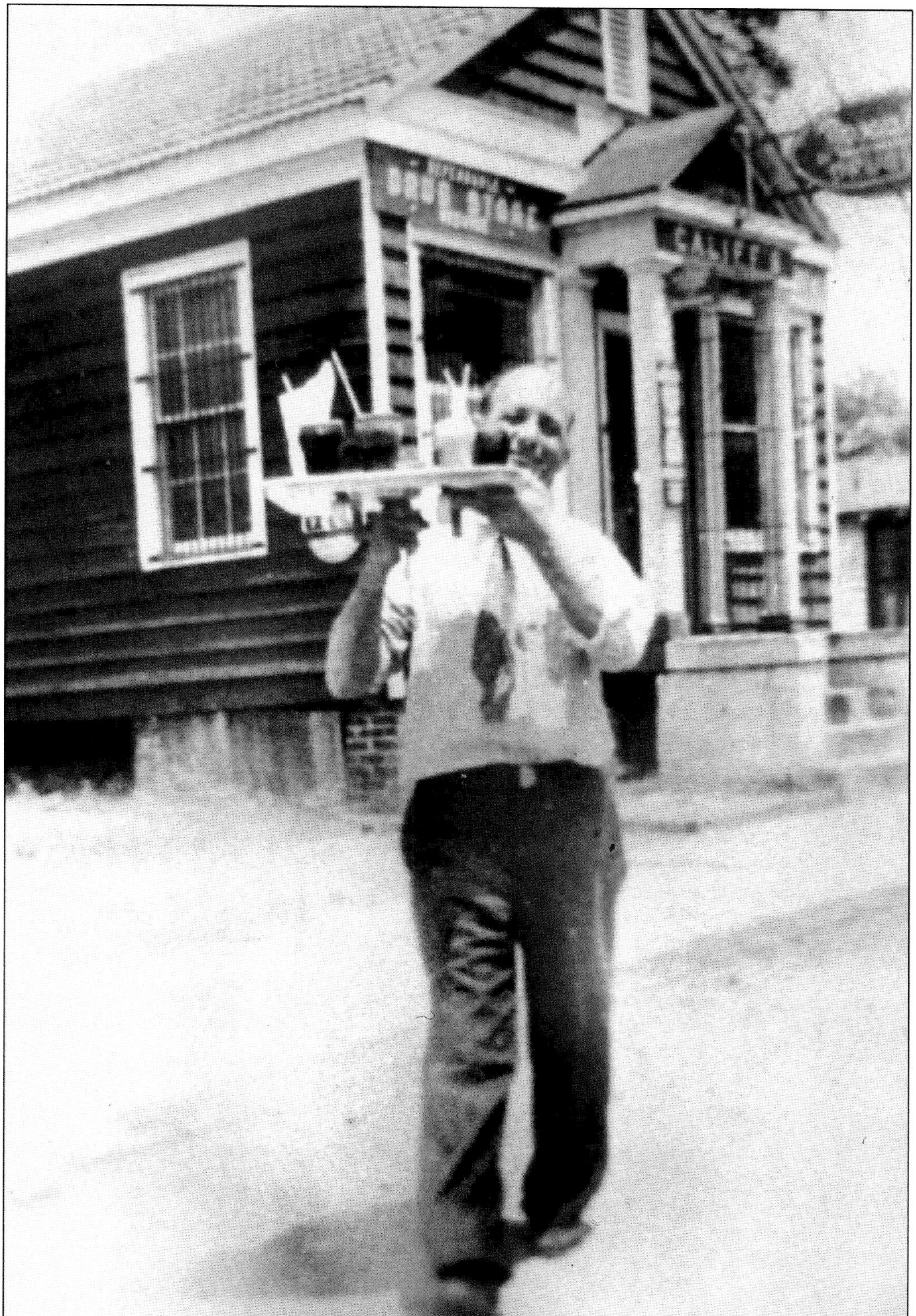

Dr. Califf delivers an order to another local merchant located on Montague Avenue. (Courtesy of Jessie Tolbert.)

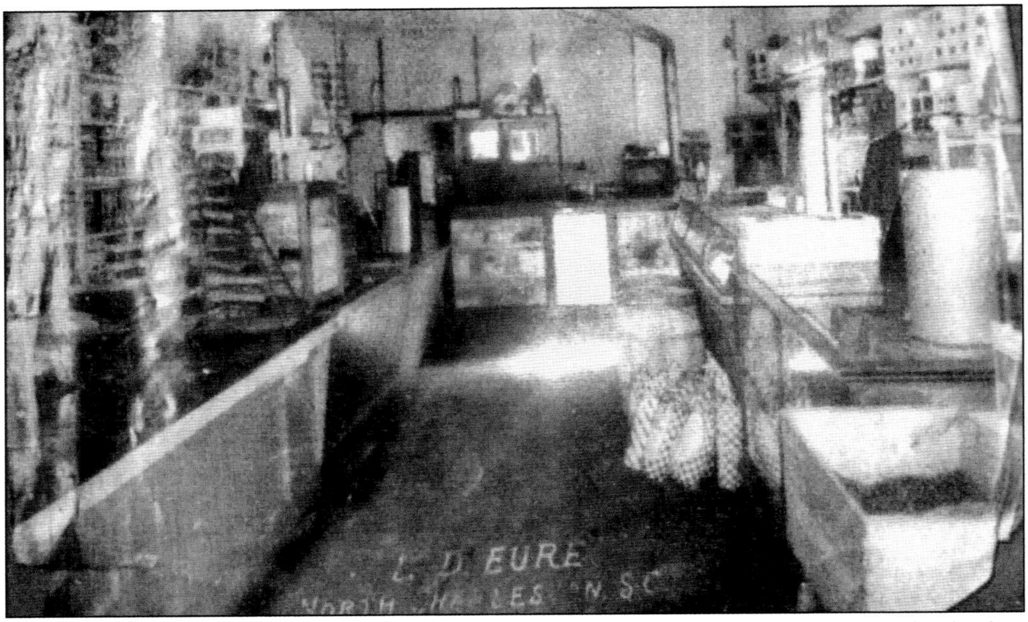

Eure's Grocery Store was located a few doors from O'Hear Avenue. It was thought to be the first store located in North Charleston. (Courtesy of the City of North Charleston.)

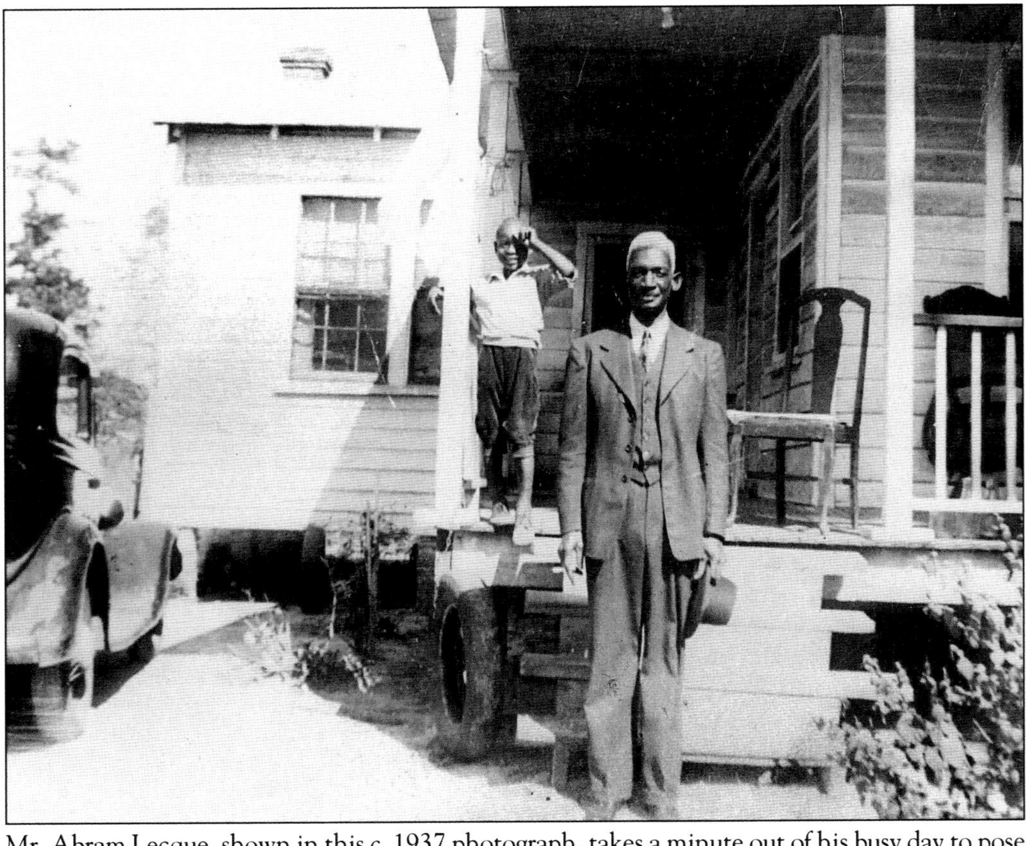

Mr. Abram Lecque, shown in this c. 1937 photograph, takes a minute out of his busy day to pose outside his Liberty Hill home on Montague Avenue. (Courtesy of Carolyn Lecque Collins.)

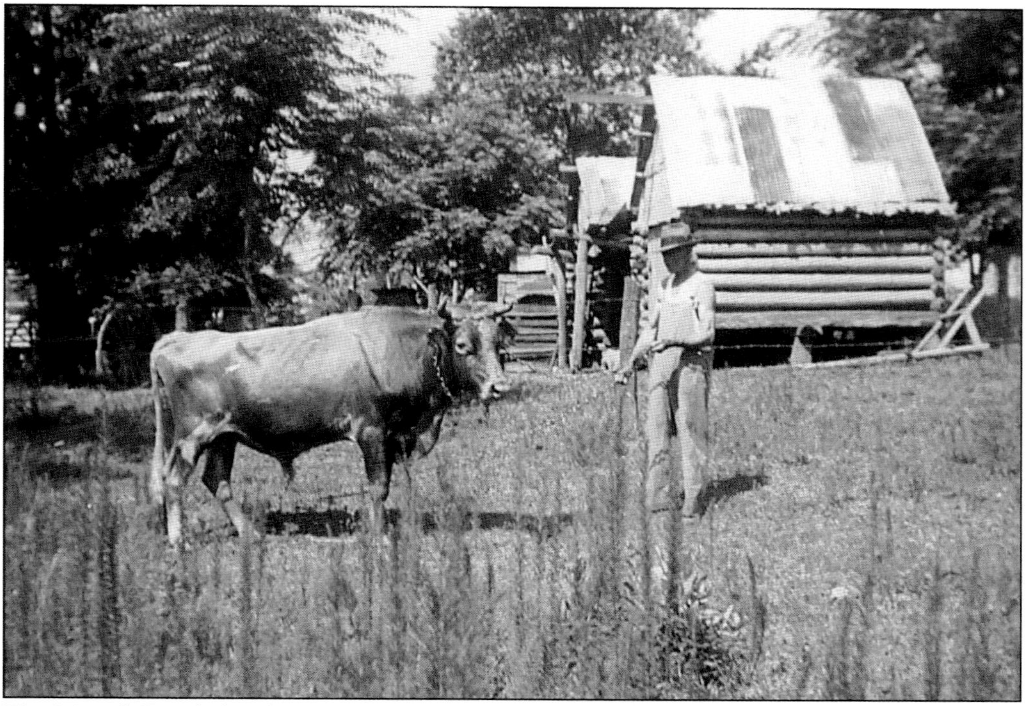

The Mazyck Family lived in a log cabin located in the Midland Park Area between Ashley Phosphate Road and Midland Park Road. Edward P. Mazyck is pictured here with the family bull on his farm where cotton was the main crop. Taken in the early 1930s, the photo shows the log cabin where the family lived. (Courtesy of Bill Mazyck.)

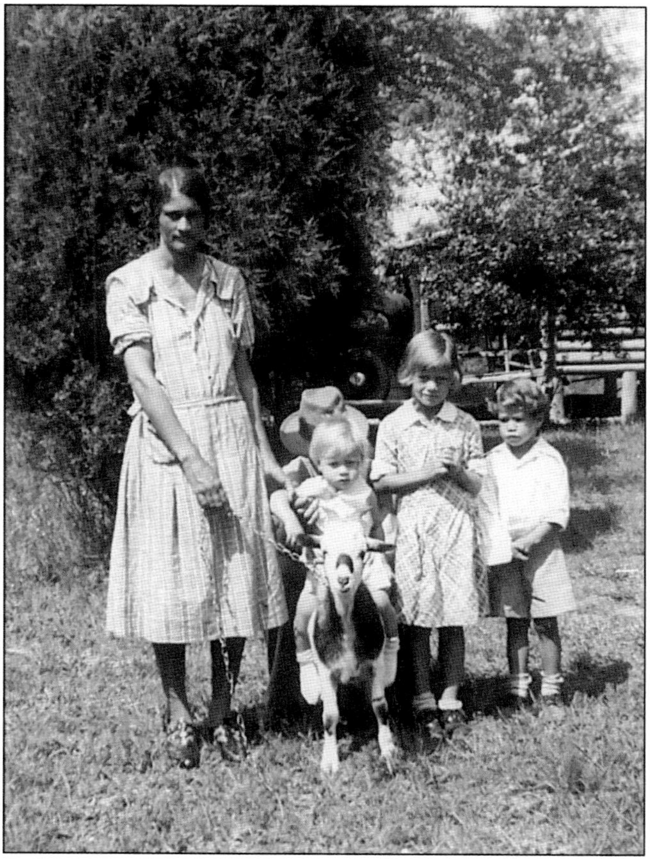

The Mazyck children pose for a picture with their pet goat on the family farm. Pictured are mother Doris Mazyck, her son James on the goat, Ida Mazyck, and Bill Mazyck. Father Edward P. Mazyck, whose face is hidden, holds James on the goat. Bill and Ida Mazyck still live on the property today. (Courtesy of Bill Mazyck.)

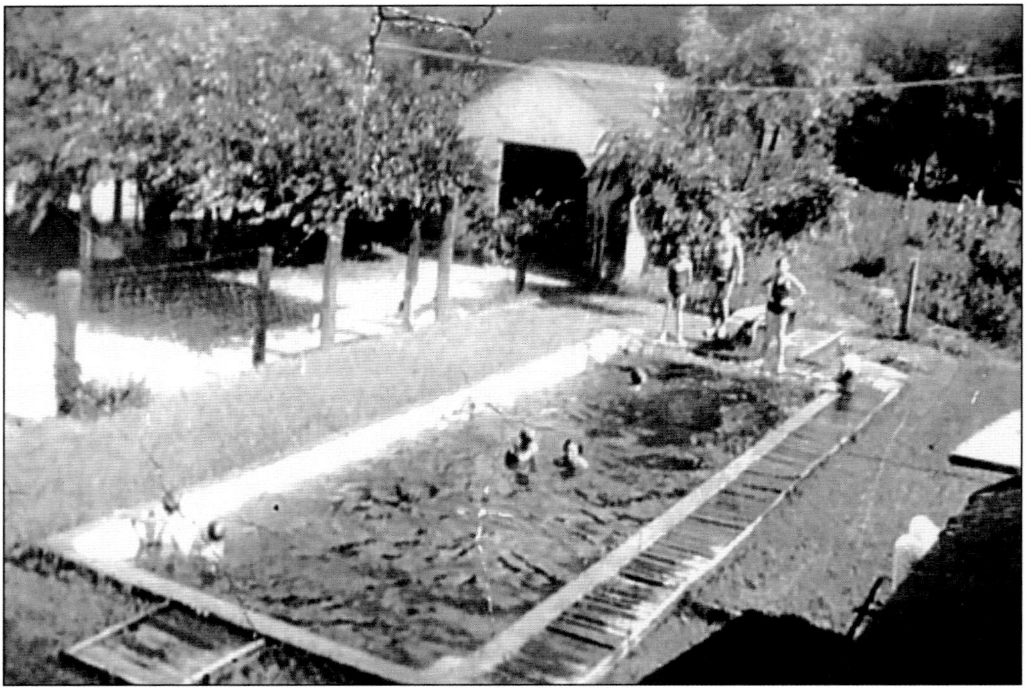

Twelve-year-old Q.P. Brooks Jr. built the first swimming pool in North Charleston behind his parents' house on O'Hear Avenue in 1934. It took him a year to dig the 36-foot by 13-foot pool. His father had it cemented and young Q.P. charged kids five cents to swim. He obtained his pool supplies from the YMCA and drained the pool weekly. (Courtesy of Q.P. Brooks Jr.)

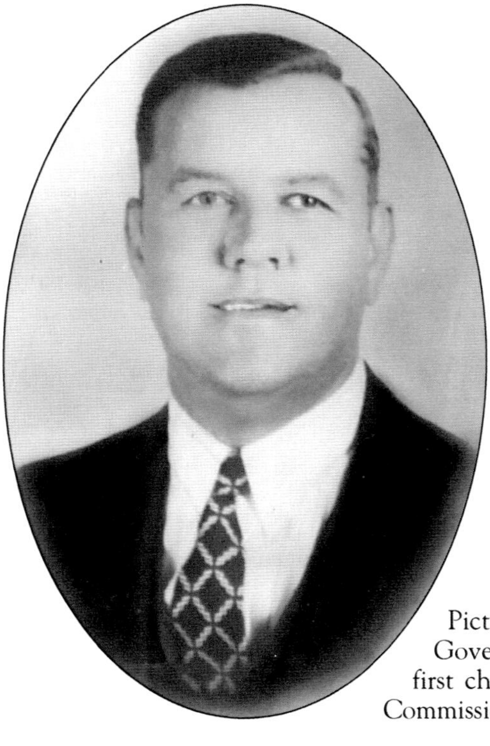

Pictured at left is H. Harrison Attaway. In 1935, Governor Olin D. Johnson appointed Attaway as the first chairman of the North Charleston Public Service Commission. (Courtesy of Eleanor Attaway Fuller.)

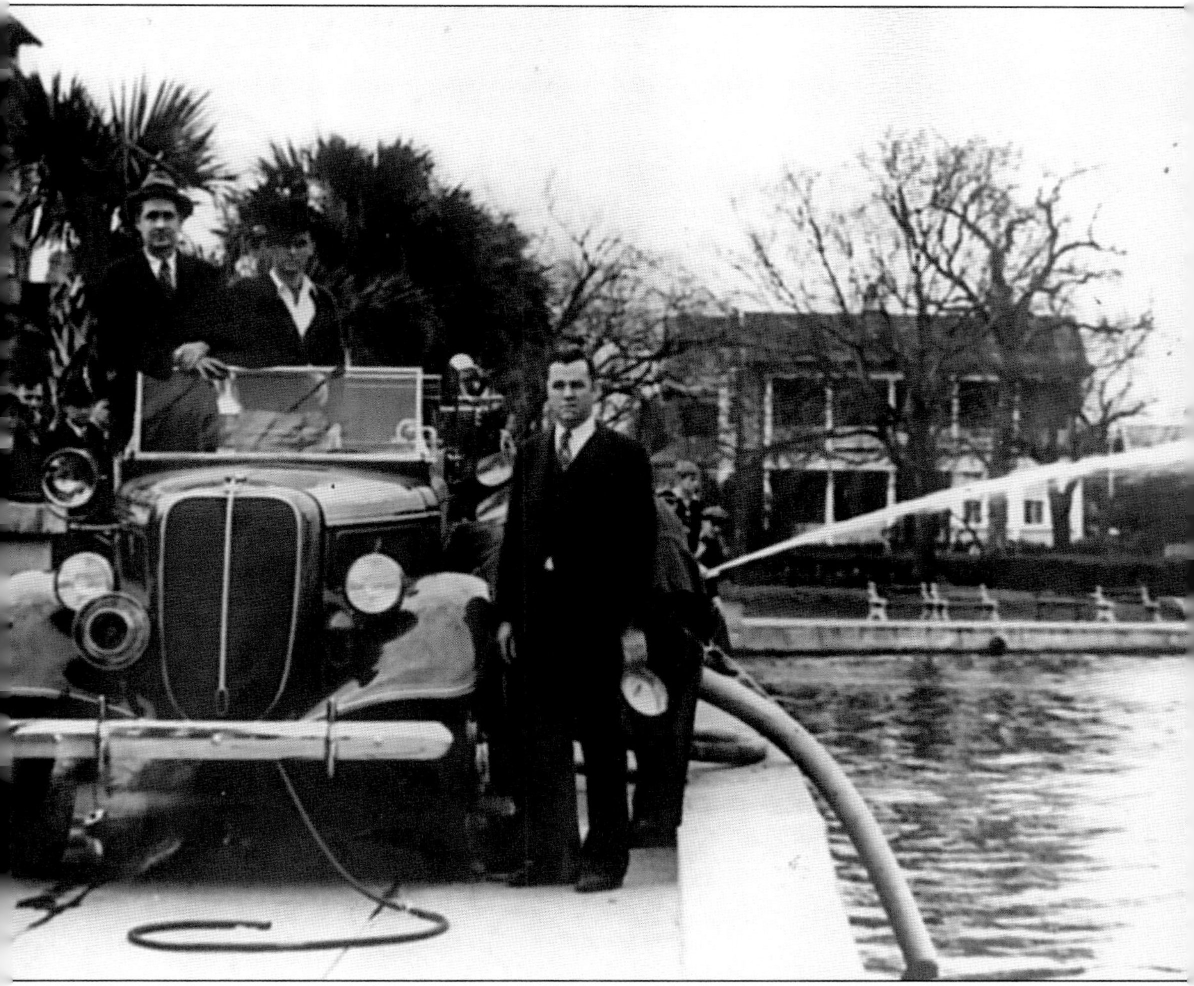

As the first chairman of the Public Service Commission, Attaway and his fellow commissioners were instrumental in obtaining fire protection, garbage disposal, sewerage, and street lights for the North Area. He is pictured in this 1935 photograph with Chief L.P. Baker and E.W. Maxwell in front of the city's first fire truck. (Courtesy of Eleanor Attaway Fuller.)

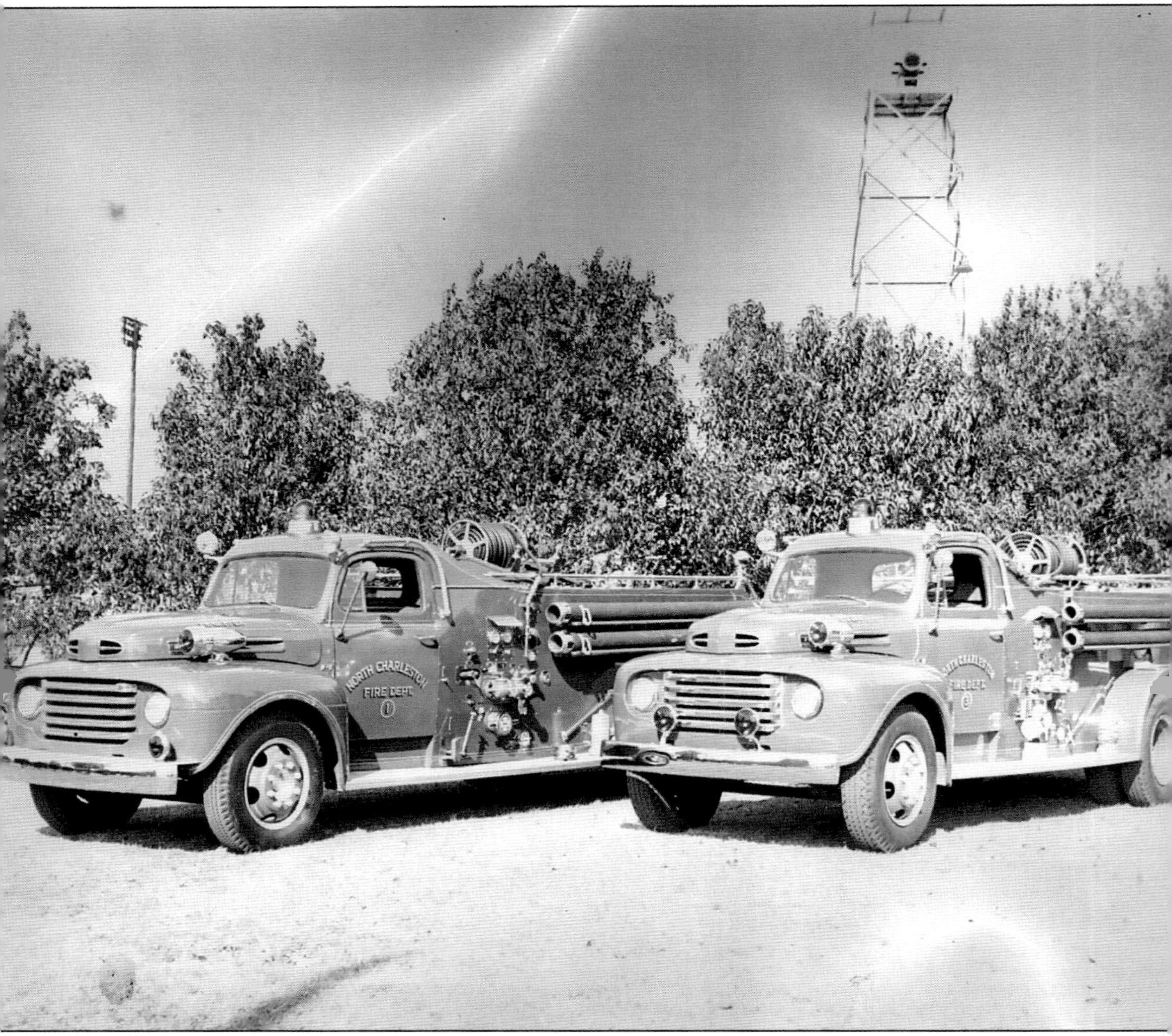

Pictured above are two North Charleston Fire Department trucks in 1937. (Courtesy of Dr. Thomas Martin.)

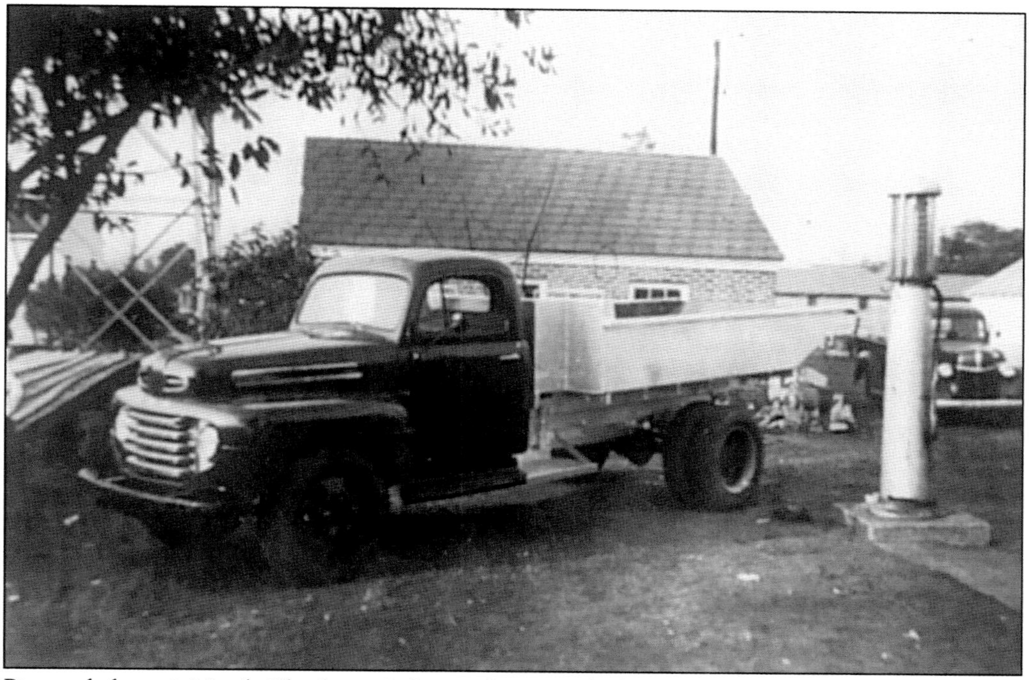

Pictured above is North Charleston's first garbage truck. (Courtesy of Eleanor Attaway Fuller.)

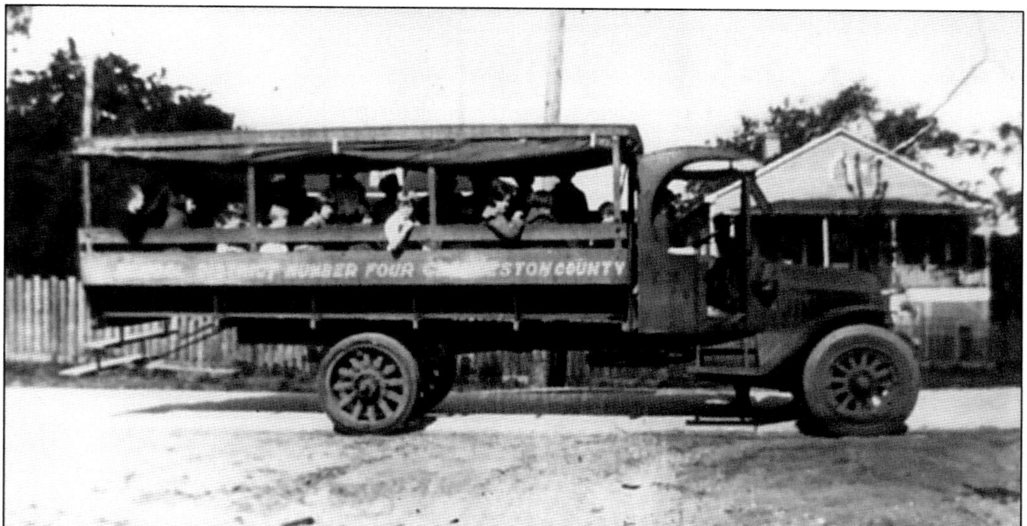

North Charleston's first school bus is seen in this 1925 photograph. H.H. Attaway owned and operated school buses in School District Number Four as well as the St. Paul's District. (Courtesy of Eleanor Attaway Fuller.)

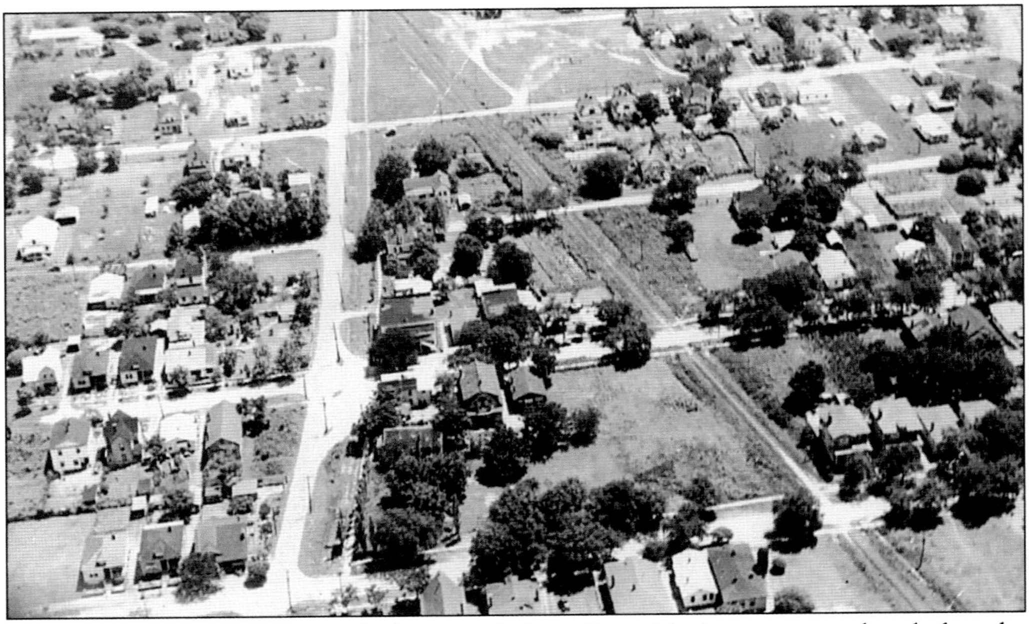

This view of the Chicora area looking south from Reynolds Avenue was taken before the construction of Spruill Avenue along the railroad track. (Courtesy of Jesse Tolbert.)

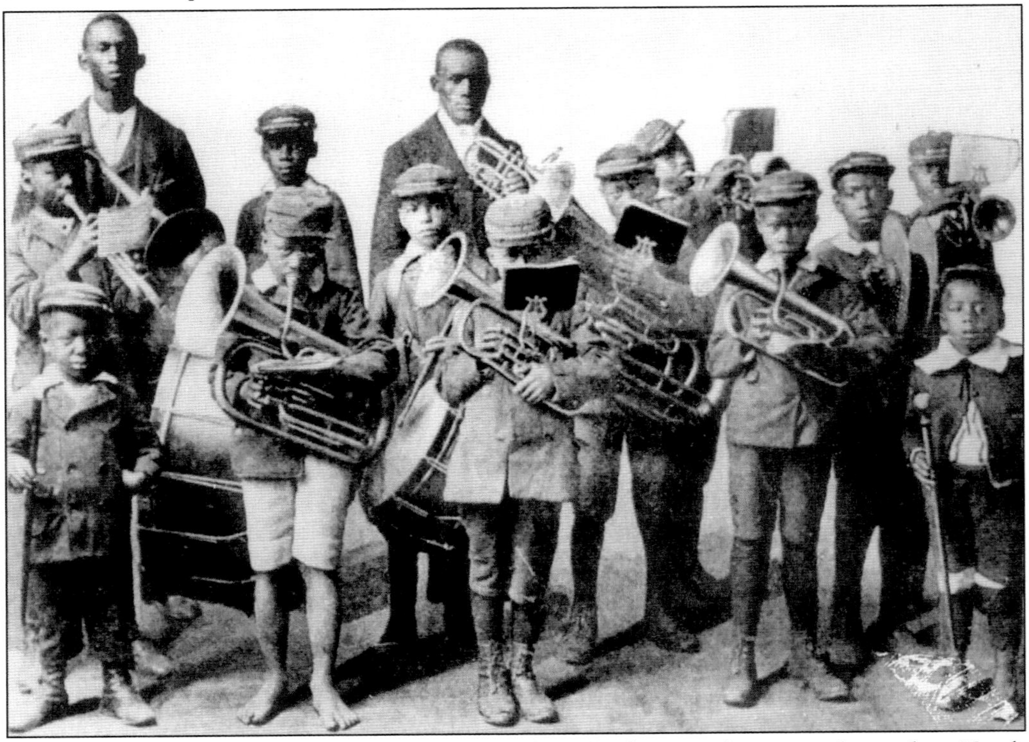

Rev. Daniel Joseph Jenkins, founder of the Jenkins Orphanage that was relocated to North Charleston, formed the Jenkins Orphanage Band as a means of raising urgently needed funds for his institution. The band also taught residents a skill they could use in the future. Jenkins focused on brass instruments because he felt blowing would help protect members from tuberculosis, which was epidemic. Pictured are the band members in the 1930s.

Three

A World War II Boomtown

More and more homes were constructed in North Charleston as the Buckfield and Chicora areas became more developed. West Virginia Pulp and Paper Company (WESTVACO) was established along the Cooper River and created more jobs for north area residents. As World War II and the military's presence increased, people flocked to the area. Major government housing developments were built to accommodate the navy yard workers. Liberty Homes, John C. Calhoun Homes, Palmetto Gardens, the Tom McMillan Homes, Ben Tillman Homes, and George Legare Homes formed new communities in North Charleston. The USO buildings at Park Circle and Liberty Hill, along with the prevalence of ships and sailors, added to the area's military appearance. The Navy Yard and the surrounding area became the center of the town and it was known as Navy Yard, South Carolina. Many high-ranking government officials visited North Charleston to promote the war effort and boost residents' morale. More schools and churches were built to provide outlets for learning and worship, as well as entertainment. Variety shows, beauty contests, sports, and various other productions were featured at the schools and churches. Supporting the military became a community effort. Civilian jobs ran the gamut from shipbuilding to serving as air raid wardens. After the war, many people opted to stay in the area and the population grew tremendously.

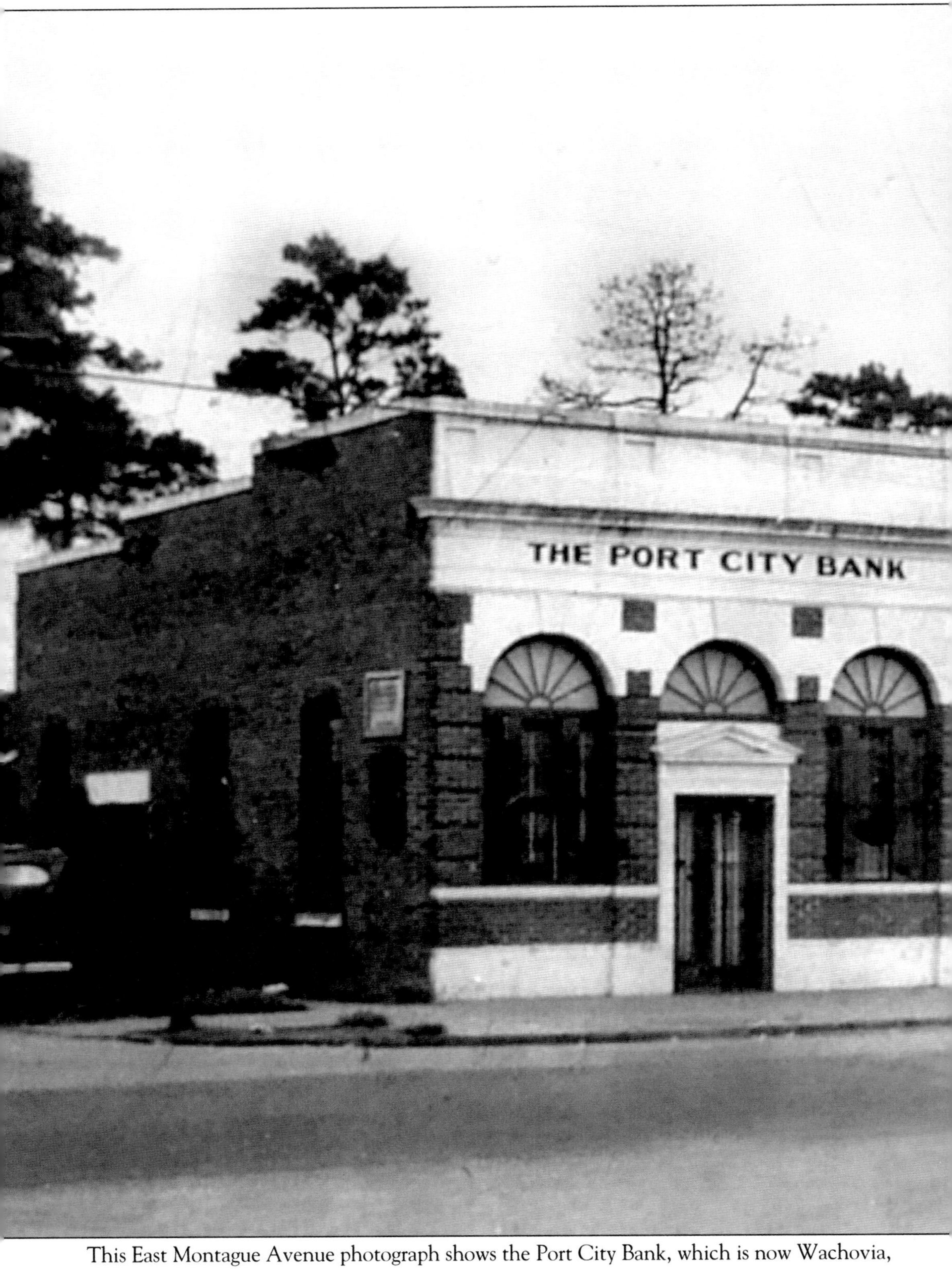

This East Montague Avenue photograph shows the Port City Bank, which is now Wachovia,

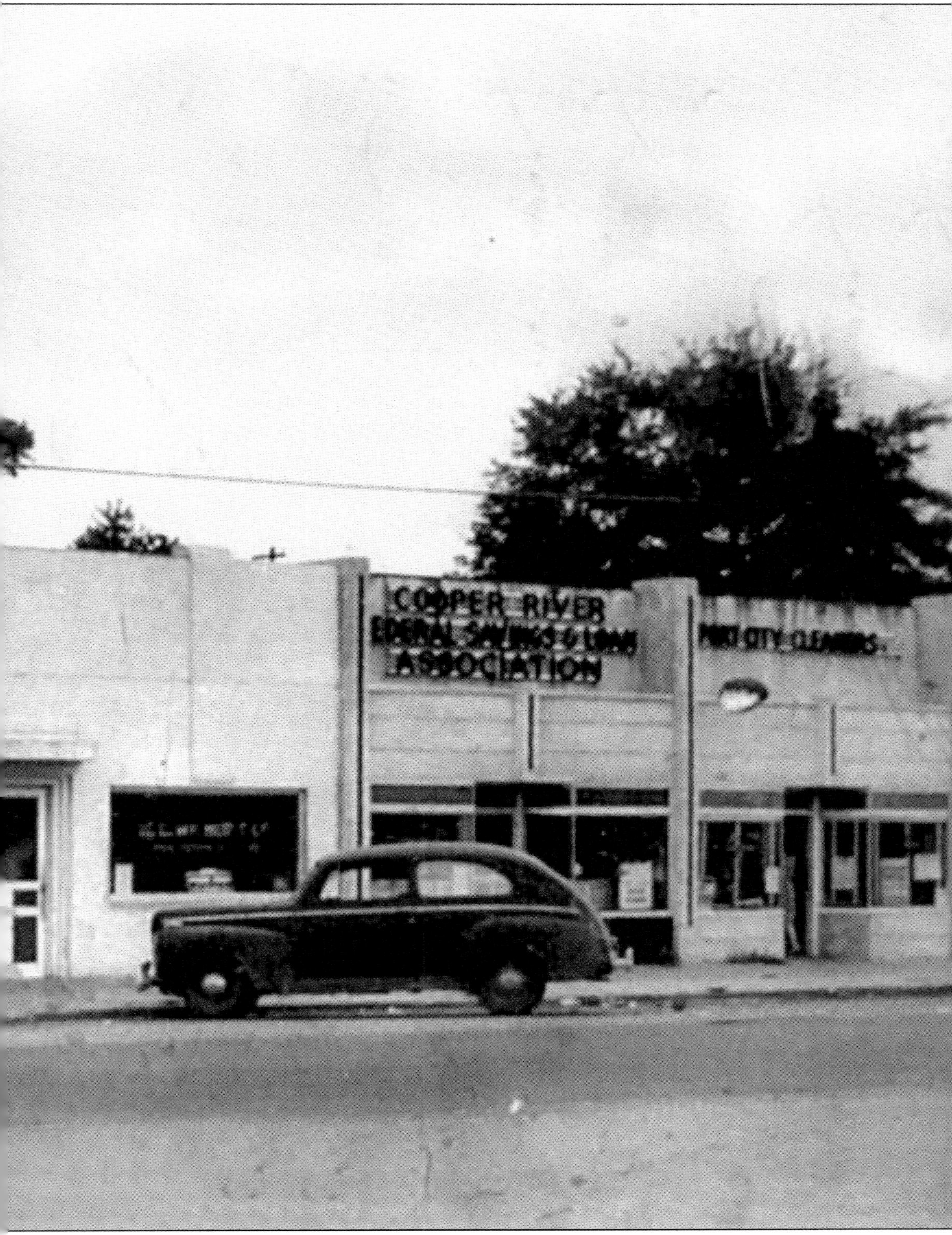

and W.C. Wilbur, which still exists. (Courtesy of the City of North Charleston.)

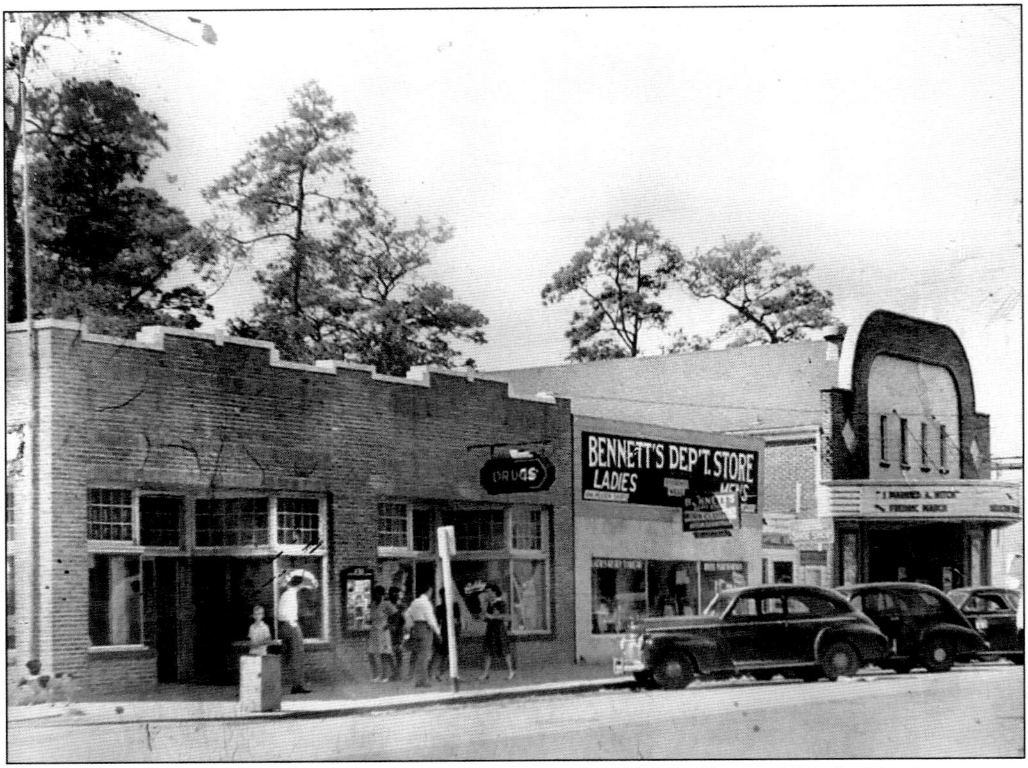

The Olde Village of North Charleston is pictured above in the 1940s. Neither Bennett's Department Store nor the Port City Theater exist today. (Courtesy of the North Charleston Heritage Corridor.)

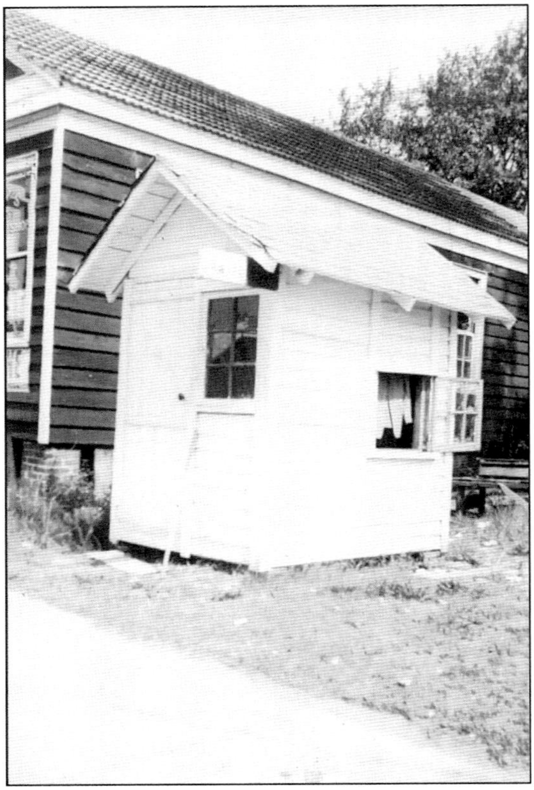

In the early 1940s, Edward D. Friday opened his law office in this little building on East Montague Avenue. Later he moved to the future location of the city's first City Hall Building. (Courtesy of Eleanor Attaway Fuller.)

Daire Griffith, the Navy Yard Recreation Association Beauty Contest winner, was chosen to be featured in this poster used nationwide during World War II. (Courtesy of Helen Blanton.)

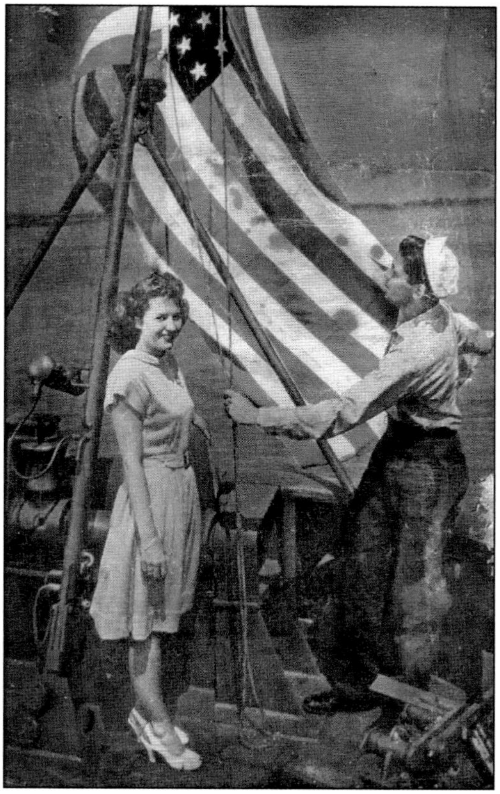

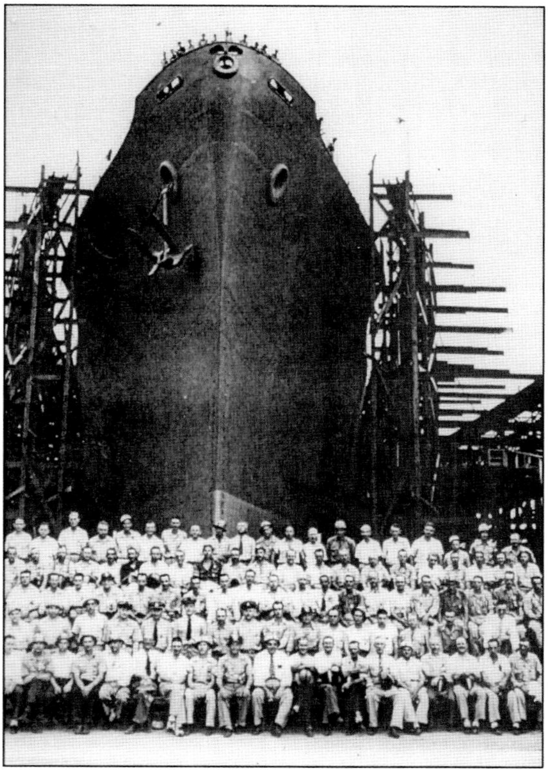

Before and during World War II, the Charleston Navy Yard experienced a long period of sustained growth. The expansion meant an increase in productivity and the construction of new ships. Pictured here are shipbuilders with a new ship. (Courtesy of The City of North Charleston.)

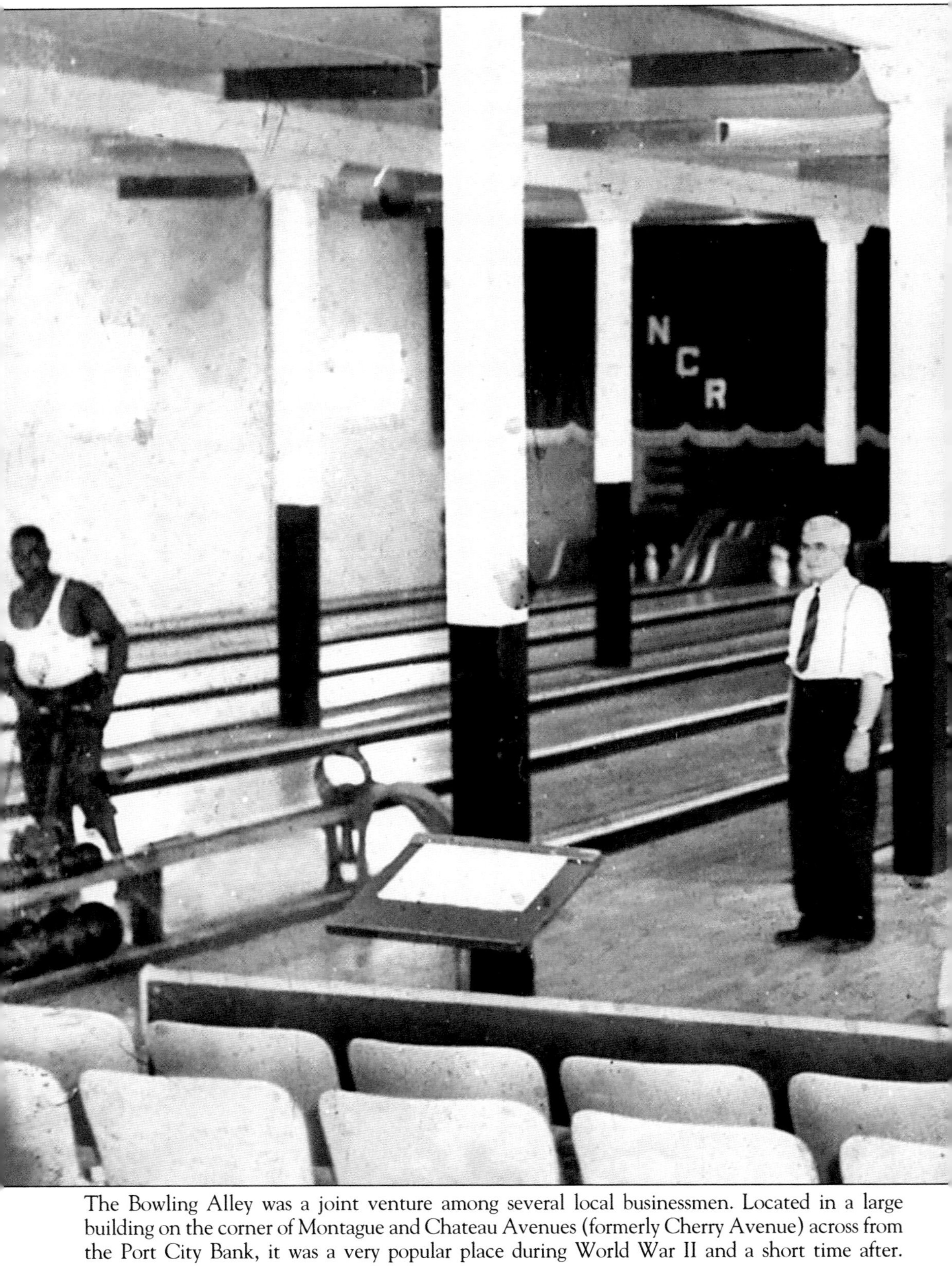

The Bowling Alley was a joint venture among several local businessmen. Located in a large building on the corner of Montague and Chateau Avenues (formerly Cherry Avenue) across from the Port City Bank, it was a very popular place during World War II and a short time after.

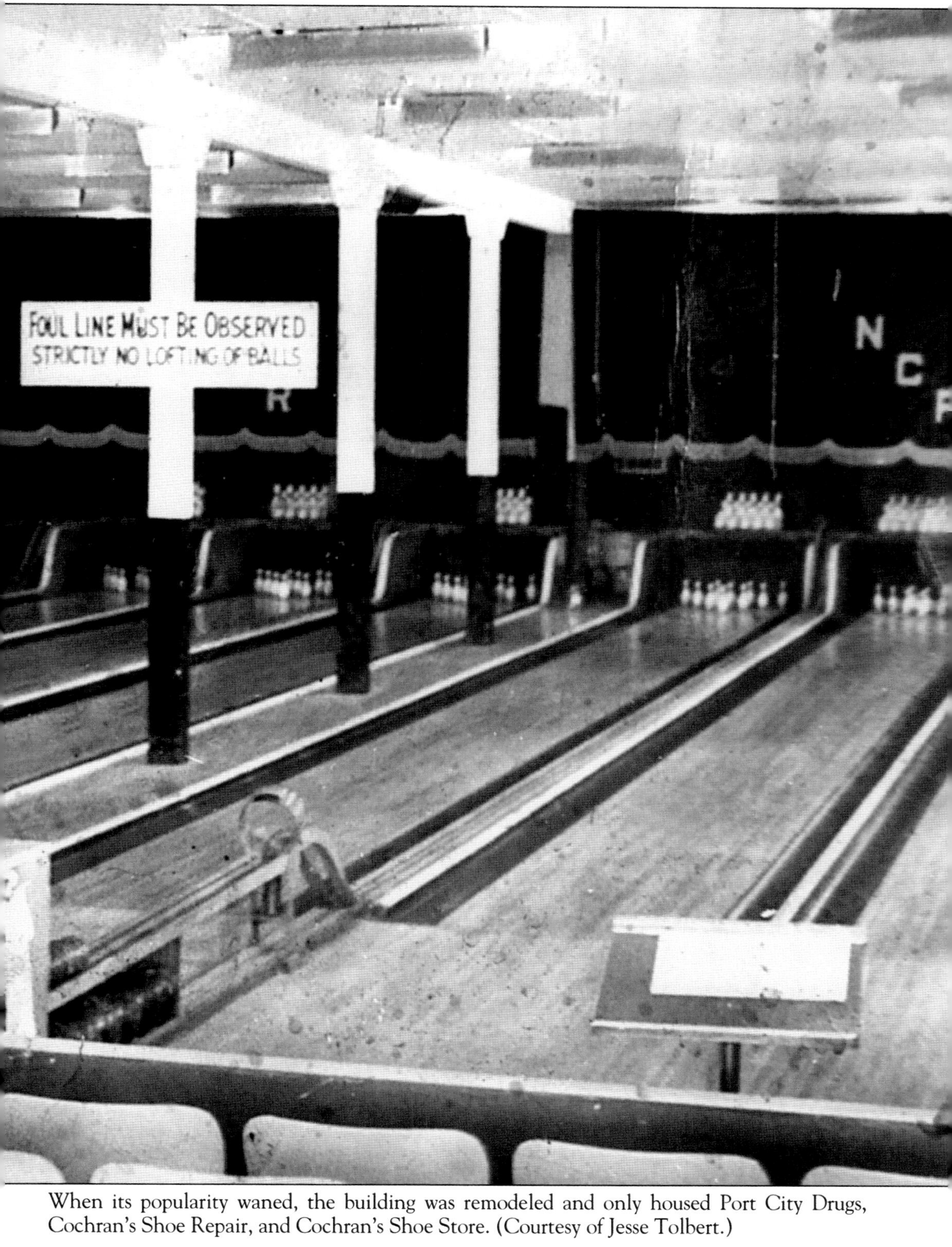

When its popularity waned, the building was remodeled and only housed Port City Drugs, Cochran's Shoe Repair, and Cochran's Shoe Store. (Courtesy of Jesse Tolbert.)

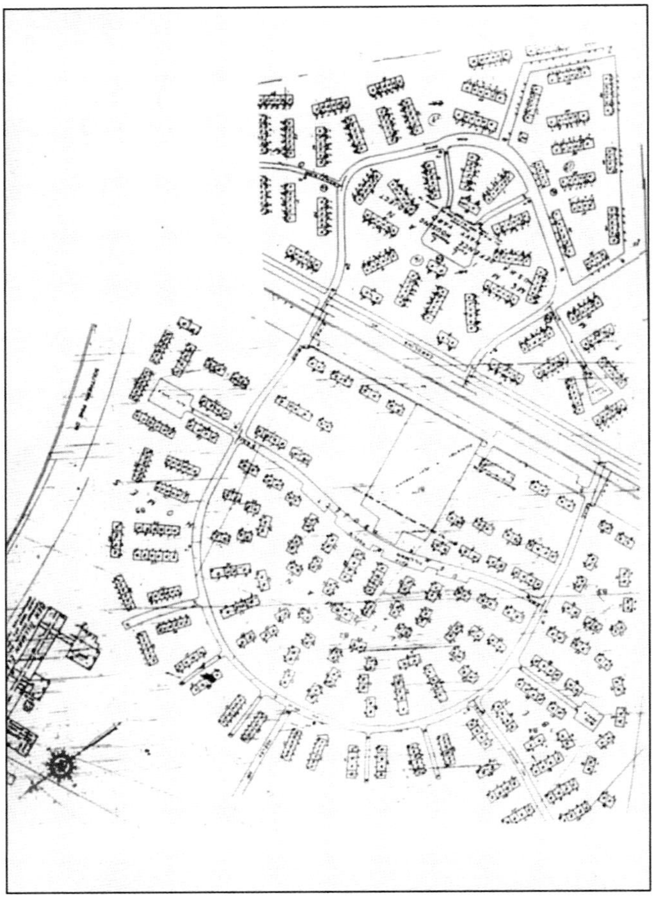

The Tom McMillan and Ben Tillman Homes were built to house many of the Navy Yard's employees during World War II. This 1941 map shows where each of the homes were located. (Courtesy of the City of North Charleston.)

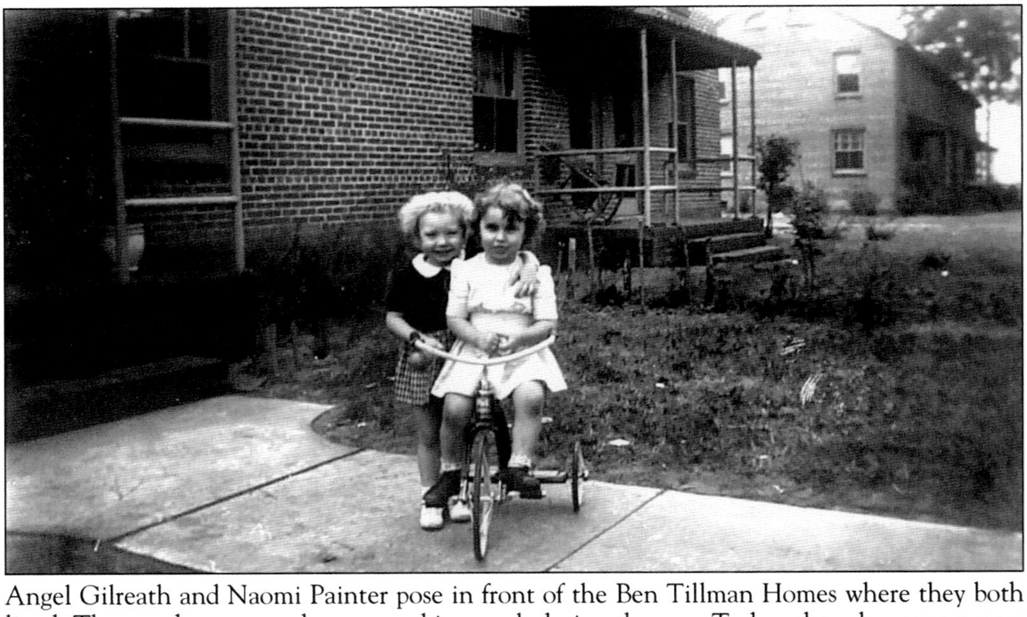

Angel Gilreath and Naomi Painter pose in front of the Ben Tillman Homes where they both lived. Thousands came to the area seeking work during the war. Today, these houses are now the River Place Apartments. (Courtesy of Edith Painter.)

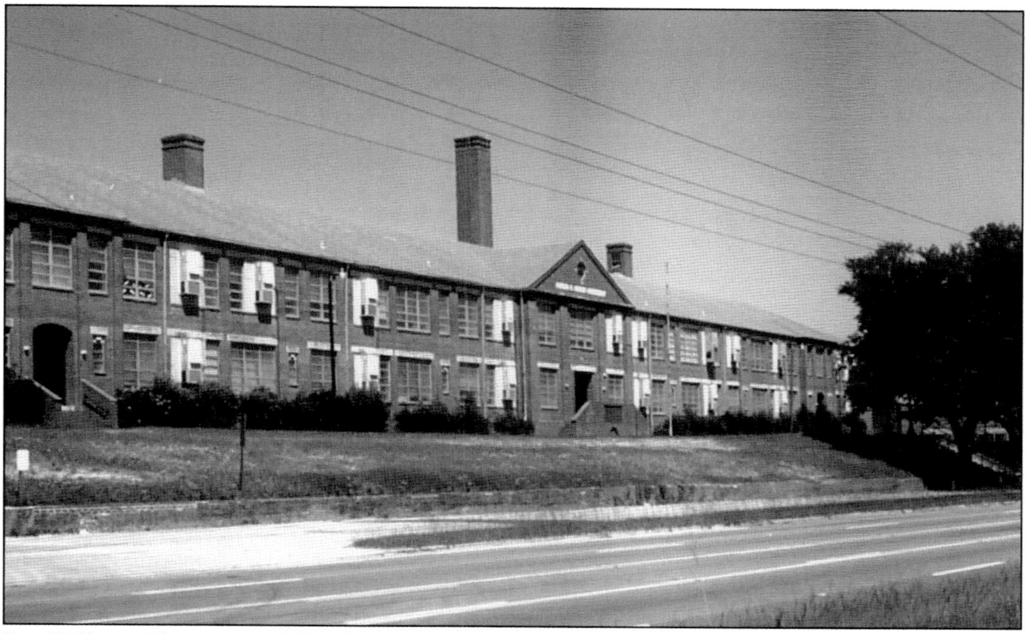

Ben Tillman Elementary School opened in 1943 and was the center of the community, since its large auditorium was used for many meetings, shows, and other public events. (Courtesy of the City of North Charleston.)

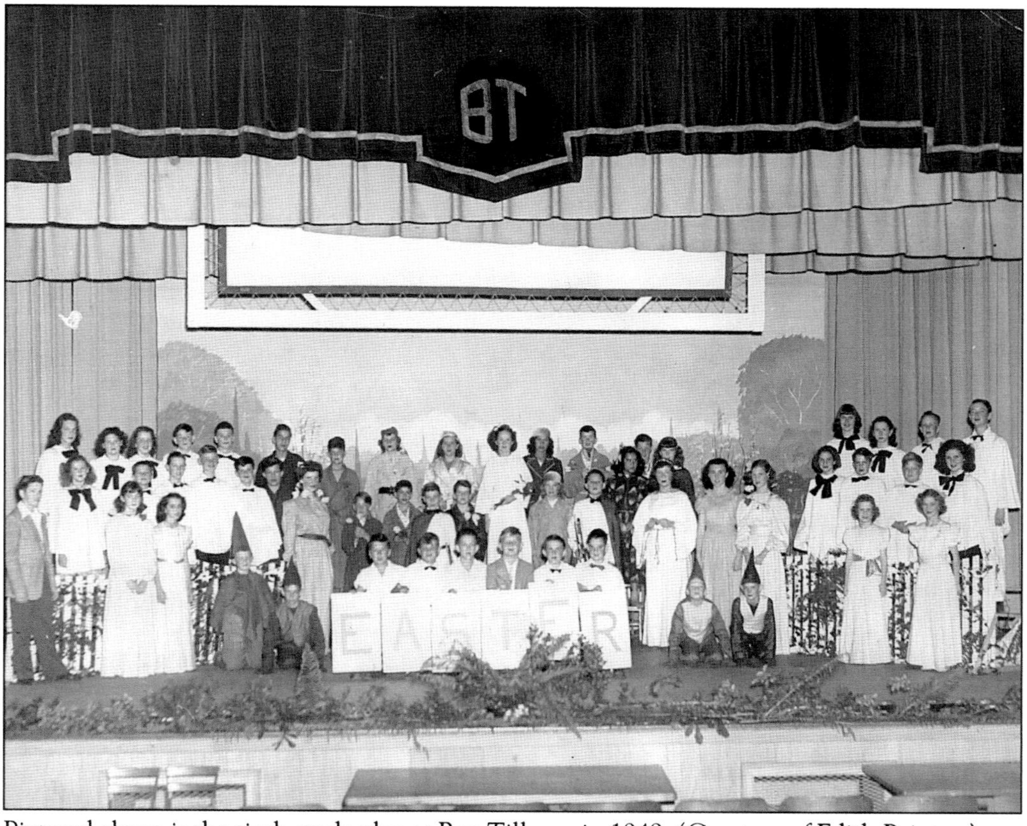

Pictured above is the sixth grade play at Ben Tillman in 1949. (Courtesy of Edith Painter.)

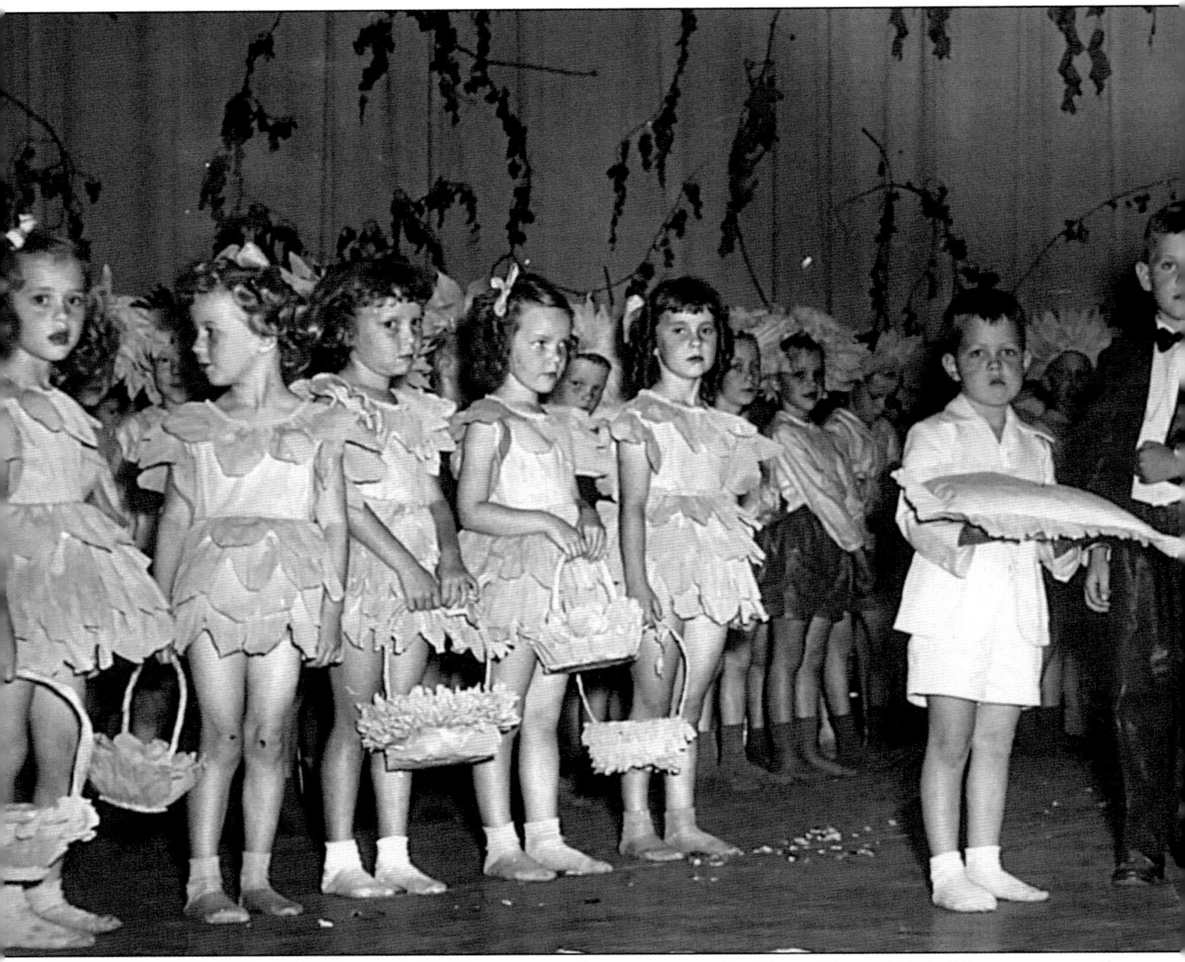

The children in the photograph above are taking part in the Tom Thumb Wedding presented

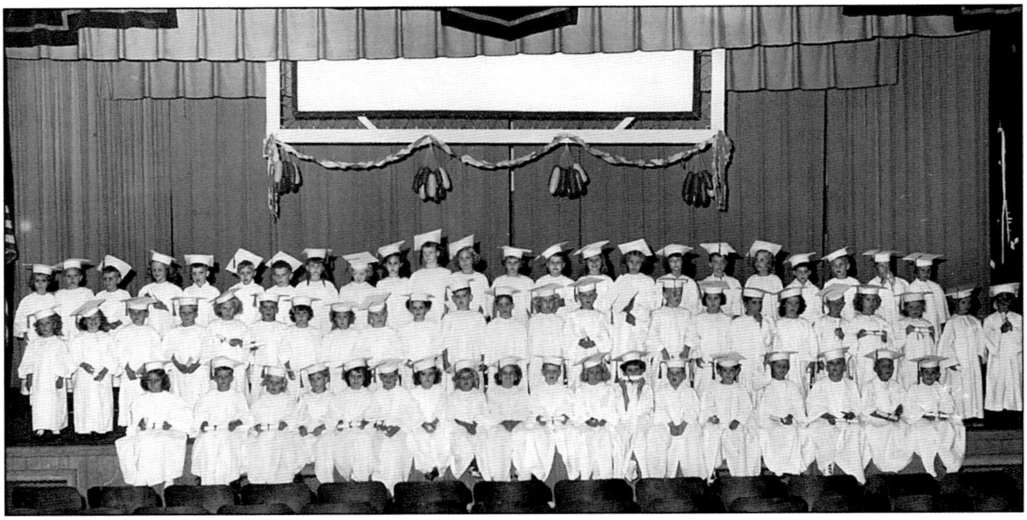

The George Legare Kindergarten graduation is seen above in this late 1940s photograph. (Courtesy of Edith Painter.)

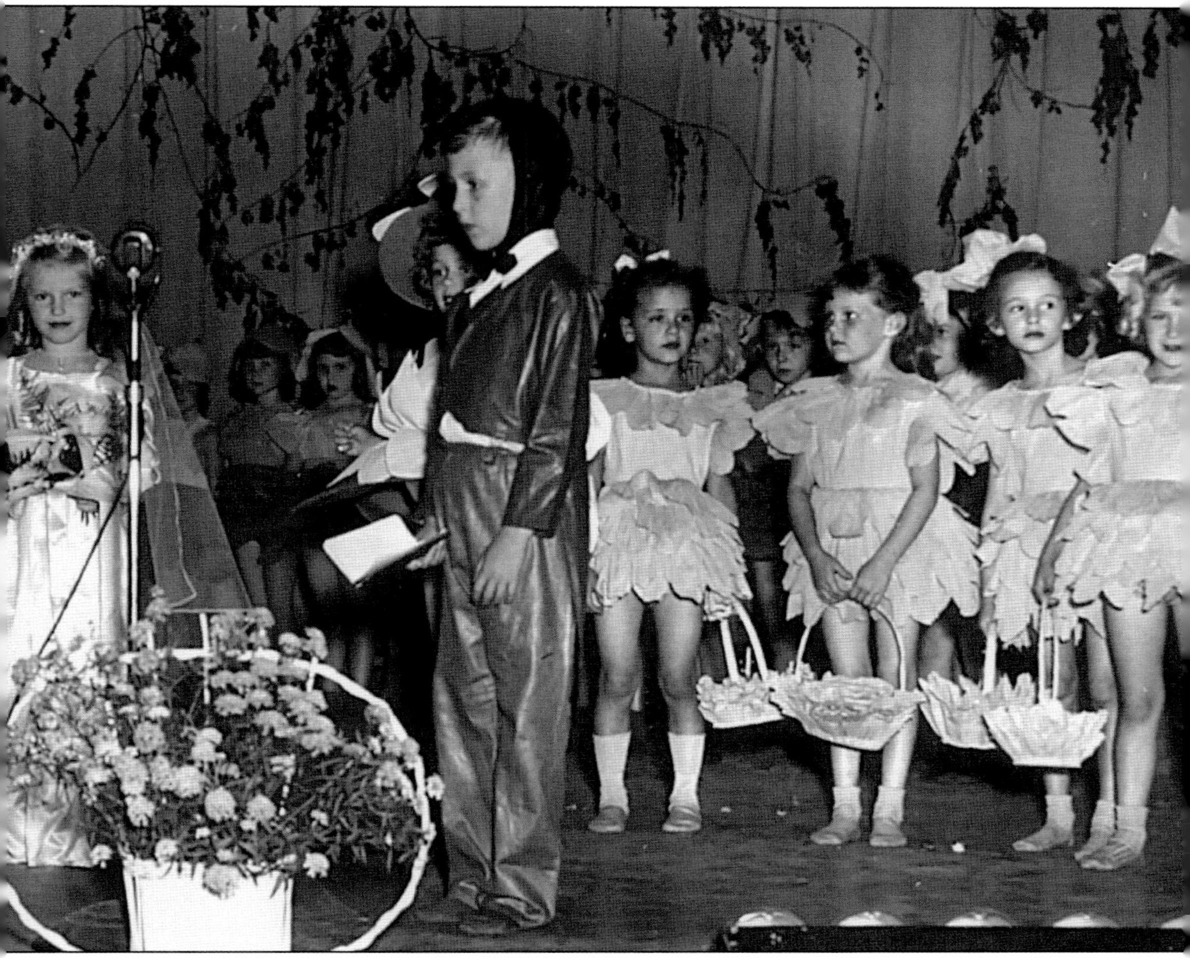

by the Ben Tillman school. (Courtesy of Edith Painter.)

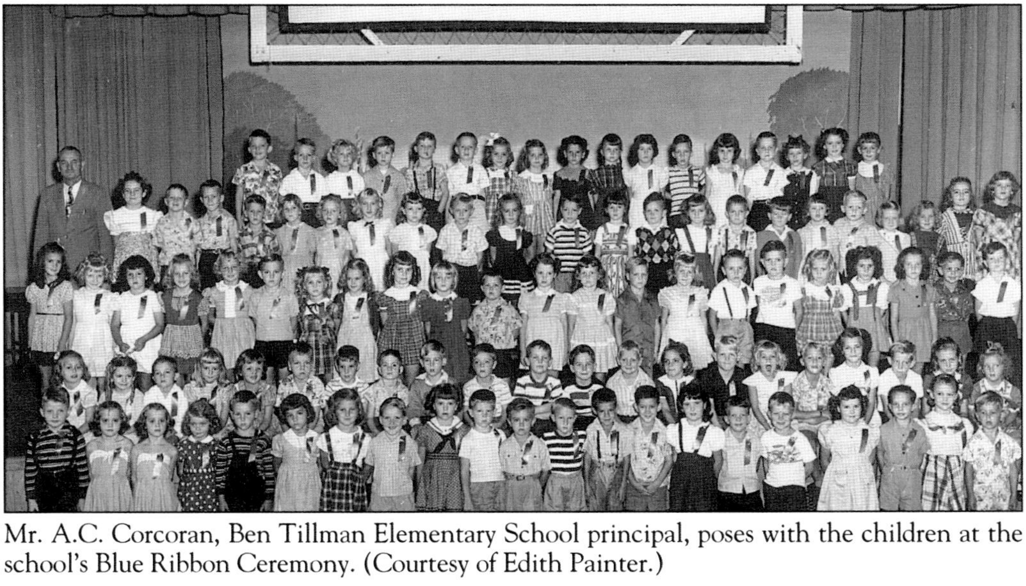

Mr. A.C. Corcoran, Ben Tillman Elementary School principal, poses with the children at the school's Blue Ribbon Ceremony. (Courtesy of Edith Painter.)

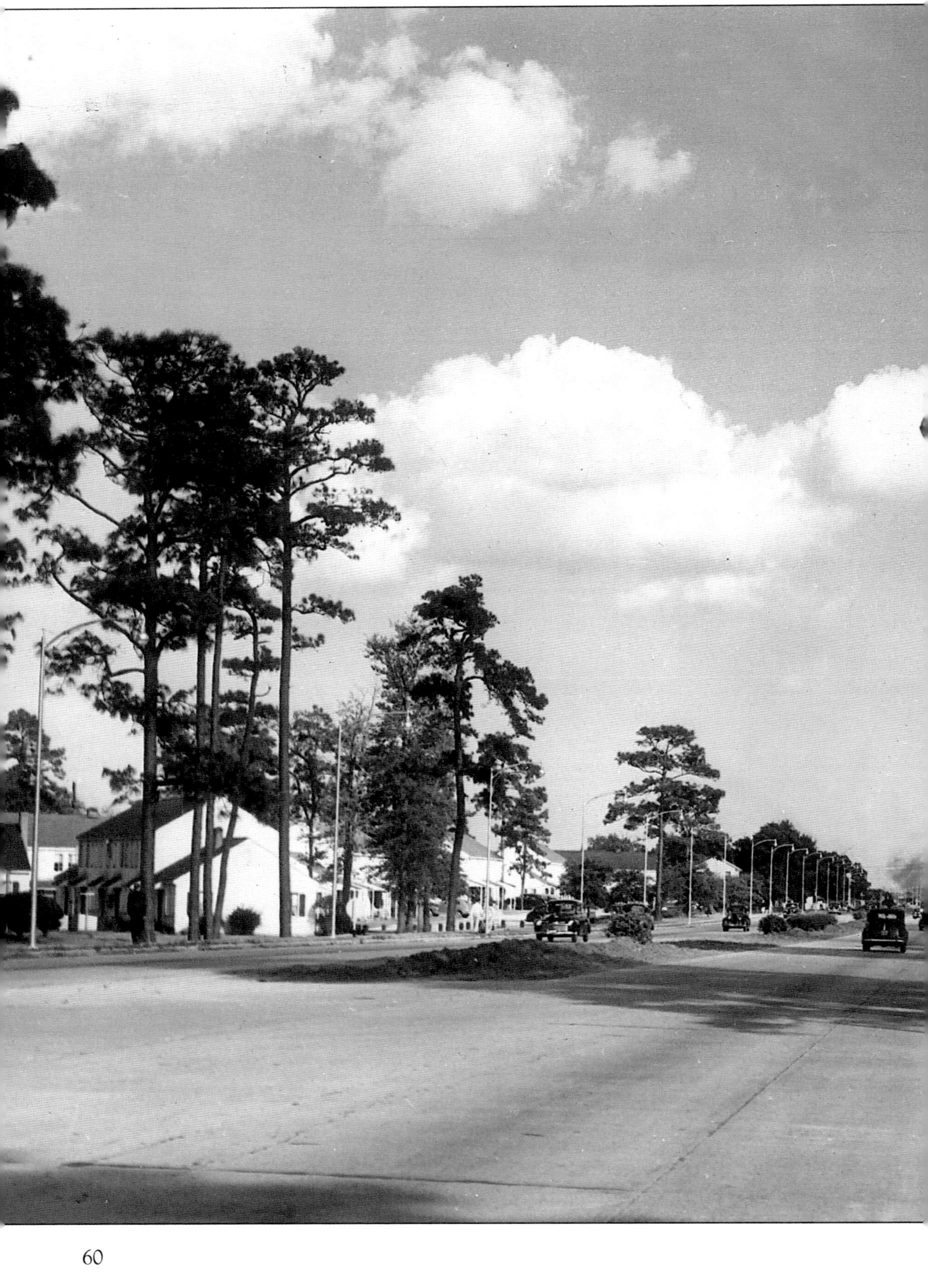

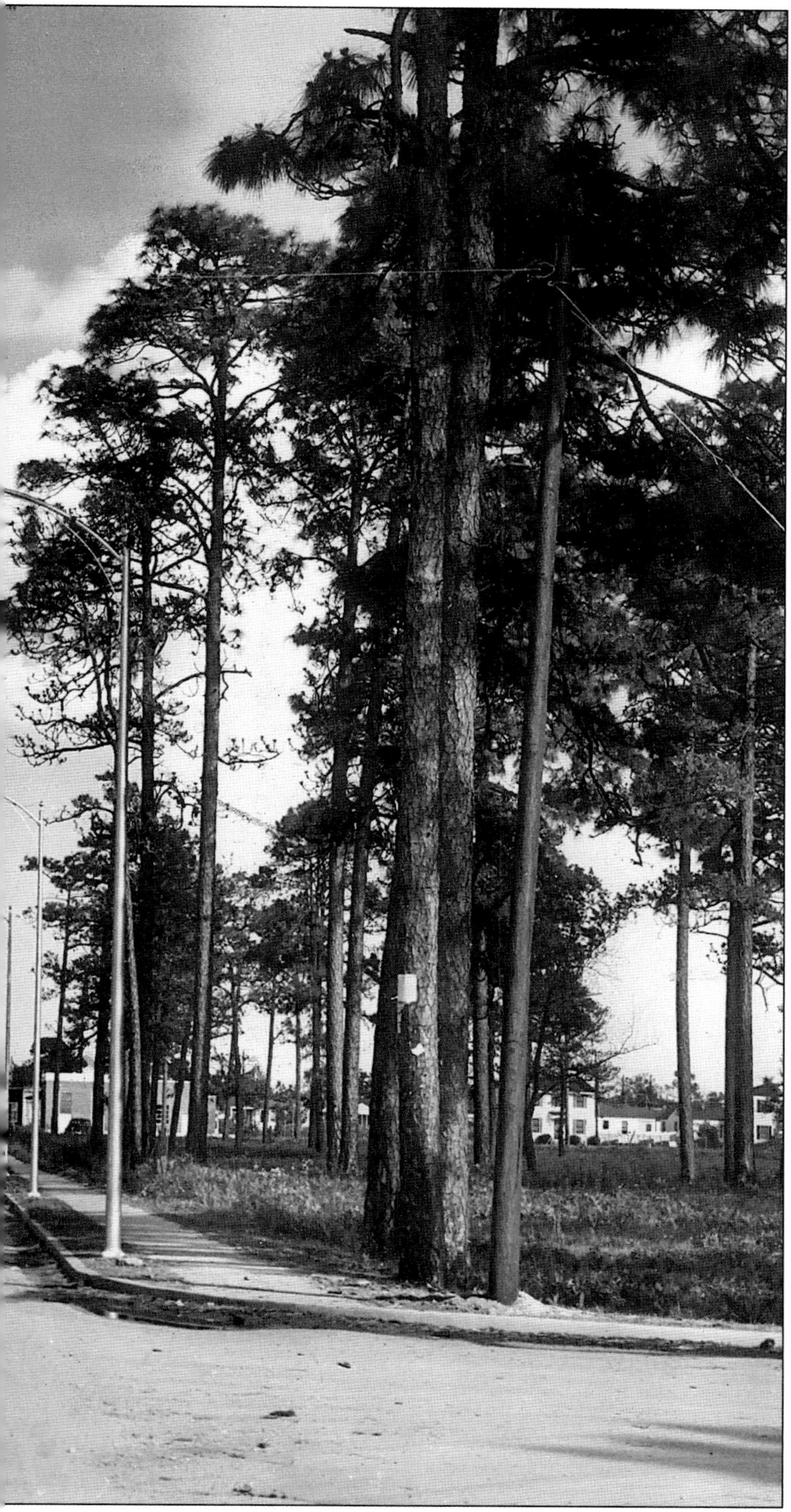

After streetlights were installed in the early 1940s, people referred to Rivers Avenue as "The Great White Way." Pictured is the corner of Rivers and McMillan Avenues. Note the Tom McMillan Homes on the left. (Courtesy of Helen Blanton.)

The North Charleston
Junior Chamber of
Commerce

Presents

Big Stage Show

MINSTRELS and FOLLIES

One Hundred "100" Local Talent

For Benefit of

Cooper River District Band

Ben Tillman School---Two Nights April 21 & 22

Professionally Staged and Produced by Lew Van
of New York City

Occasionally, the Junior Chamber of Commerce employed the use of the Ben Tillman School as a location for benefits. This flyer was used at a show, organized by the chamber, that helped the Cooper River District Band.

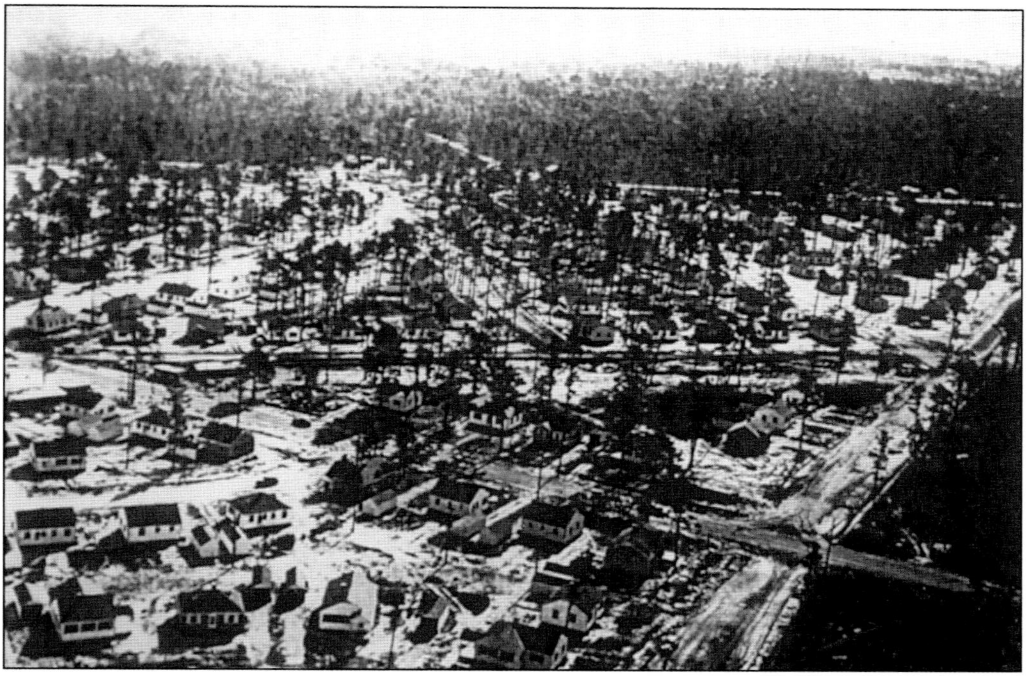

Palmetto Gardens was developed as military housing during World War II. Many of the servicemen continued to live and work in the area after the war and purchased these homes. Palmetto Gardens was then integrated as a neighborhood into the larger Park Circle area. (Courtesy of Ruth Cupp.)

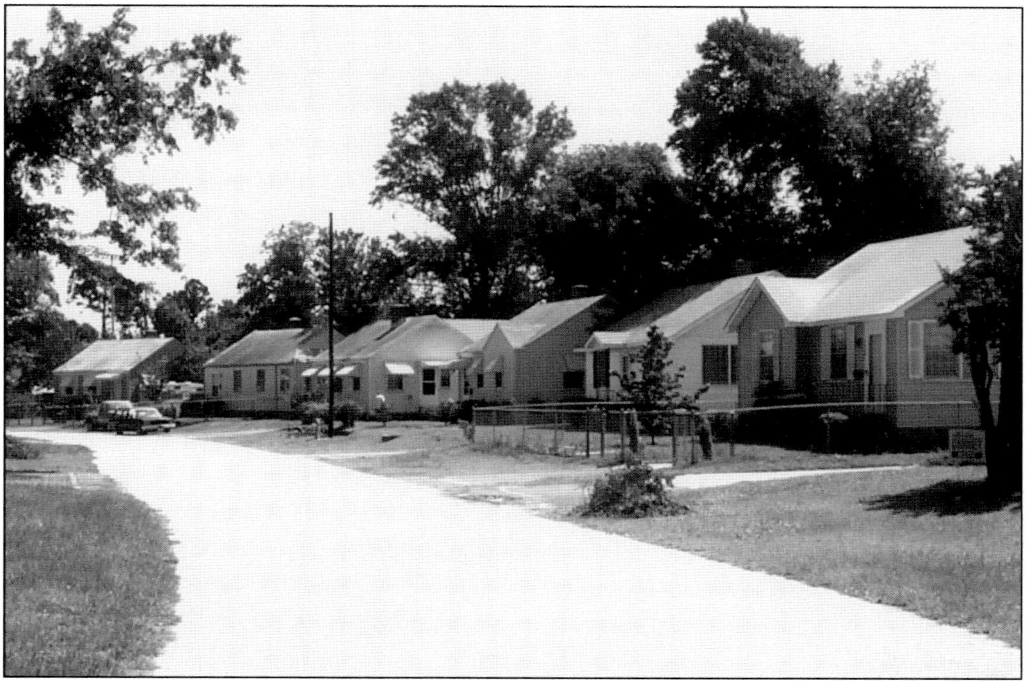

Pictured above are houses in the Palmetto Gardens area today. Many of the original buyers still live here. (Courtesy of Ruth Cupp.)

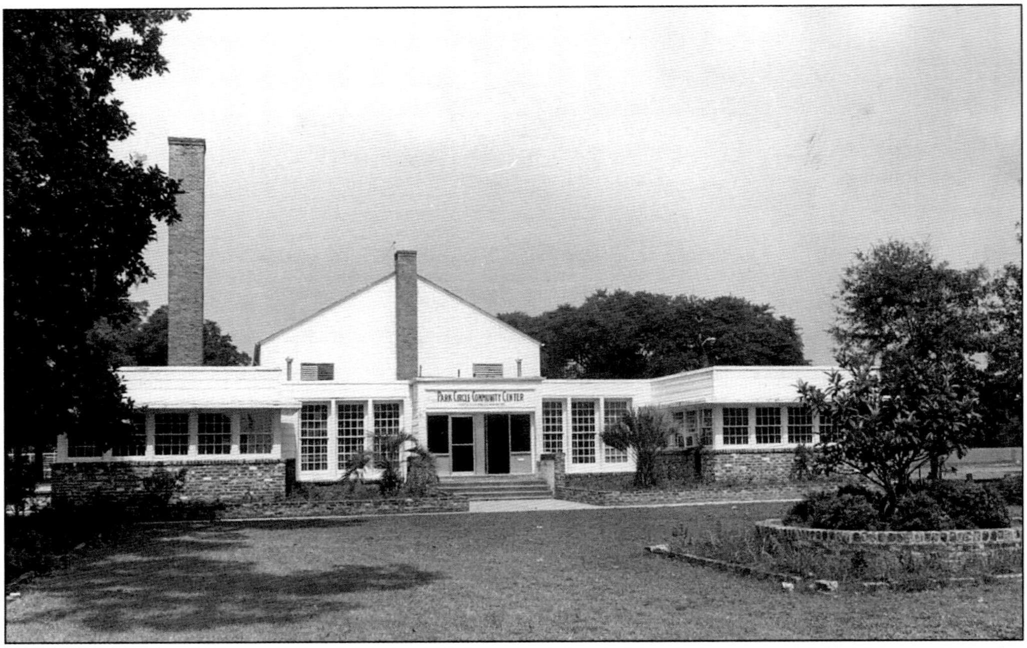

Erected in 1942 at Park Circle, the USO operated as an entertainment and fellowship center for military men and their families. Cooper River Parks and Playgrounds Commission bought it in 1945. It was remodeled in 1962 and again in 1990 after Hurricane Hugo. Later named the Felix Davis Community Center, it is still the hub of many social and community activities and houses the North Charleston Recreation Department. (Courtesy of *The Post and Courier*.)

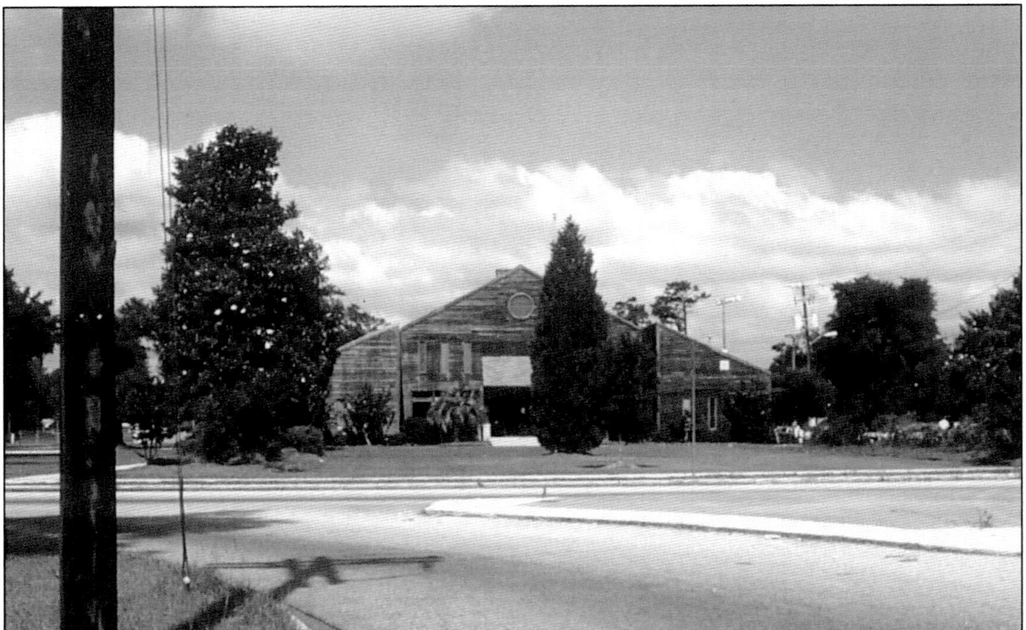

The Felix Davis Community Center is shown as it appears today. Because Hurricane Hugo severely damaged the building in 1989, it was remolded by the Air Force Reserve. (Courtesy of the City of North Charleston.)

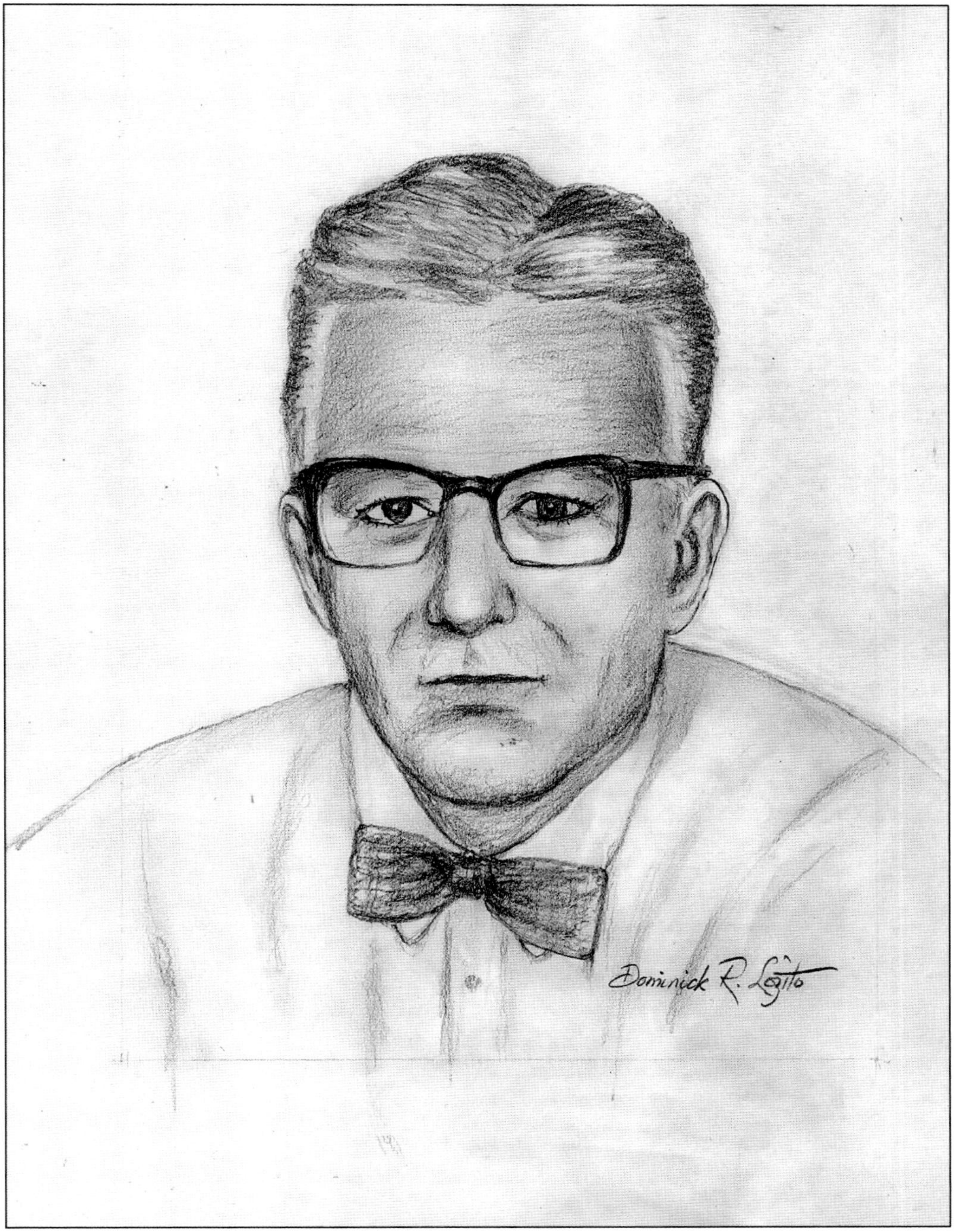

Danny Jones, pictured in this drawing by Dominick Lozito, served for many years as the recreation director of the Cooper River Parks and Playgrounds Commission beginning in 1945. (Courtesy of the North Charleston Recreation Department.)

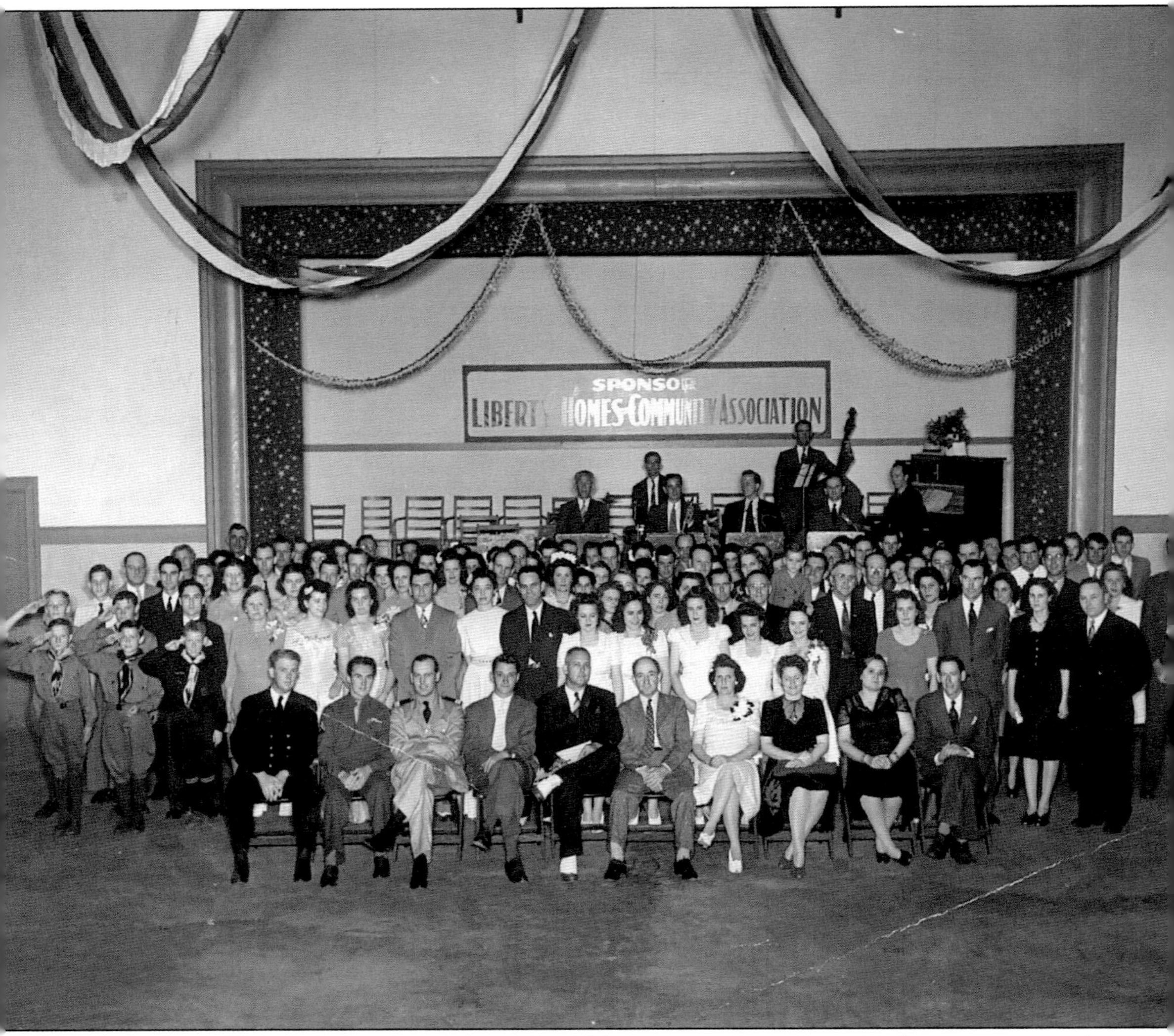

Liberty Homes was constructed during World War II as a government housing project for shipyard workers. It was later sold to the Liberty Homes Corporation, a group comprised of people who lived in the dwellings. The Liberty Homes Community Association is pictured above in the 1940s. In the early 1990s, Liberty Homes was sold and is now privately owned. The new owners eventually changed the development's name to Century Oaks. (Courtesy of Rosemary Moore.)

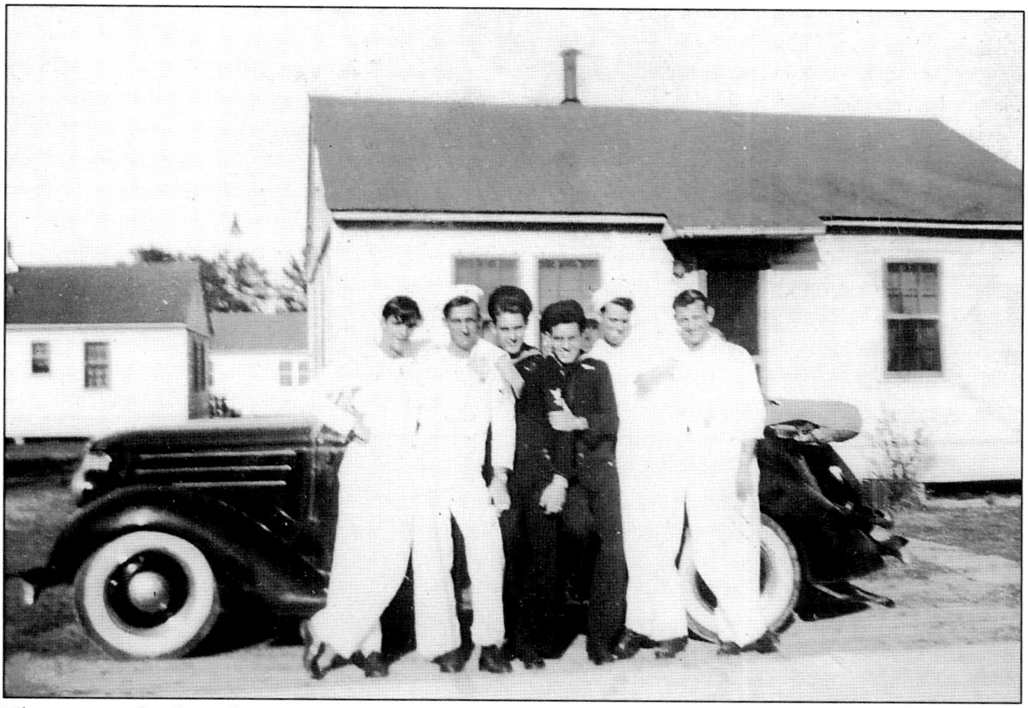

The group of sailors above were stationed at the Charleston Naval Base during the war. They are pictured in front of the Liberty Home that one of them occupied during their stay. (Courtesy of Ellen Lewin.)

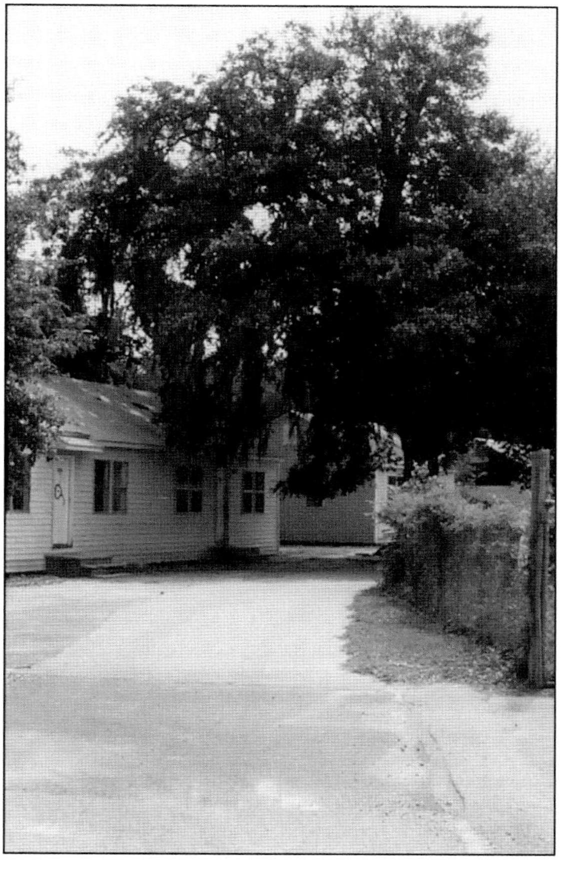

Pictured on the right is the Century Oaks subdivision today. (Courtesy of the City of North Charleston.)

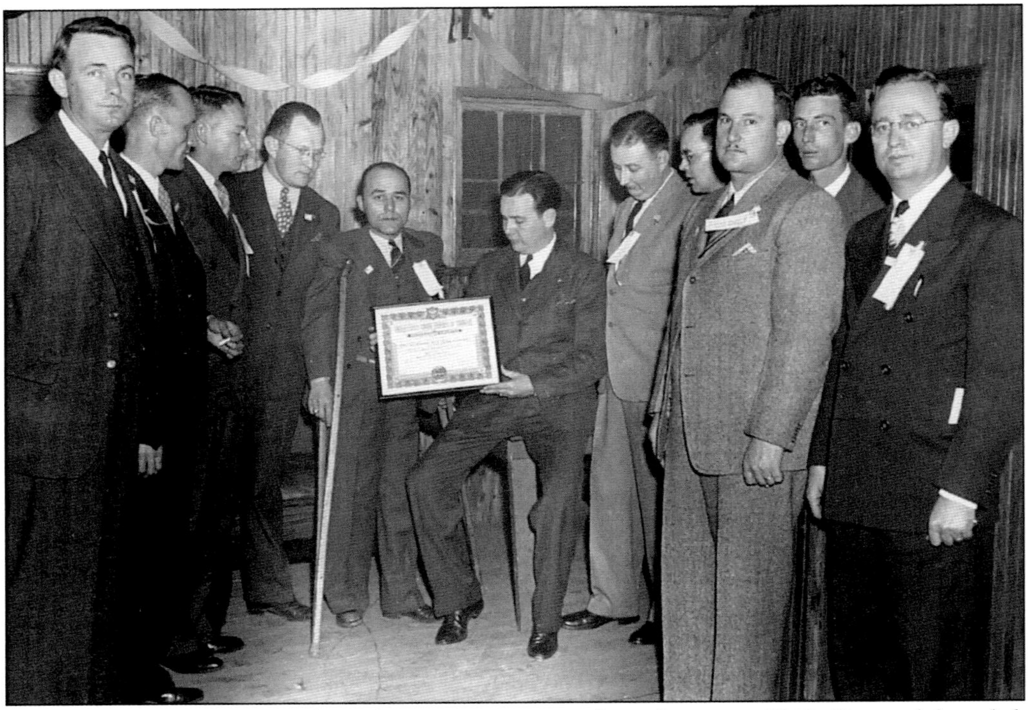

The Suburban Junior Chamber of Commerce received its charter in 1943. Pictured from left to right are J.W. Stewart, financial secretary; E.P. Blanton, second vice president; D.E. Likes, recording secretary; W.L. Spruill, treasurer; R. Harry Morse, first vice-president; Arthur H. Burton, president; E.C. Hough, State Jaycee president; W.L. Poplin, Daniel G. Varner, and Joseph Sullivan, directors; and H.L. Corder, national councilor. (Courtesy of Helen Blanton.)

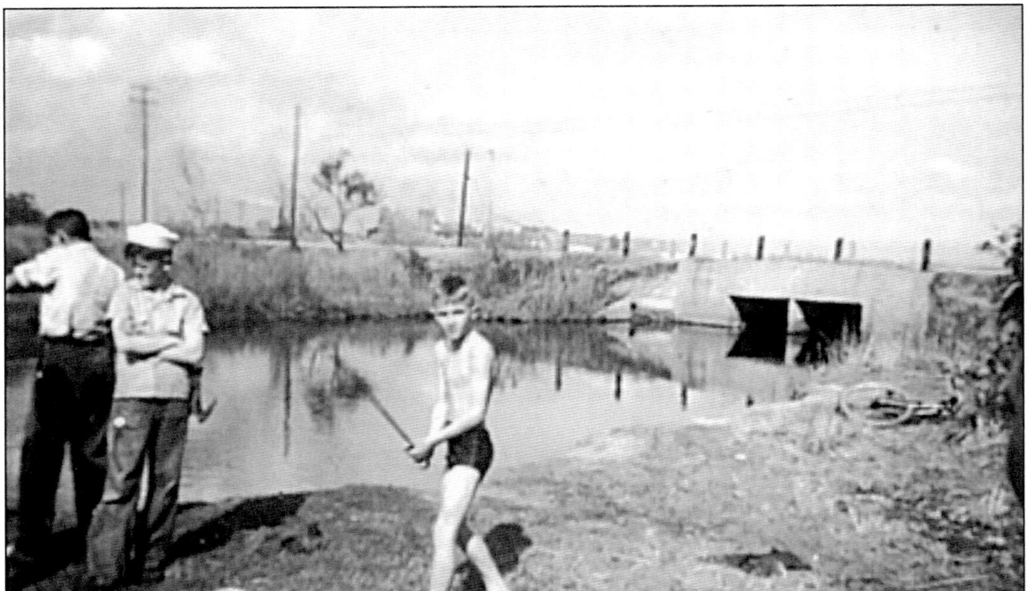

North Charleston had several swimming holes in the 1940s. Young Bobby Ashby's choice for a cool dip was Reed's Creek during the summer of 1942. Many chose this particular spot when the dock at Oak Dean Compress was too busy for swimmers. (Courtesy of Ruth Cupp.)

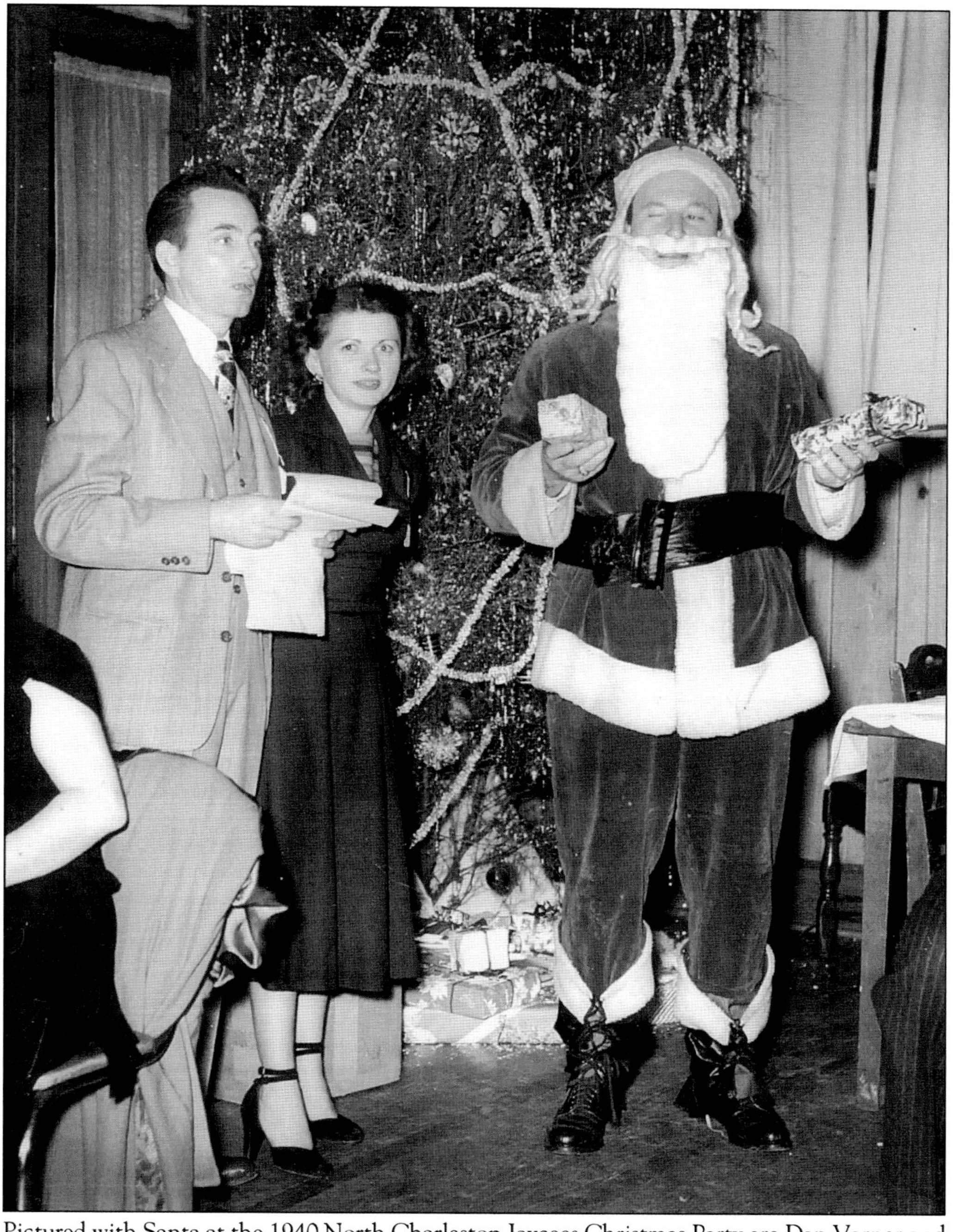

Pictured with Santa at the 1940 North Charleston Jaycees Christmas Party are Dan Varner and Dorothy Pop. (Photo Courtesy of Helen Blanton.)

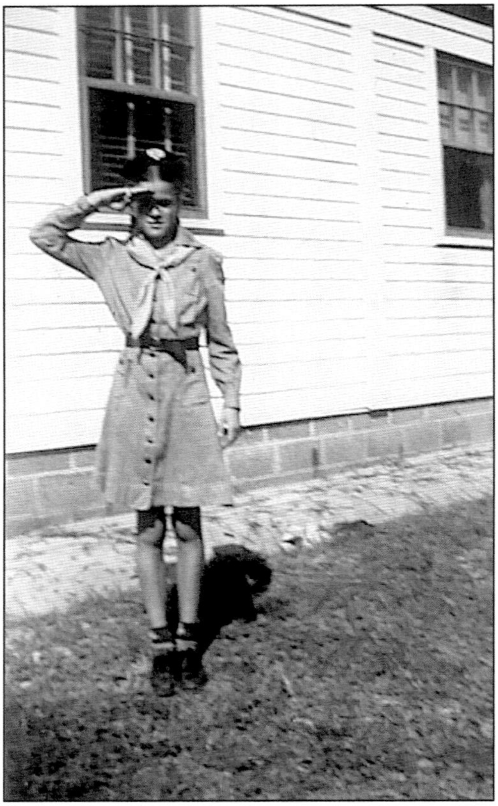

Former City Councilwoman Patsey Hughes salutes for the camera in her Girl Scouts uniform in the early 1940s beside the John C. Calhoun Homes. (Courtesy of Ruth Cupp.)

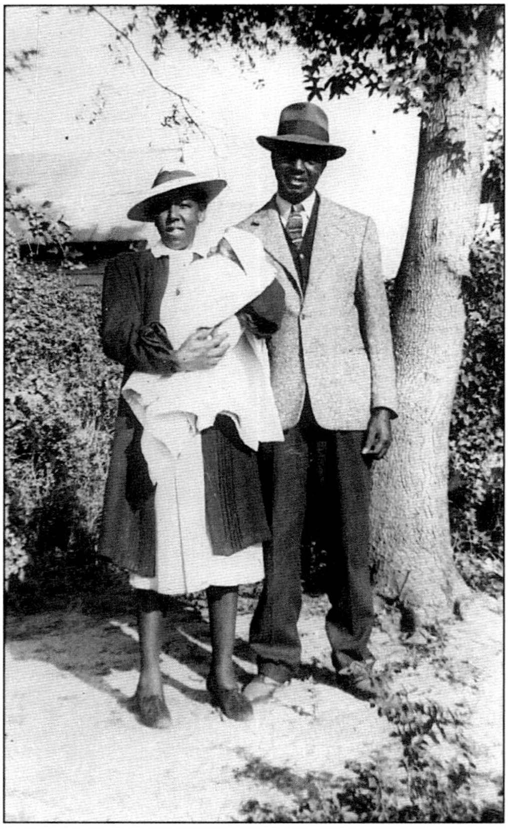

Arnold and Wilhelmena Lecque pose with their newest child, Carolyn, at Liberty Hill in 1941. (Courtesy of Carolyn Lecque.)

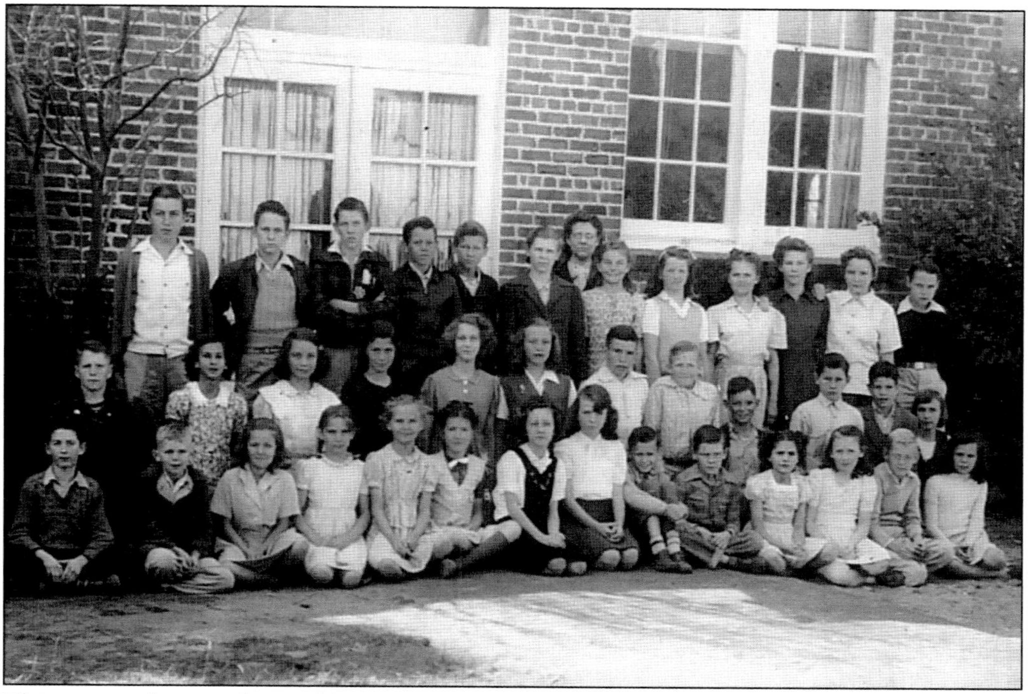

This picture shows a class in 1941 at Midland Park Elementary, which is still operating today. (Courtesy of Bill Mazyck.)

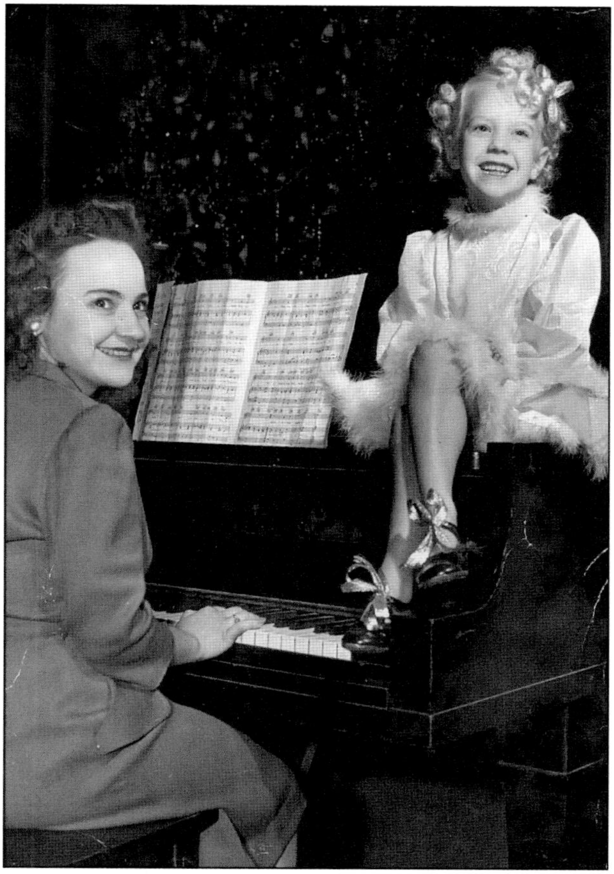

In 1944, many local talents performed for the men and their families stationed in North Charleston. Pictured are Mrs. Ruby Moore and her daughter Rosemary as they entertain at Sterret Hall on the former Naval Base. (Courtesy of Rosemary Moore.)

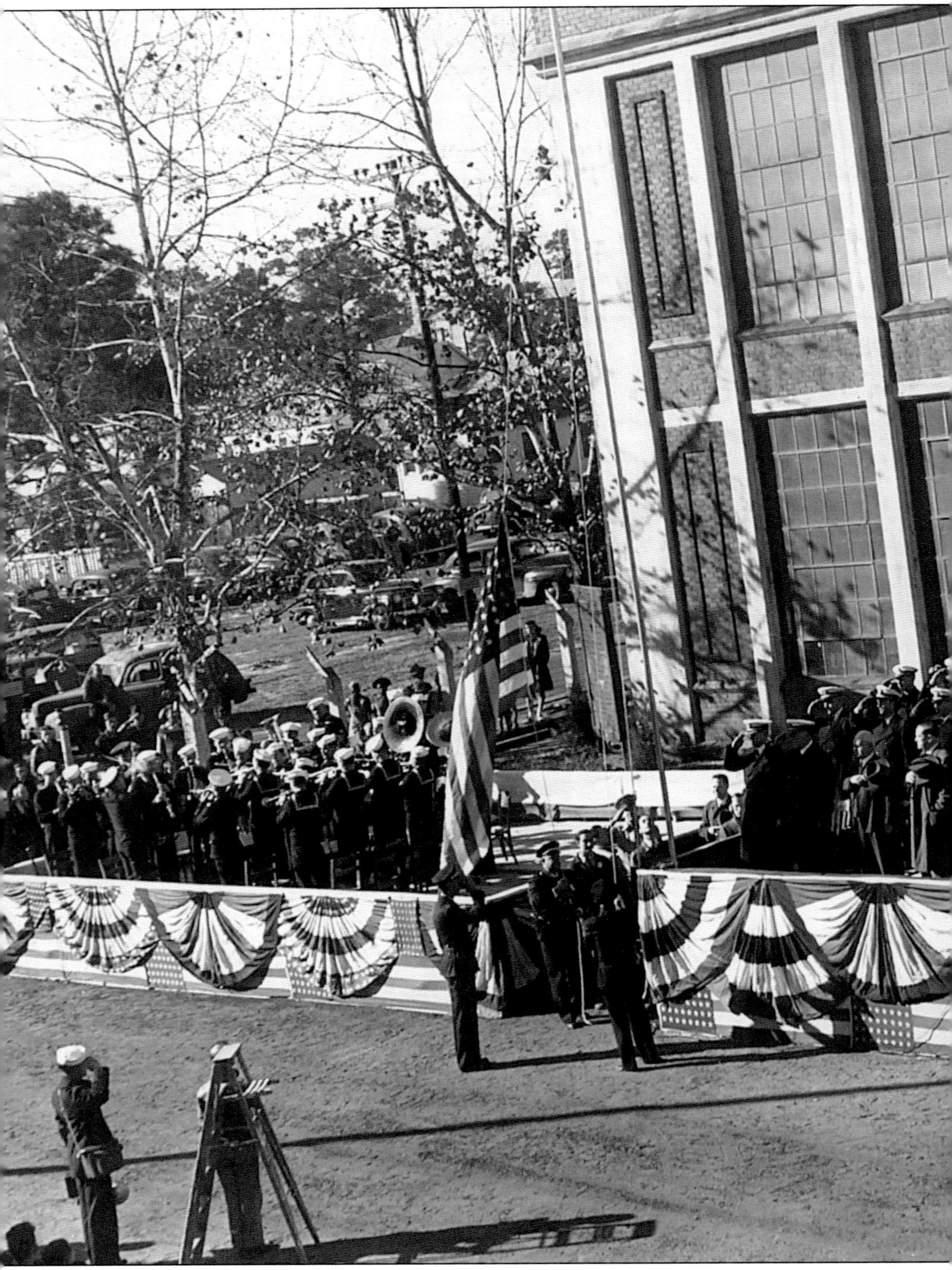

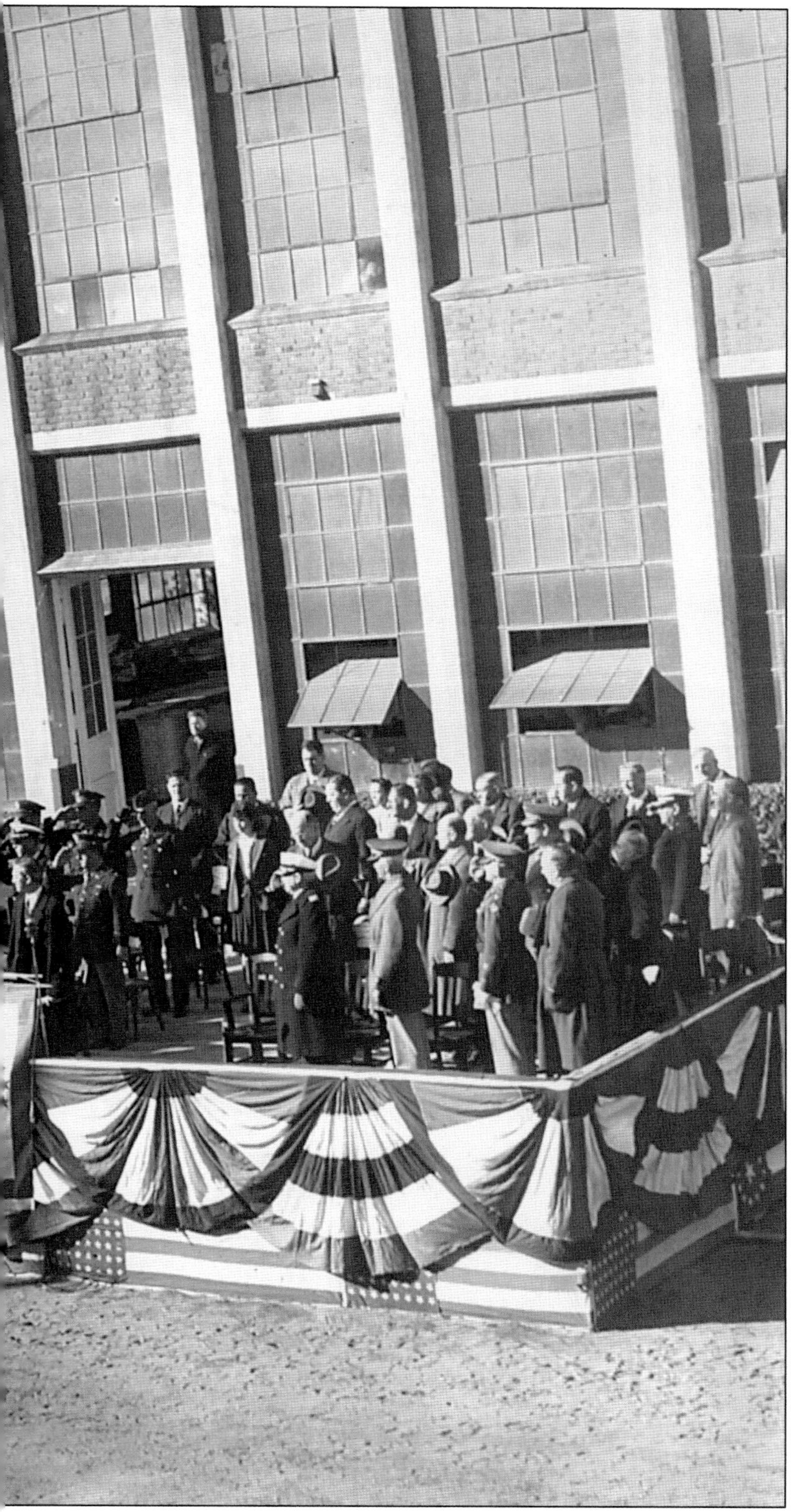

Garco received the Army/Navy "E" Award for their performance during World War II. (Courtesy of Launa Thompson.)

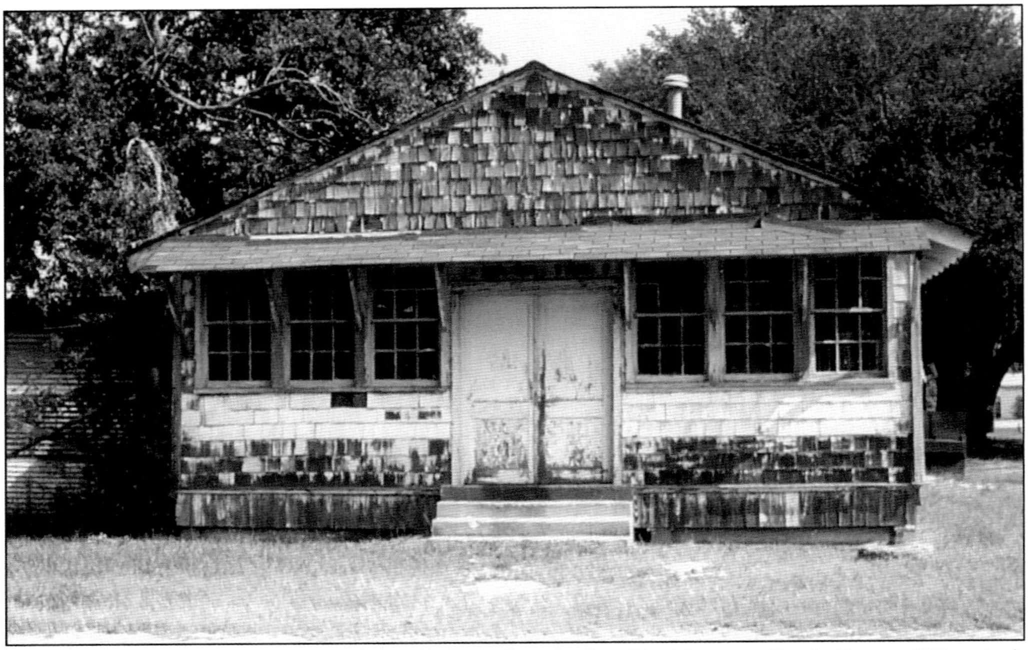

During World War II, the Army literally built hundreds of buildings at Stark General Hospital. Pictured above is one of the Stark Army Hospital's buildings. Many of the buildings still stand and are used today at Stark Industrial Park. (Courtesy of the City of North Charleston.)

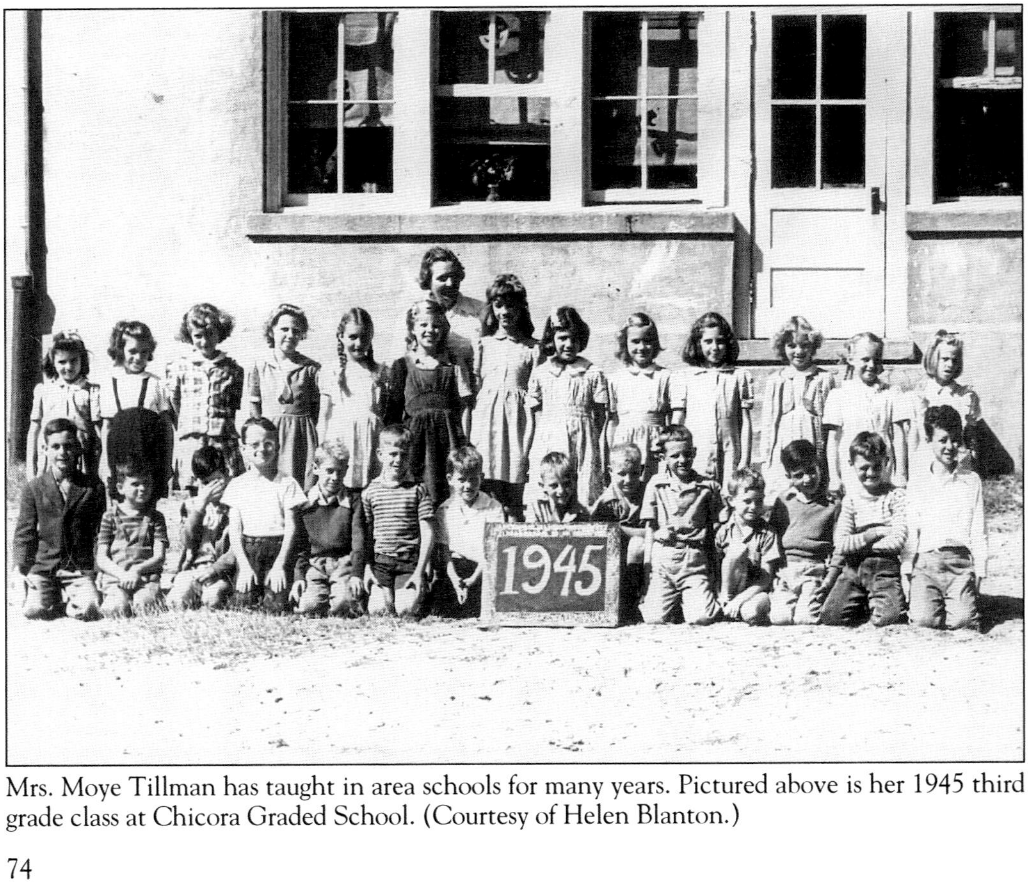

Mrs. Moye Tillman has taught in area schools for many years. Pictured above is her 1945 third grade class at Chicora Graded School. (Courtesy of Helen Blanton.)

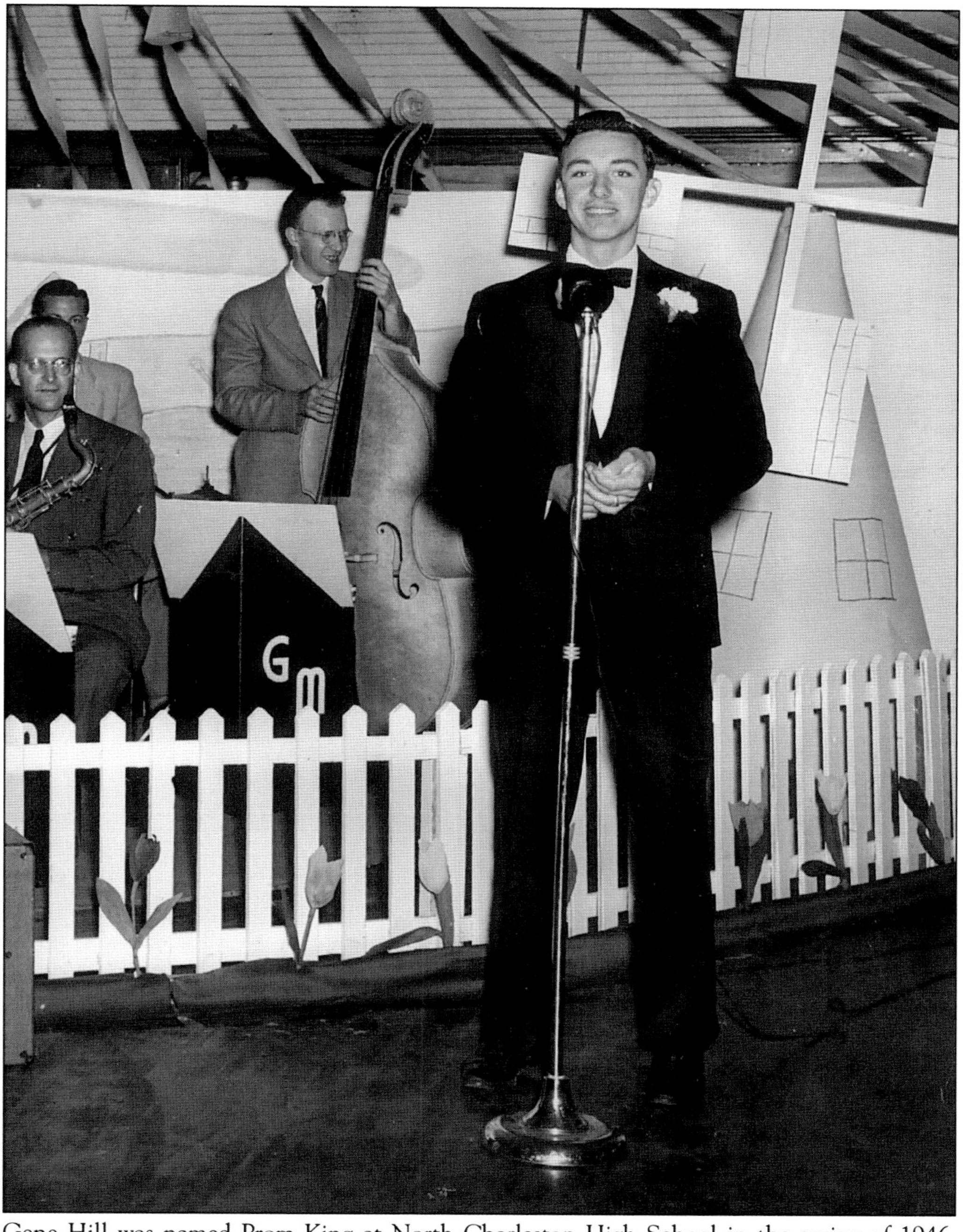

Gene Hill was named Prom King at North Charleston High School in the spring of 1946. (Courtesy of Ruth Cupp.)

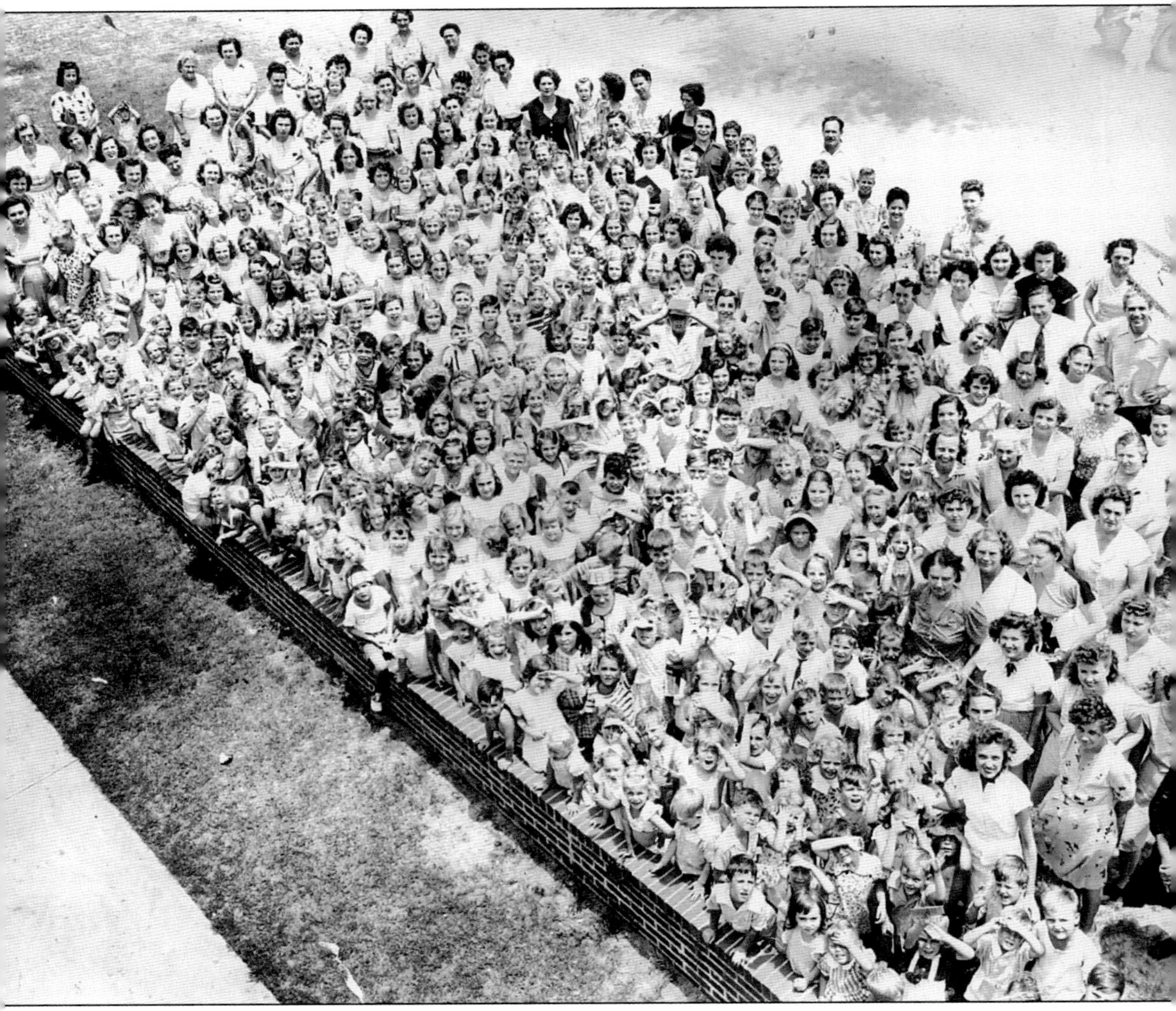

In the summer of 1946, hundreds of children attended Vacation Bible School at Charleston Heights Baptist Church. (Courtesy of Edith Painter.)

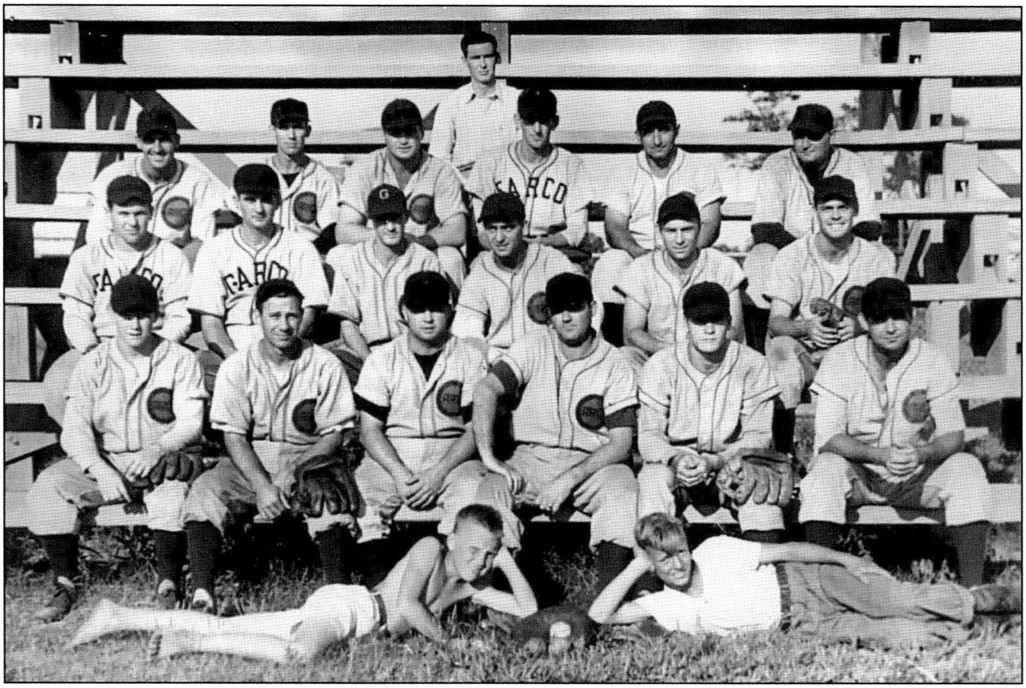

The South Carolina Semi-Professional Champions of 1946 came from the GARCO Team in North Charleston. (Courtesy of Ruth Cupp.)

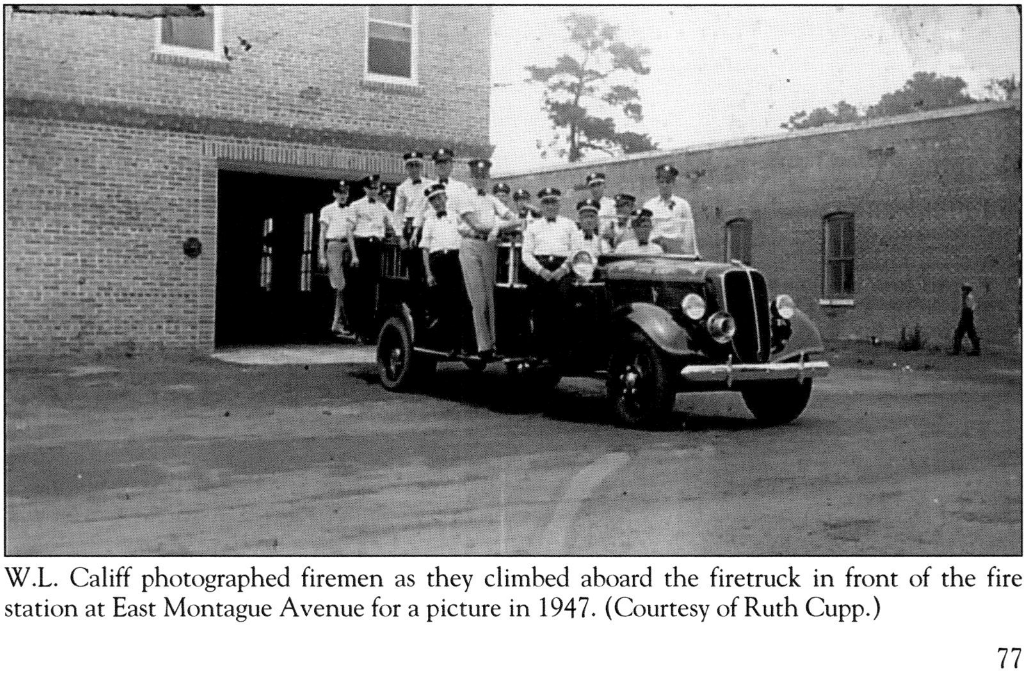

W.L. Califf photographed firemen as they climbed aboard the firetruck in front of the fire station at East Montague Avenue for a picture in 1947. (Courtesy of Ruth Cupp.)

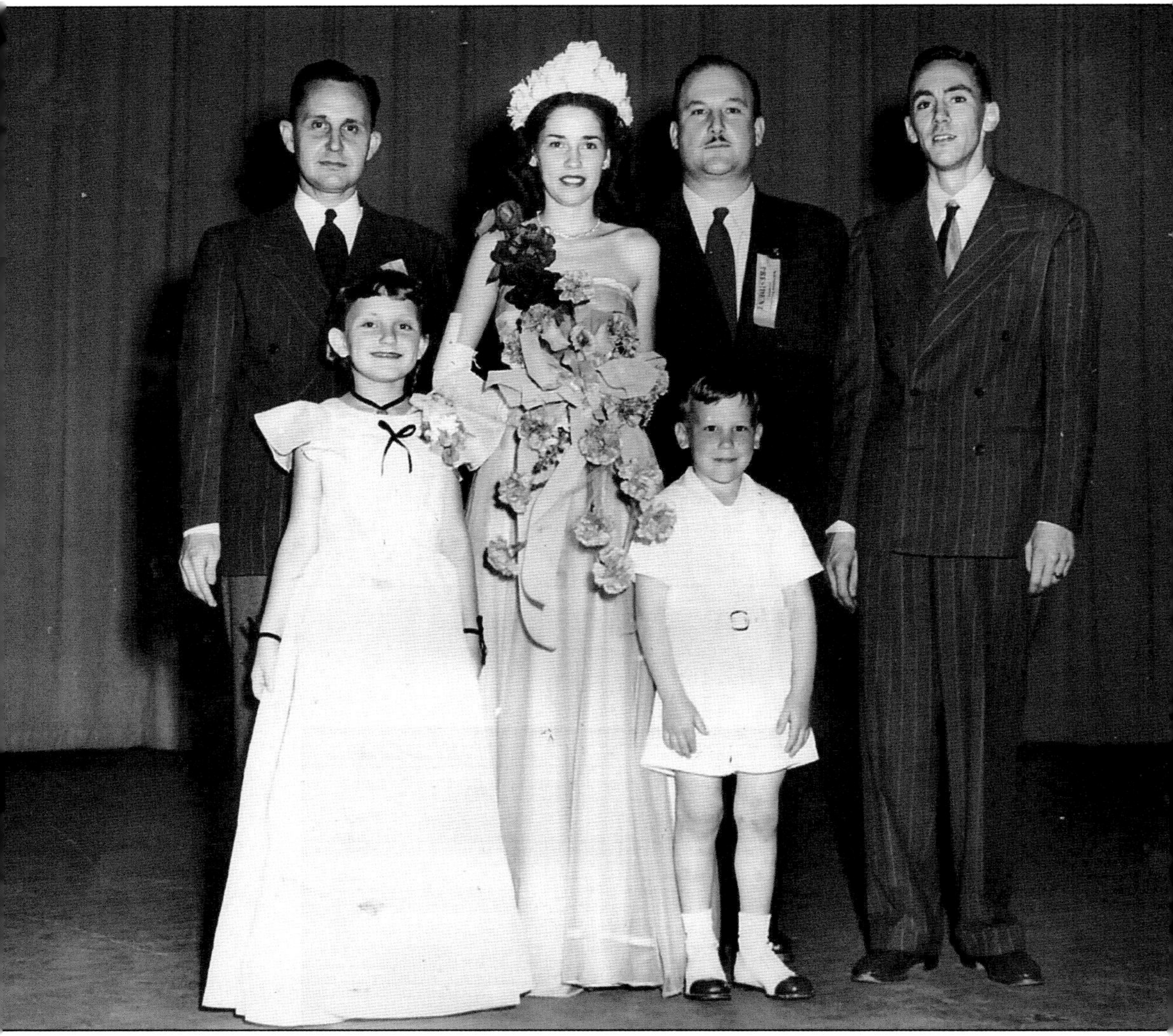

The 1948 Beauty Queen Elimination Contest was held on March 12 at Ben Tillman Elementary School auditorium at Navy Yard, South Carolina. Pictured from left to right are George T. Walker, committee chairman; Brenda Walker, flower girl; Miss North Charleston Betty McMillan; Daniel Varner Jr., crown bearer; Daniel G. Varner, Jaycee President; and Mr. Trayner Ferillo. (Courtesy of Helen Blanton.)

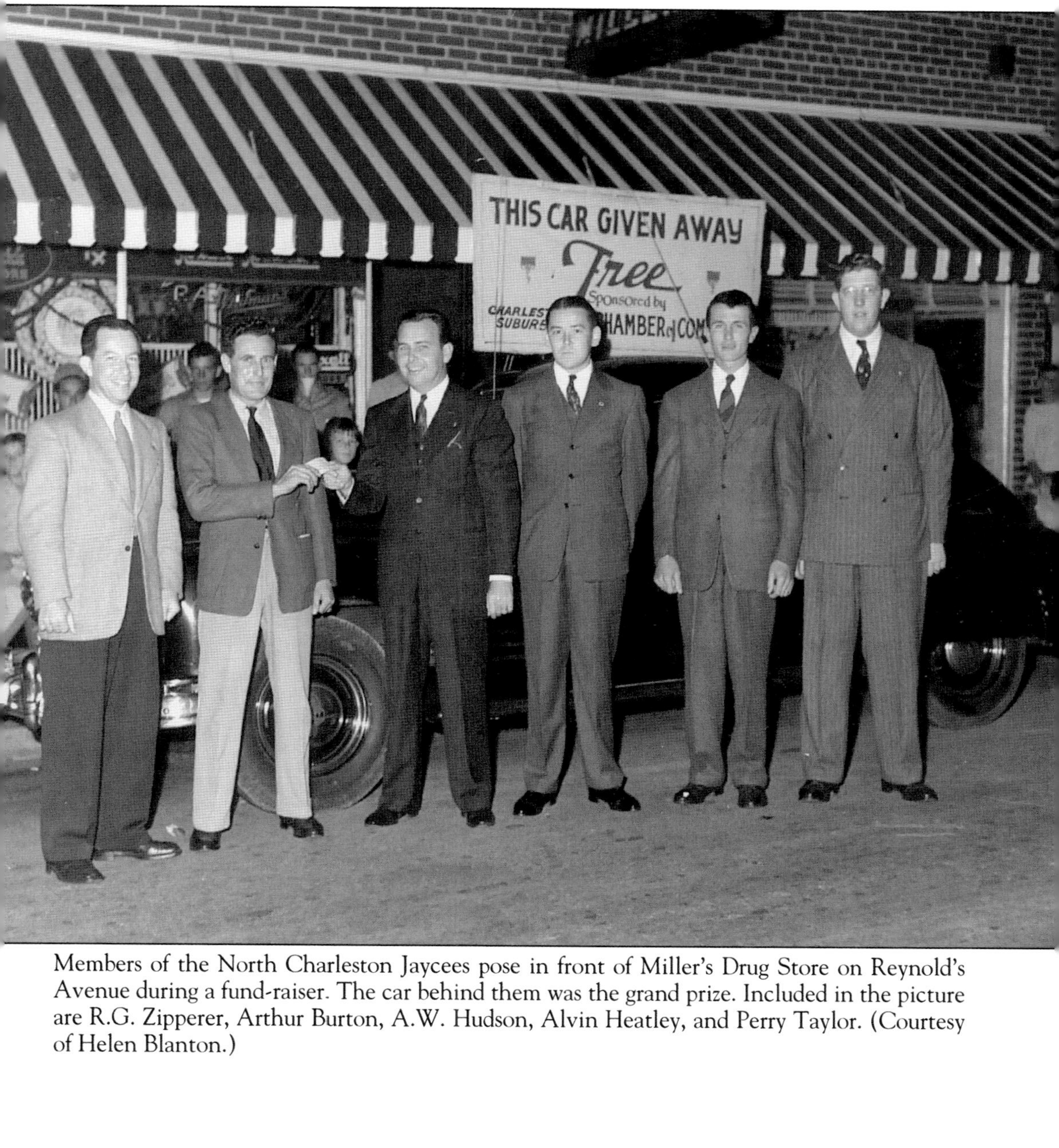

Members of the North Charleston Jaycees pose in front of Miller's Drug Store on Reynold's Avenue during a fund-raiser. The car behind them was the grand prize. Included in the picture are R.G. Zipperer, Arthur Burton, A.W. Hudson, Alvin Heatley, and Perry Taylor. (Courtesy of Helen Blanton.)

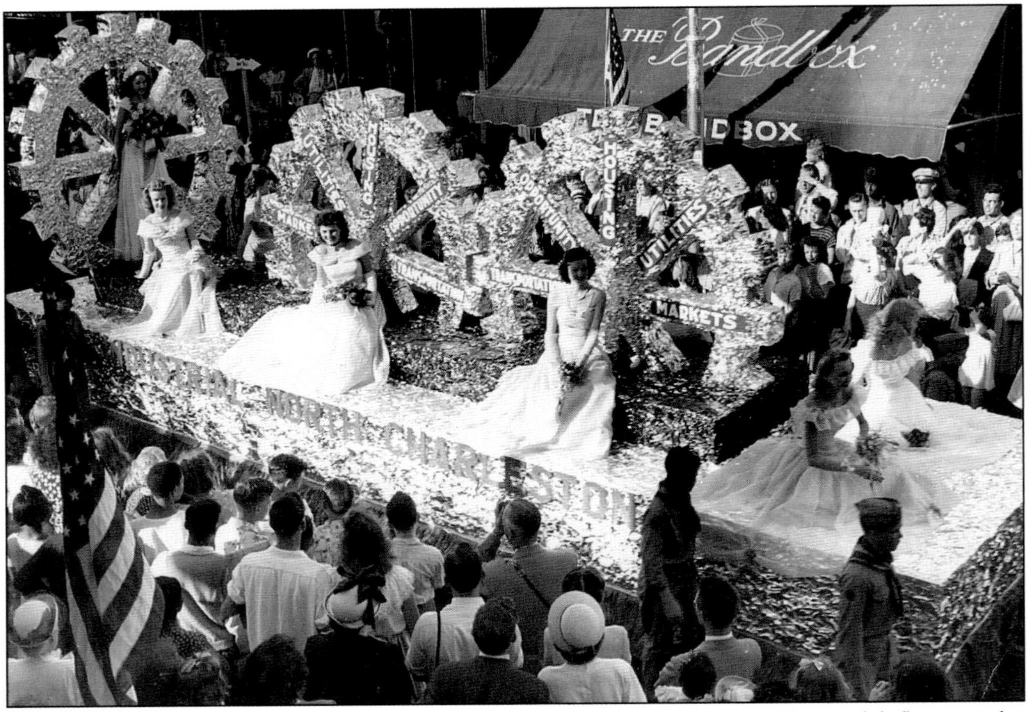

The North Charleston Junior Chamber of Commerce sponsored this beautiful float in the Azalea Parade held in the late 1940s in Charleston. (Courtesy of Helen Blanton.)

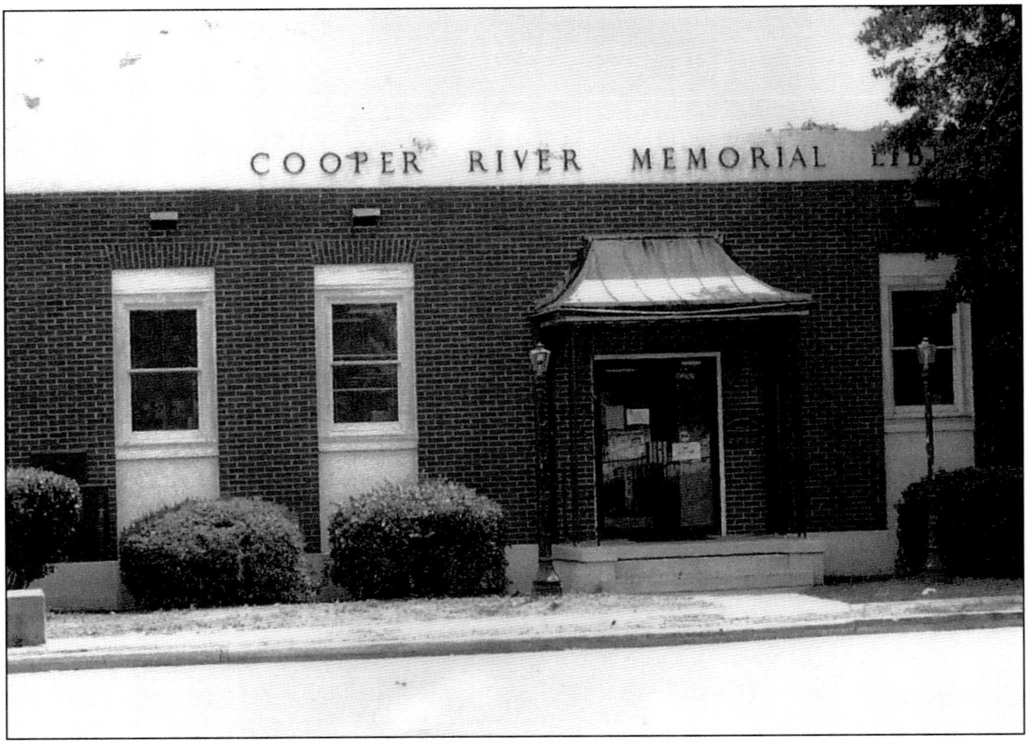

The Cooper River Memorial Library was built on the corner of Dorchester Road and Rivers Avenue, where it still stands today.(Courtesy of Helen Blanton.)

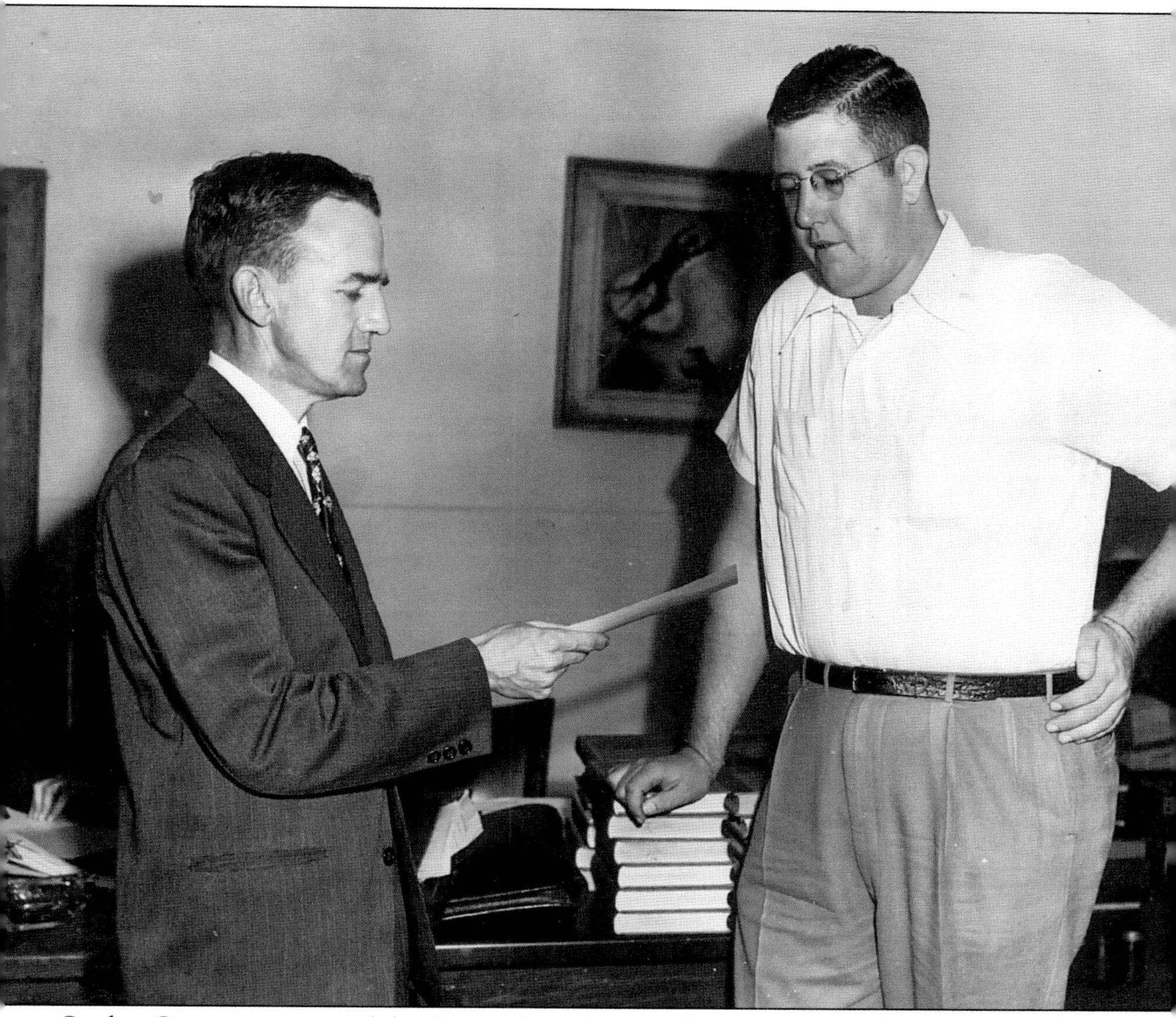

Gordon Garrett, treasurer of the Cooper River Memorial Association, is shown receiving a check from Perry A. Taylor, vice-president of the North Charleston Junior Chamber of Commerce. The money was raised to build the Cooper River Memorial Library. (Courtesy of Helen Blanton.)

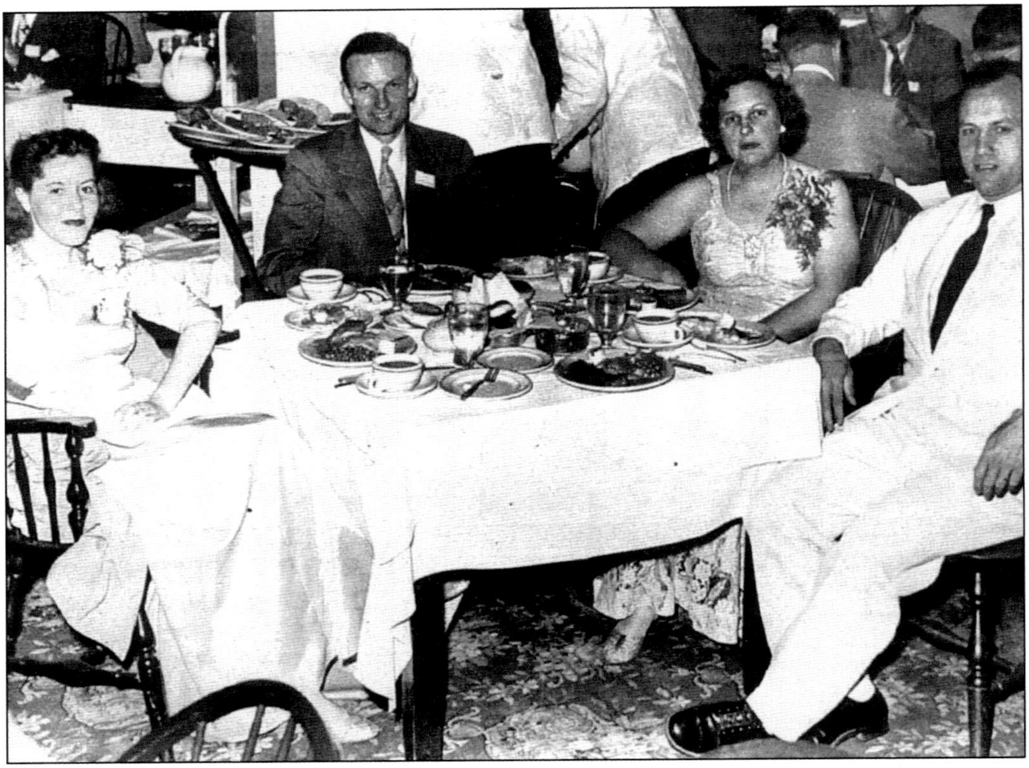

Lydia and Carl Young along with Moye and Frank Tillman attend the Chamber of Commerce State Convention. (Courtesy of Helen Blanton.)

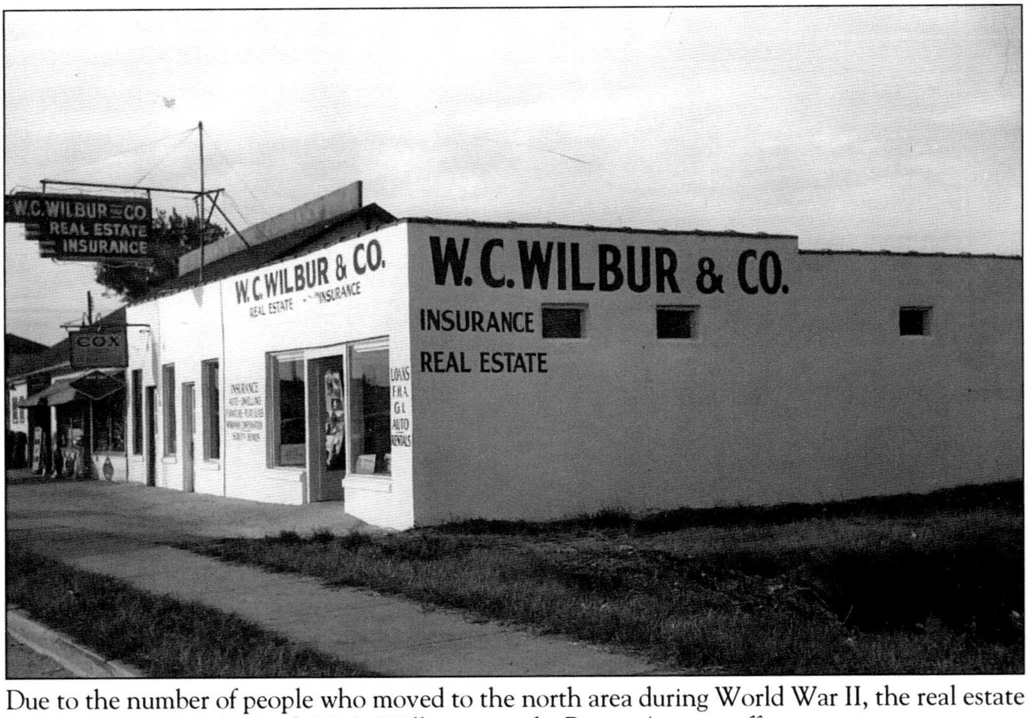

Due to the number of people who moved to the north area during World War II, the real estate business was in big demand. W.C. Wilbur opened a Rivers Avenue office.

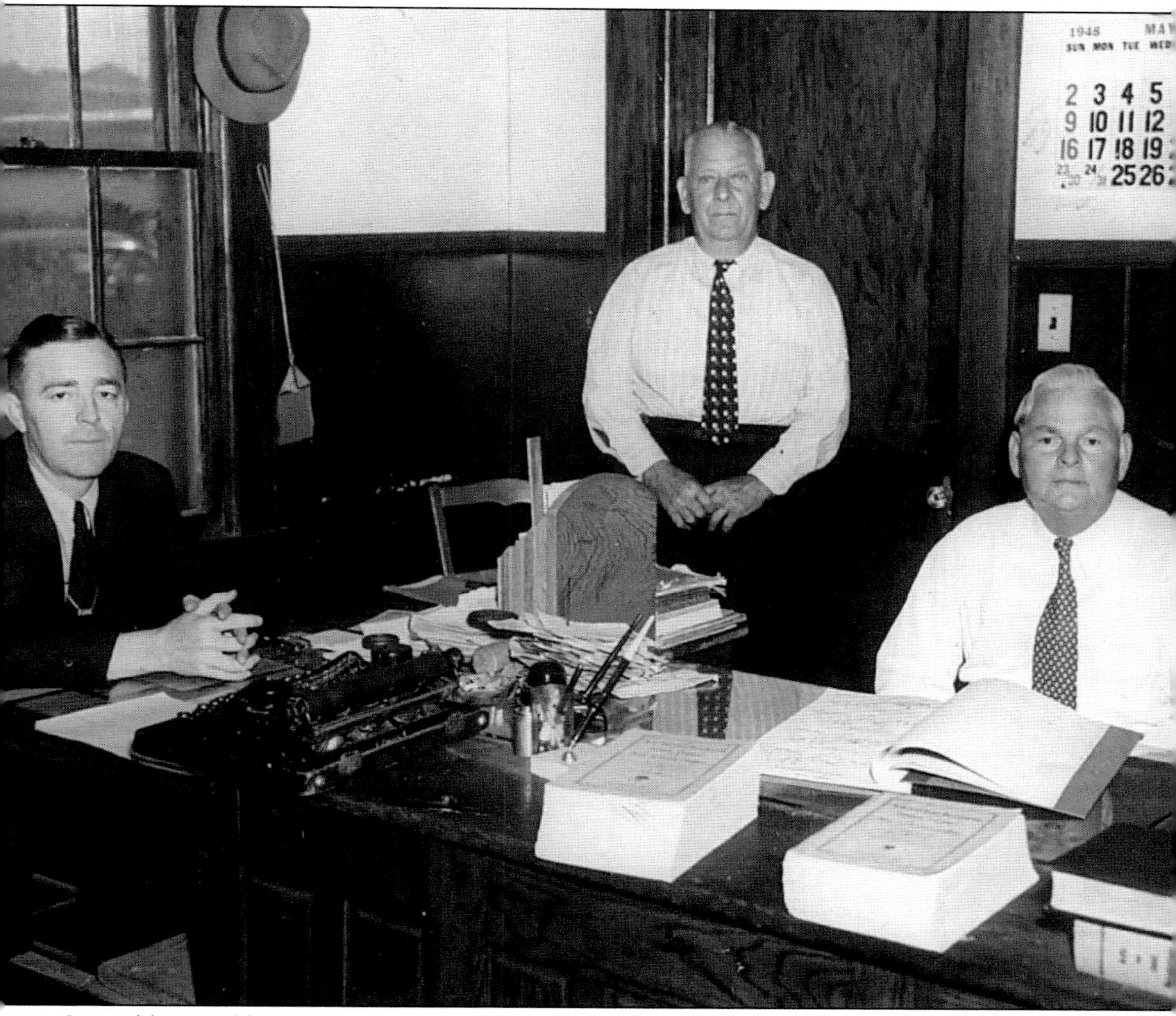

Constable Harold Fox, Ben Bowie, and Judge John R. Stall are pictured in Stall's Montague Avenue office. (Courtesy of Ruth Cupp.)

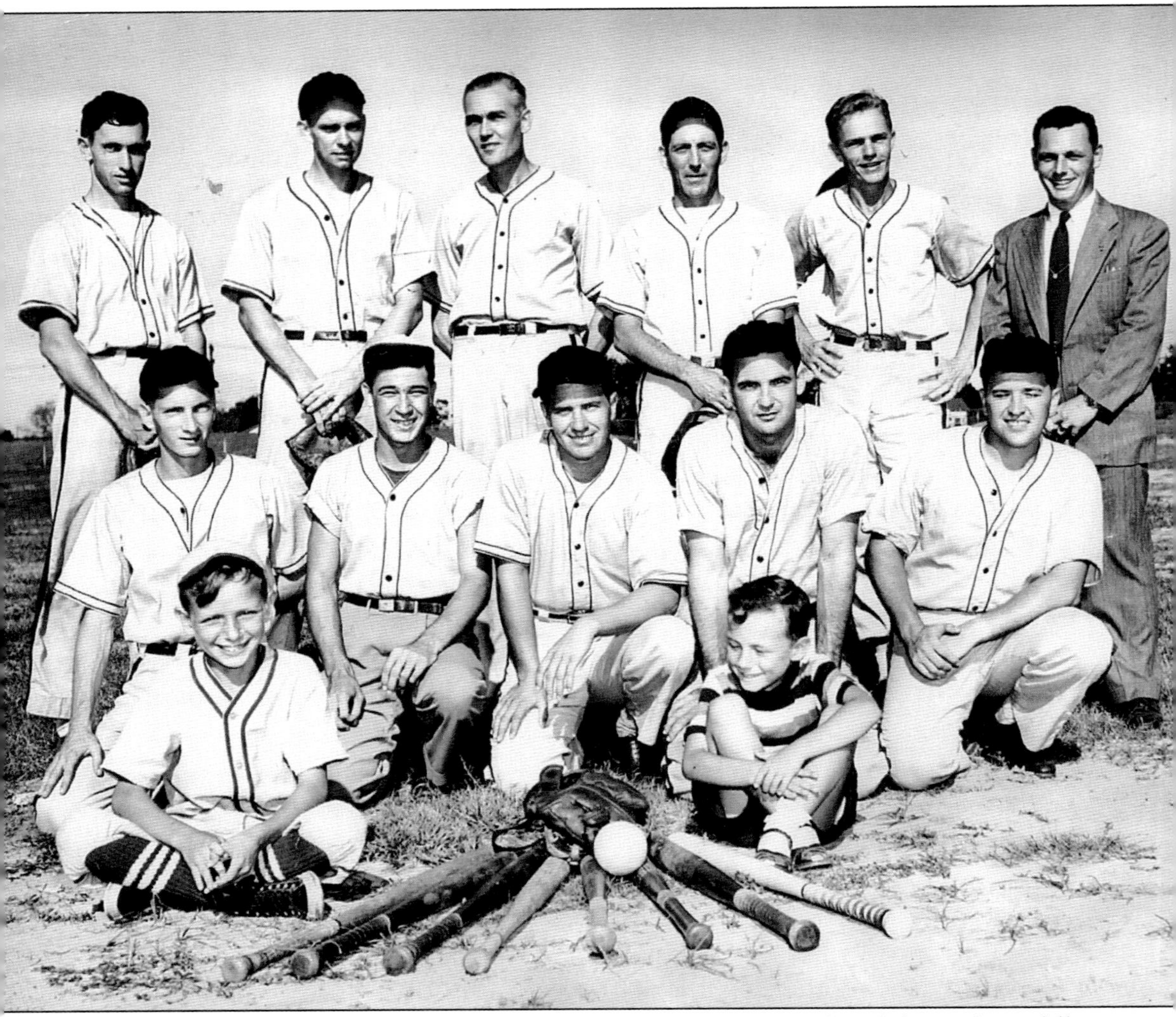

The W.C. Wilbur & Co. Fast Pitch Softball Champions of 1949 are from left to right, as follows: (row one) Bob Carter, bat boy, and Roger Carter, mascot; (row two) Bob Estes, Eddie Mizell, Ty Owens, Jesse Tolbert, and Jack Owens; (row three) Bill Dickey, John Smith, Jim Farrish, Curtis Lybrand, Tom Waden, and Harry L. Carter, sponsor. (Courtesy of Ruth Cupp and Harry L. Carter Jr.)

Four

The City of North Charleston

In the 1950s and 1960s growth continued in the north area. The increase in population prompted the community's need for more recreational outlets. Danny Jones and the Cooper River Parks and Playgrounds Commission, along with church and school activities, all gave people something to do in their spare time. A big date during this time consisted of a football game and a hamburger at one of the local drive-ins. However, many people in North Charleston were growing more unhappy with the way the city was evolving. They longed to have their own representation and control over future development of the area and to be completely out from under Charleston's control.

In 1969 an attempt to incorporate North Charleston as a city failed. John Bourne, who later became the first mayor of North Charleston, actively worked to form a group to fight for incorporation once again. An election was held in April and on June 12, 1972, the City of North Charleston was born. A police department was formed in 1973 and under the direction of Chief William Frank New Sr. the North Charleston Fire Department became an official entity.

Annexation continued the huge growth pattern for the city. By 1976, North Charleston was the third largest city in the Palmetto State. In July of 1979 the new city hall building was dedicated. The city of North Charleston celebrated its 10th anniversary in 1982, and even then it was quite apparent that it was well on its way to becoming the great city it is today.

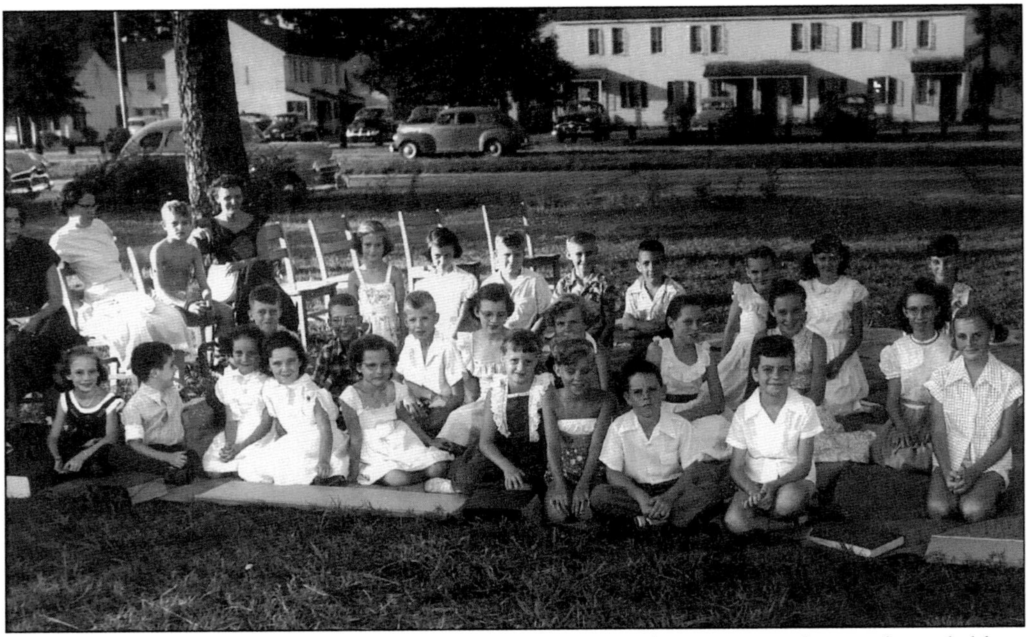

Cooper River Memorial Library held a six-week summer reading program. Pictured are children in the early 1950s who had participated. Note the Tom McMillan Homes in the background where the Charleston Naval Hospital now stands. (Courtesy of Helen Blanton.)

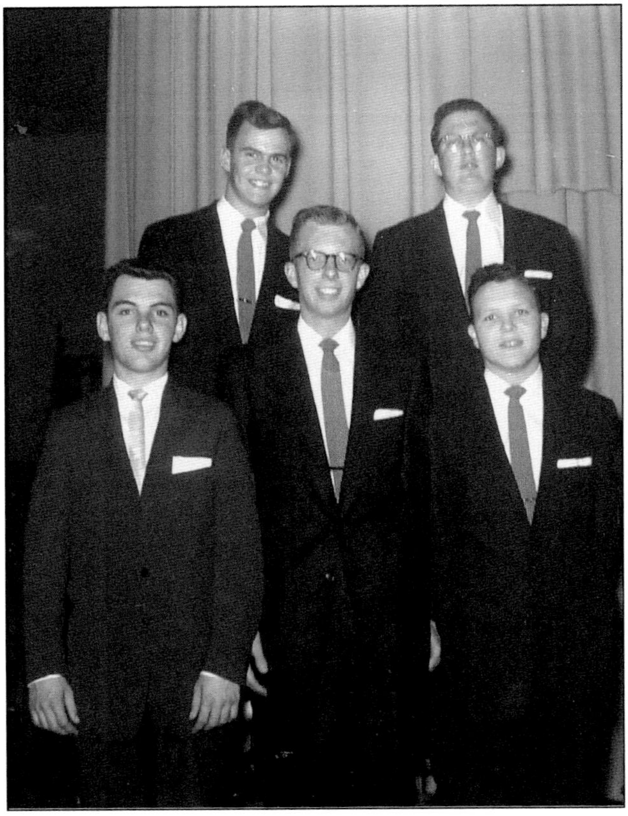

In the early 1950s the Loafers serenaded hundreds of North Charlestoners at the Park Circle Teen Club. The group started singing together as teenagers at North Charleston Methodist Church and later moved to "rock 'n roll." Pictured are Charles Gatch, Tony Davis, Bob Brown, Bob Newton, and Carlyle Singletary. In 2002, the group returned to Park Circle for the first time since 1957 and sang songs of the 1950s and '60s at a free concert sponsored by the North Charleston Cultural Arts Program. (Courtesy of Carlyle Singletary)

The North Charleston Junior Chamber of Commerce sponsored Troop 61 of the Boy Scouts. Pictured is scoutmaster Tommy Owens receiving the new charter from Troop Committee Chairman Harry W. Jarrett. (Courtesy of Helen Blanton.)

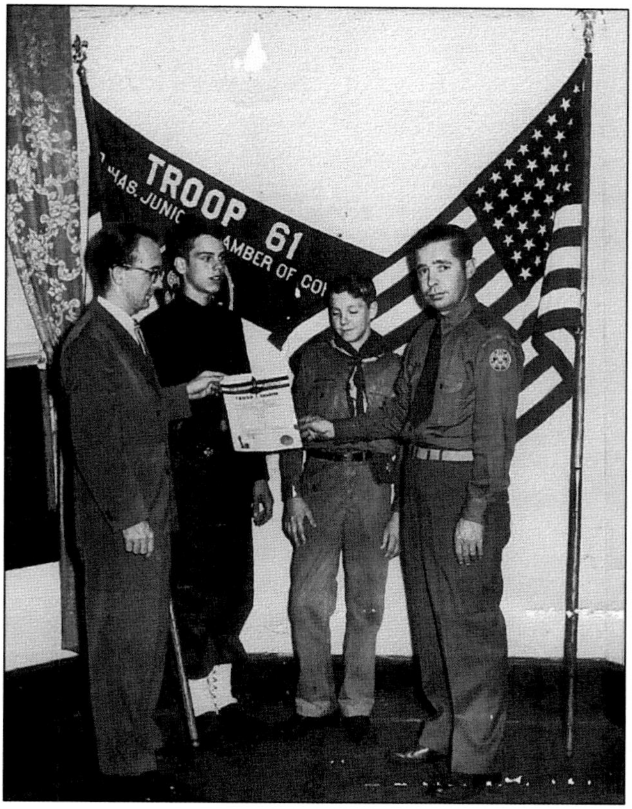

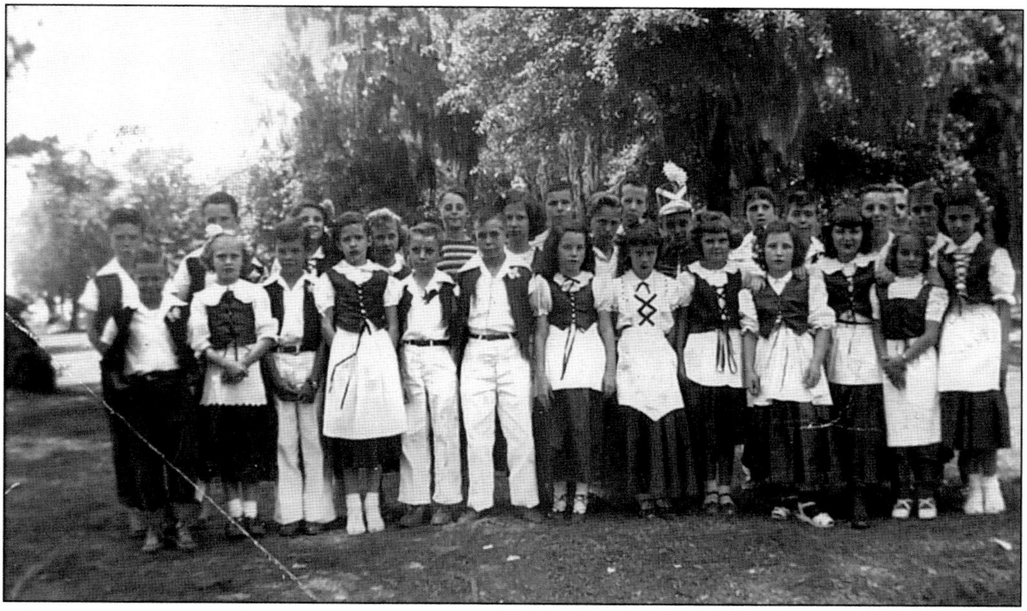

Liberty Homes School's fourth grade class held a May Day ceremony in May of 1951. (Courtesy of Priscilla Grimsley.)

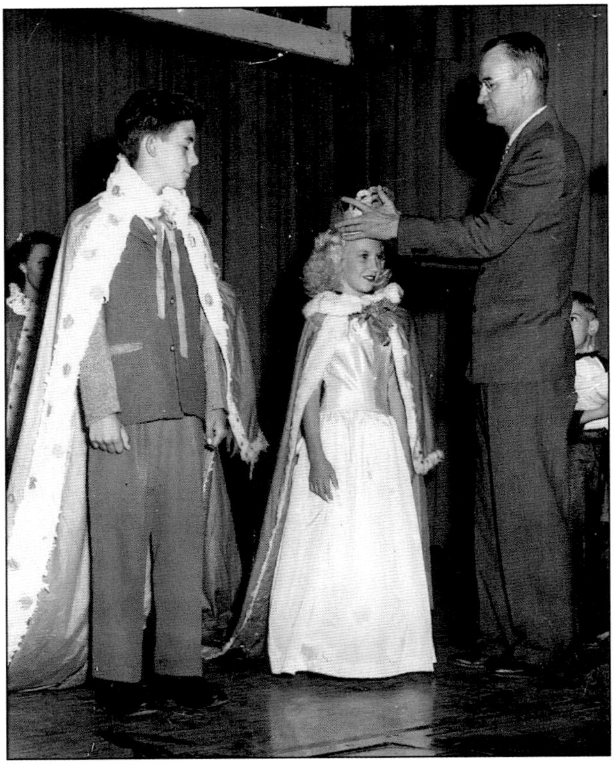

Mr. A. C. Corcoran , principal of Ben Tillman School, crowns school queen Rosemary Moore while school king Bill Veronee looks on. (Courtesy of Rosemary Moore.)

The 1952 Park Circle Small Fry Cooper River champs are pictured below. (Courtesy of Ruth Cupp.)

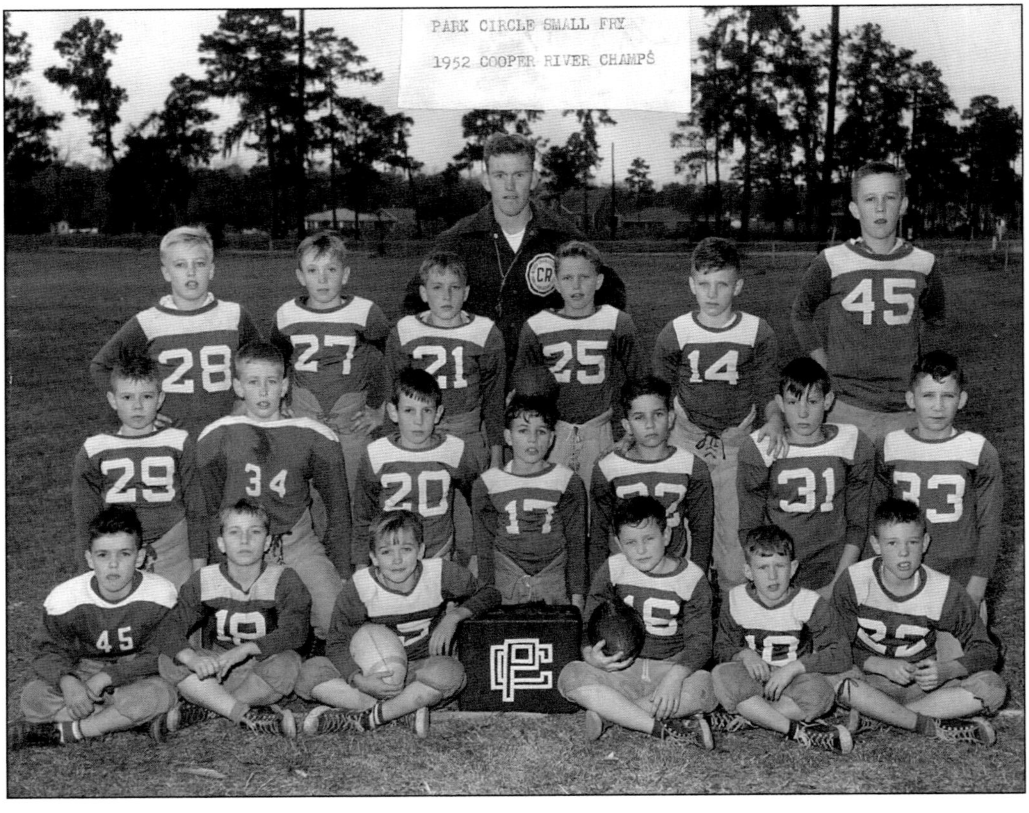

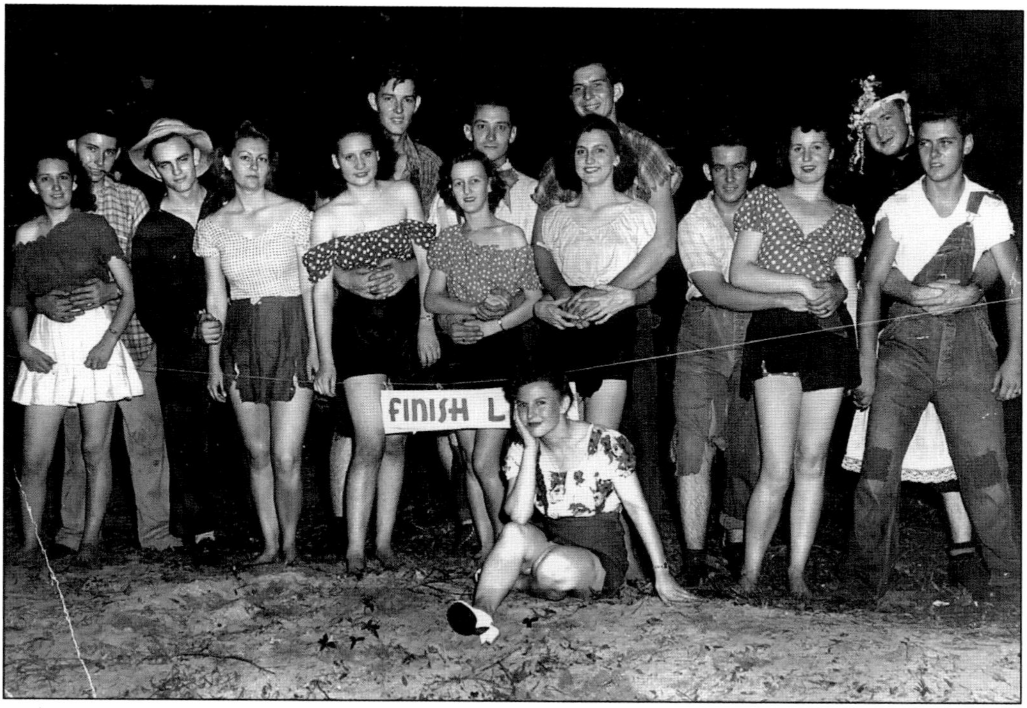

Sadie Hawkins Day is celebrated by students from Chicora High School in the early 1950s. (Courtesy of Rosemary Moore.)

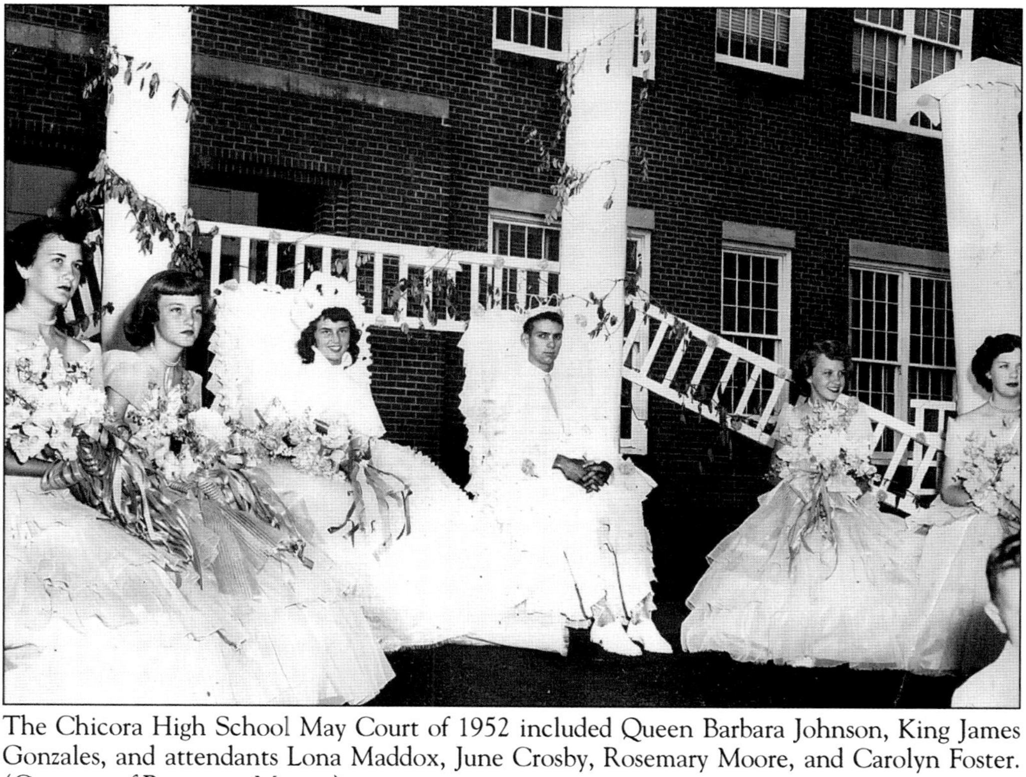

The Chicora High School May Court of 1952 included Queen Barbara Johnson, King James Gonzales, and attendants Lona Maddox, June Crosby, Rosemary Moore, and Carolyn Foster. (Courtesy of Rosemary Moore.)

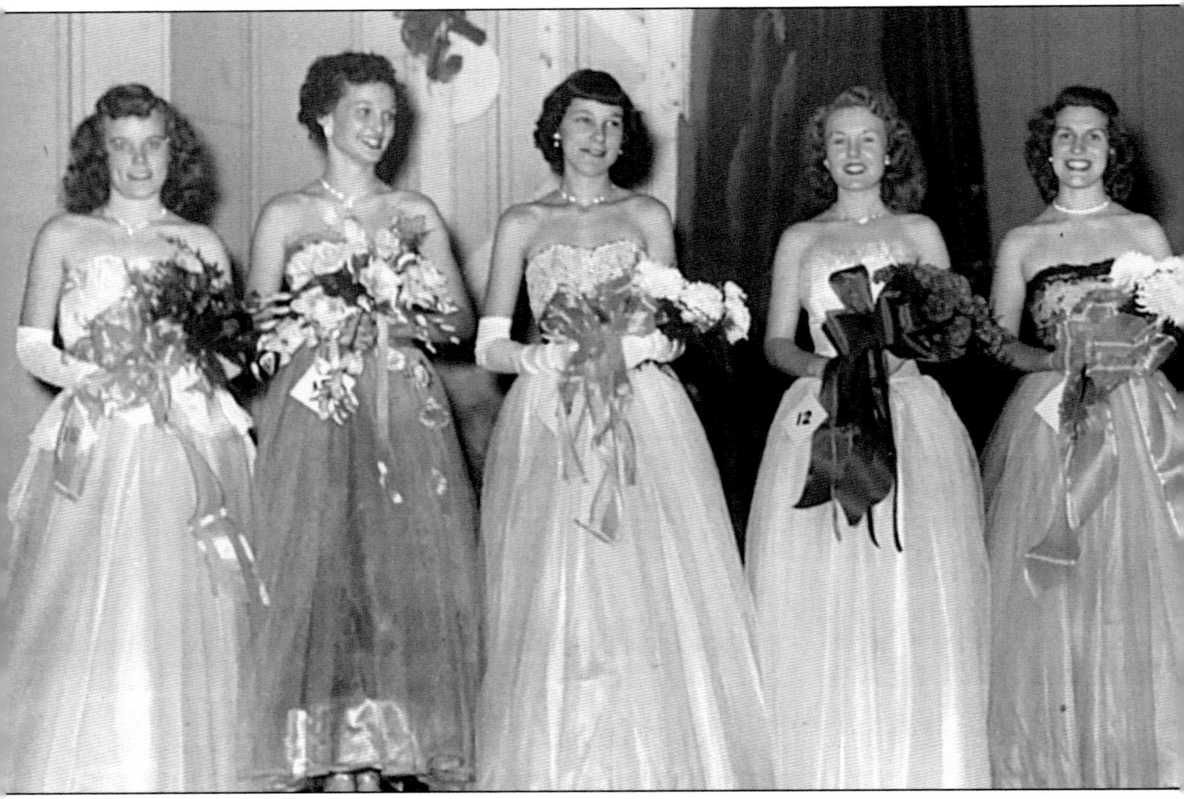

The 1950 Miss North Charleston Contestants pose for the judges. Miss Freddie Campbell, pictured fourth from the left, was selected as Miss North Charleston that year, and she

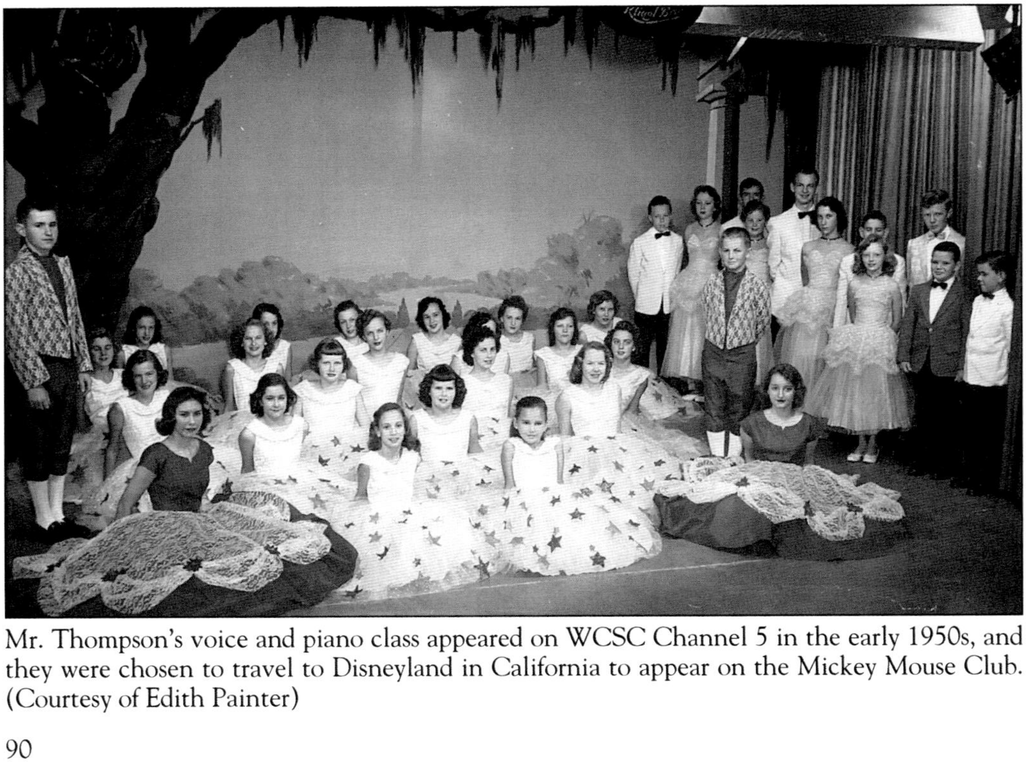

Mr. Thompson's voice and piano class appeared on WCSC Channel 5 in the early 1950s, and they were chosen to travel to Disneyland in California to appear on the Mickey Mouse Club. (Courtesy of Edith Painter)

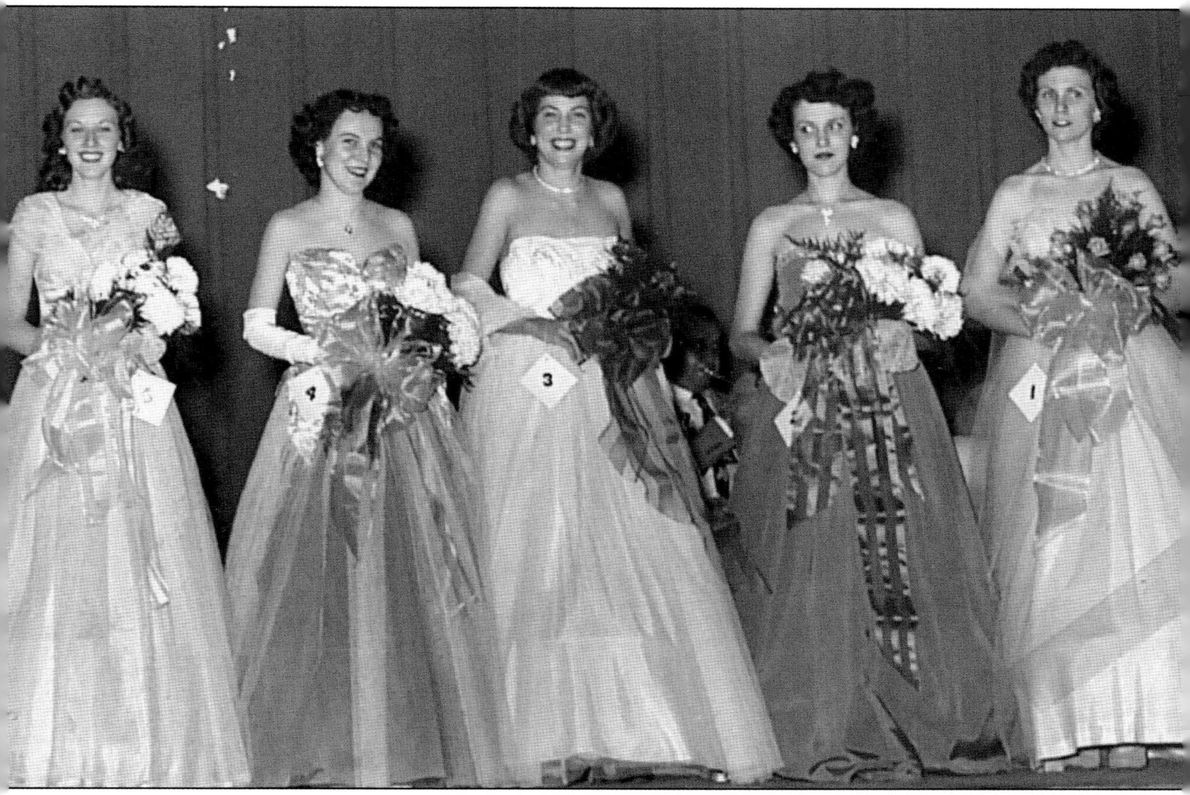

represented the area at the Azaela Festival and the Miss South Carolina Pageant. (Courtesy of Helen Blanton.)

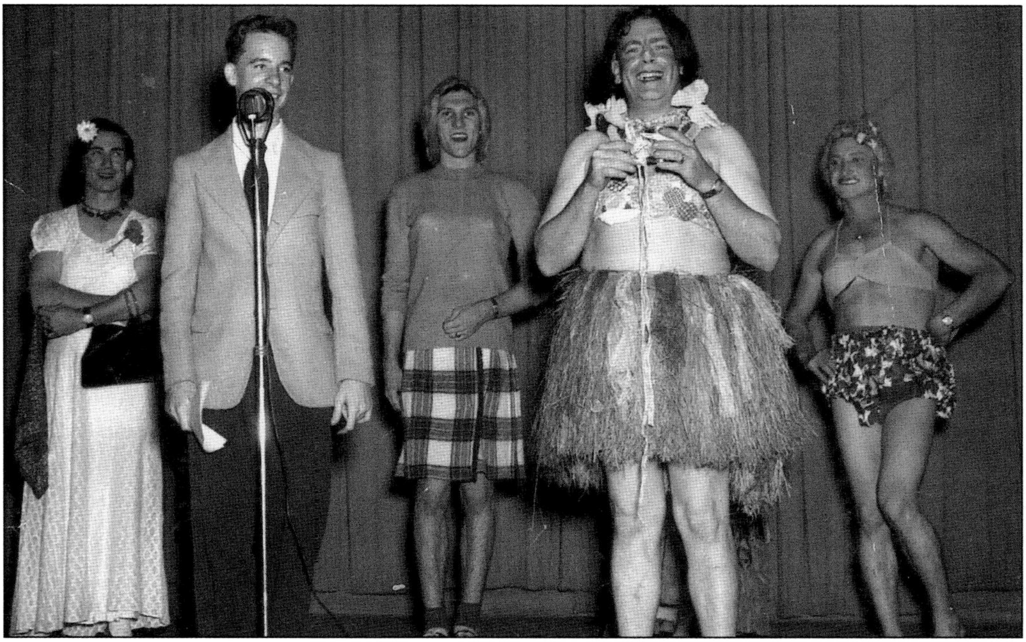

North Charleston Elementary School held an annual all-male beauty contest where the fathers of students were the contestants. (Courtesy of Rosemary Moore.)

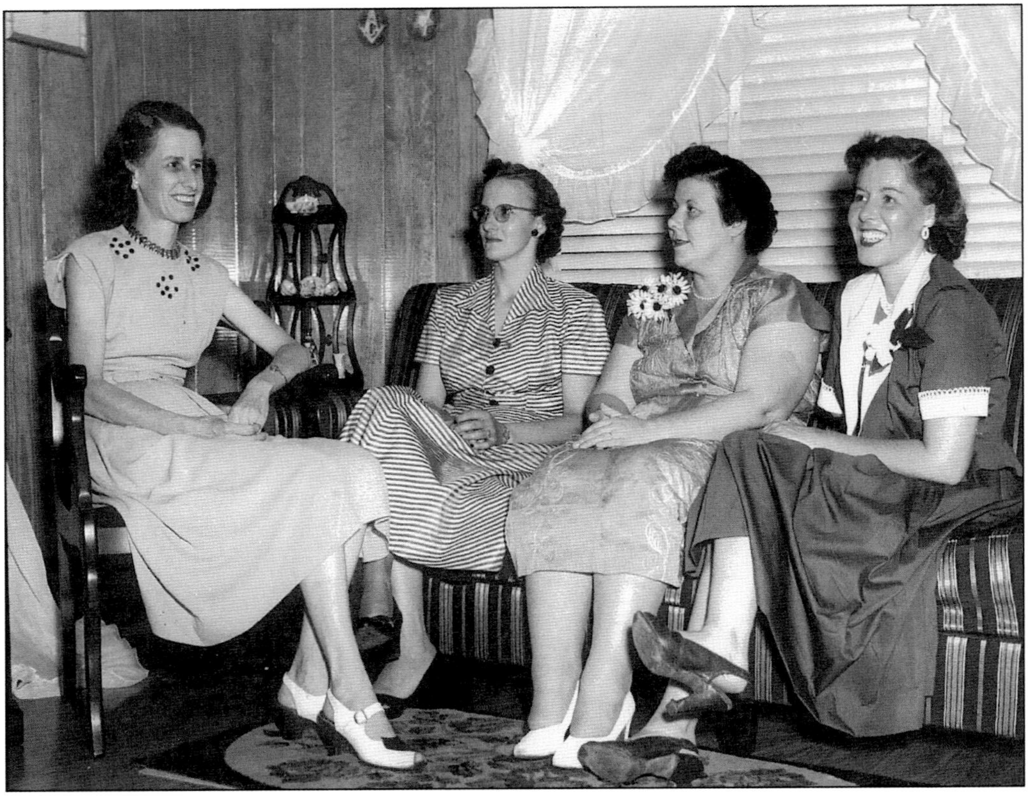

The 1952 Jaycee-ettes officers included Mrs. M.M. Russell, Mrs. J.A. Cannon, Mrs. E.B. Blanton, and Mrs. J.C. Young. (Courtesy of Helen Blanton.)

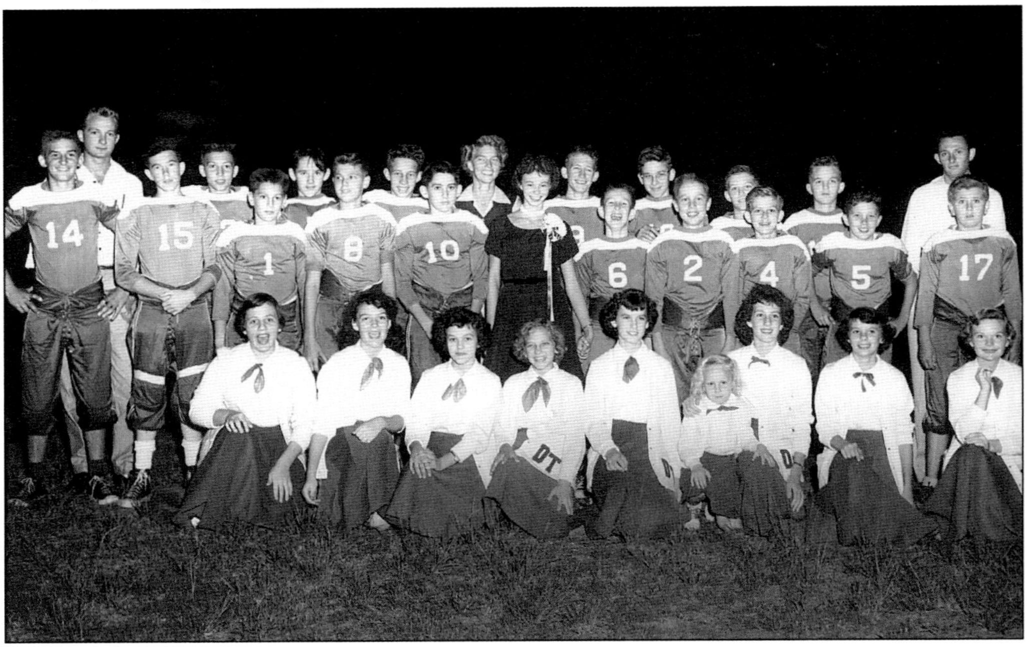

The Dorchester Terrace Midgets Football Team and cheerleaders pose for a picture in the early 1950s. (Courtesy of Helen Blanton.)

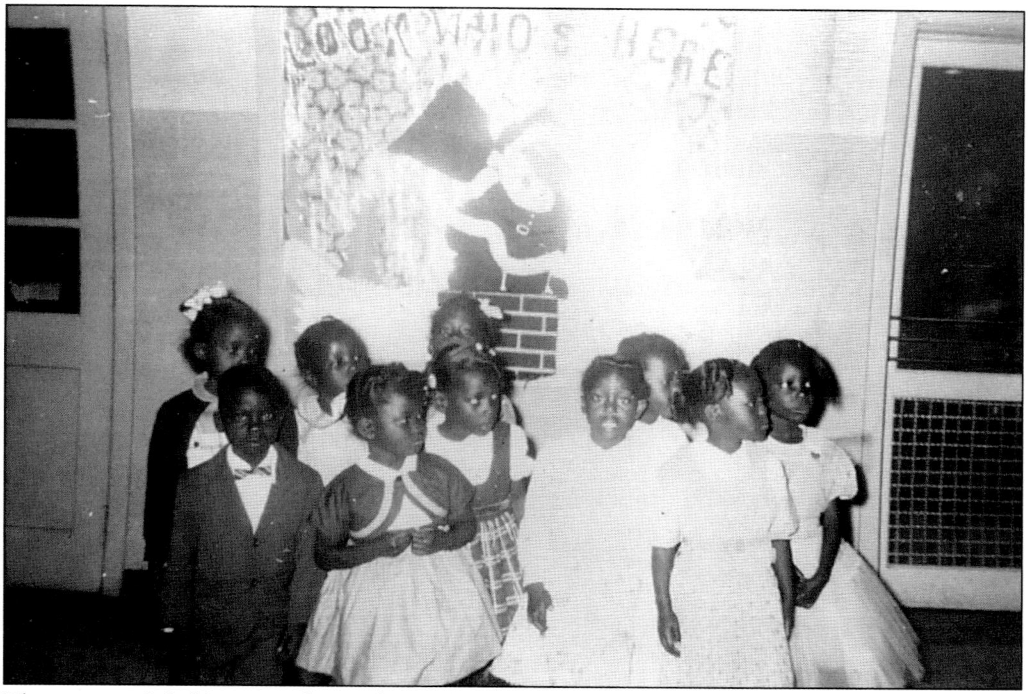

This group of children are the students of the five-year-old kindergarten class at the old USO Building at Liberty Hill. (Courtesy Carolyn Lecque Collins.)

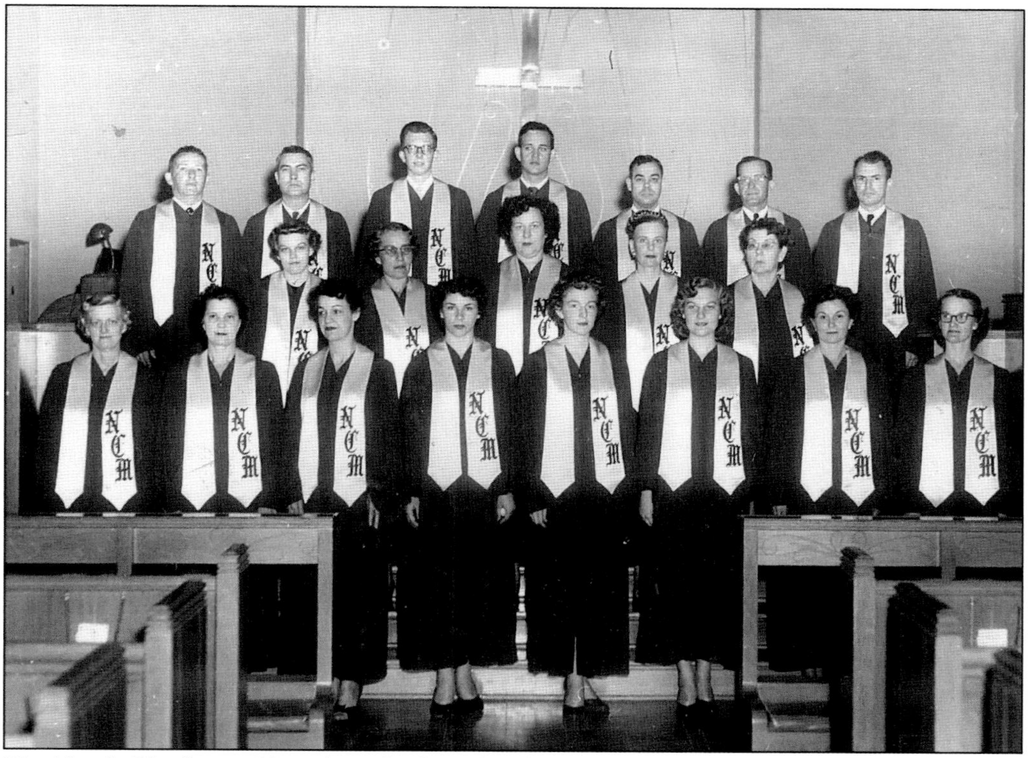

The North Charleston United Methodist Church Choir is pictured here in 1955. (Courtesy of Ruth Cupp.)

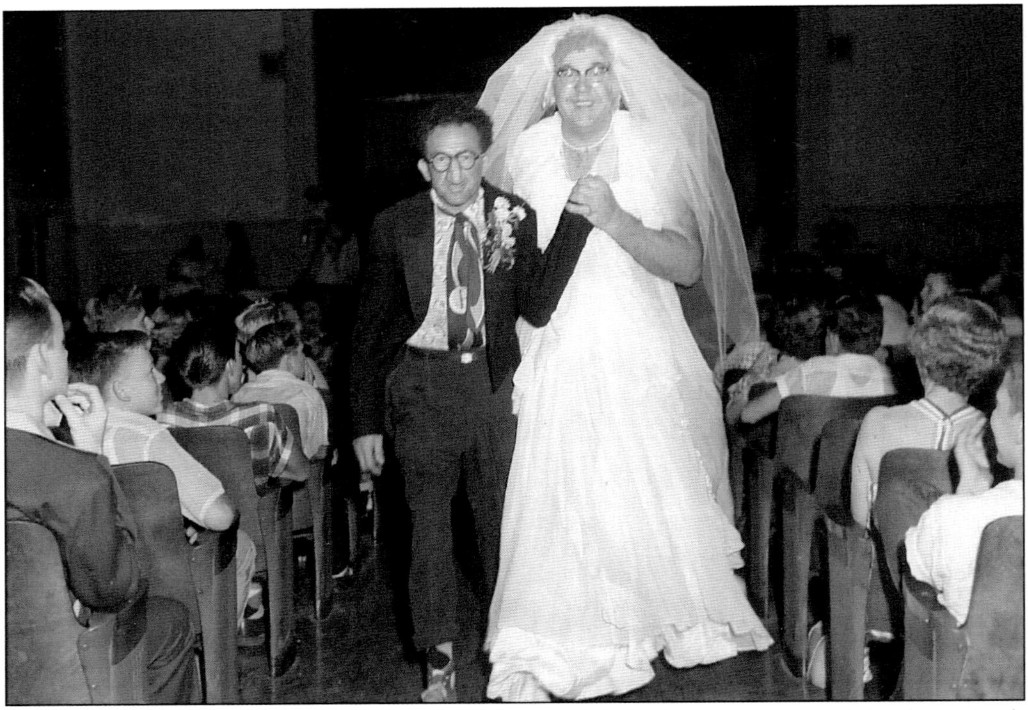

A womanless wedding was held as a fund-raiser at one of the local elementary schools in North Charleston. (Courtesy of Rosemary Moore.)

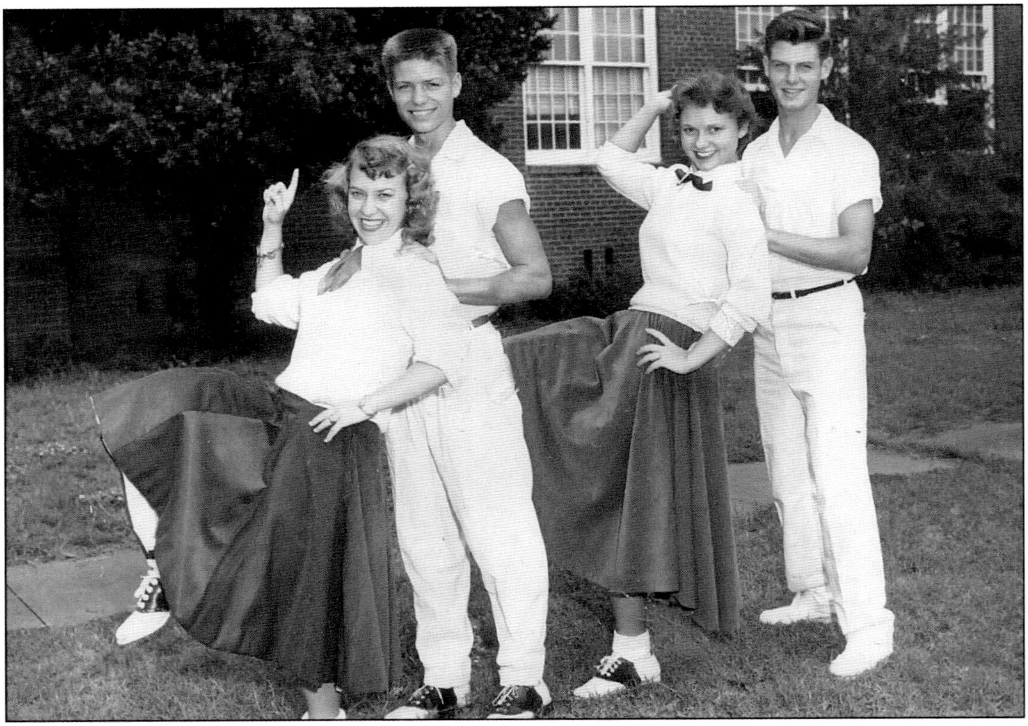

The 1955 Chicora High School cheerleaders, from left to right, are Rosemary Moore, Larry Ridgeway, Carolyn Cooper, and John English. (Courtesy of Rosemary Moore.)

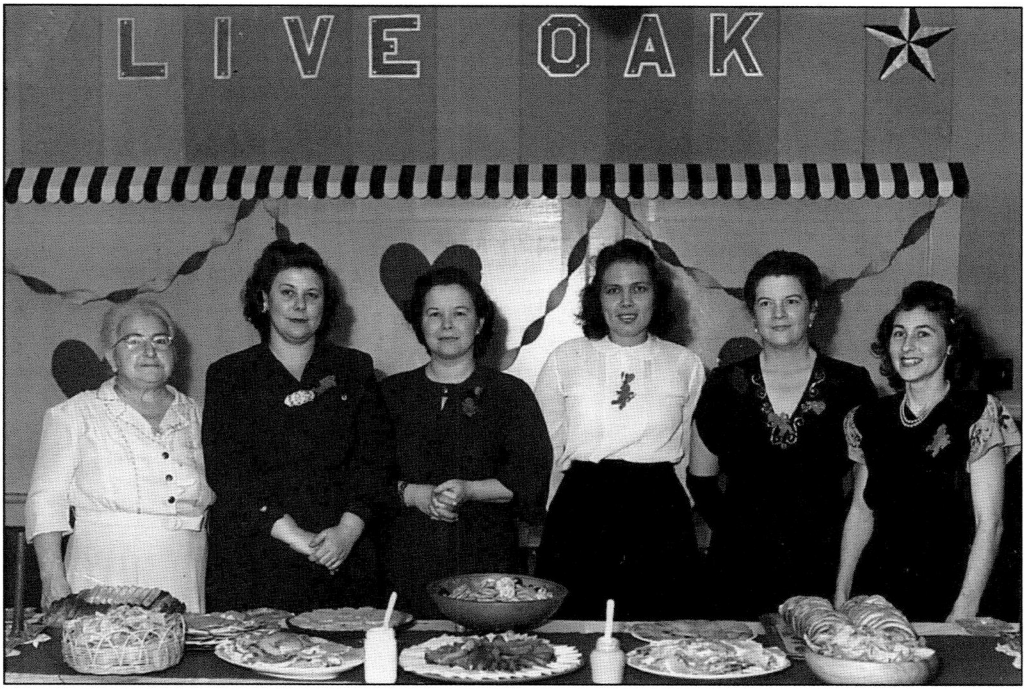

Members of the North Charleston Jaycee-ettes are pictured at a meeting at Live Oak. Pictured from left to right are Mrs. Helderfrant, Helen Blanton, Lottie Likes, Ethel Glenn, Nita Zipperer, and Marjorie Everitt. (Courtesy of Helen Blanton.)

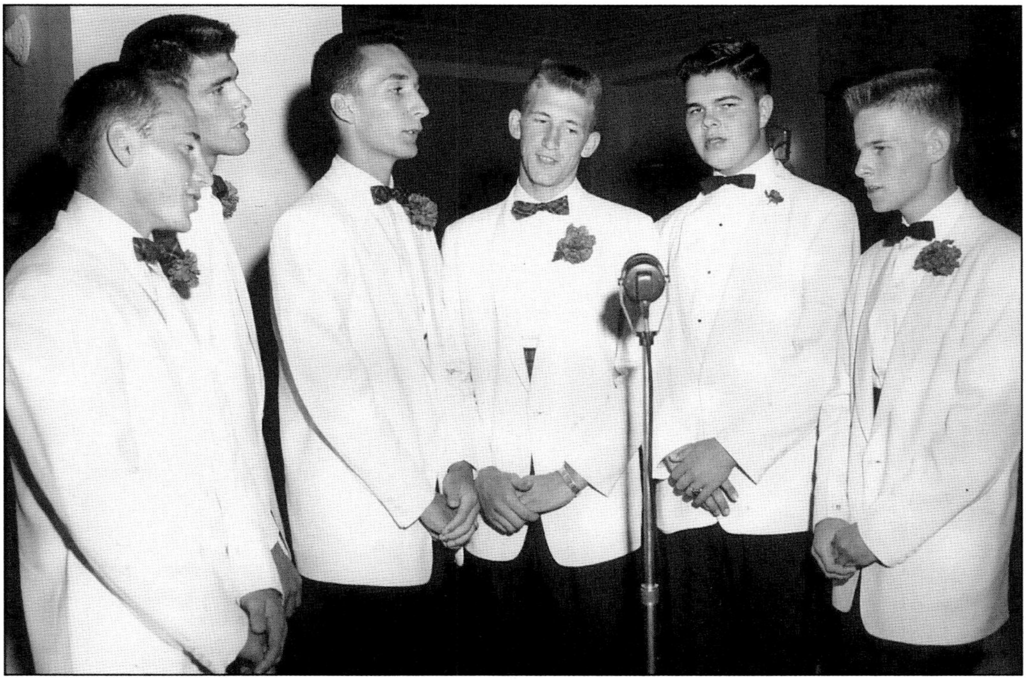
These Chicora High School students formed a singing group in 1959. Known as the "Inkie Dinks," they are, from left to right, Robert Shearer, Jerome Lipe, Pete Ayoub, Joe Bartee, Bill Poplin, and Popeye Owens. (Courtesy Ruth Cupp.)

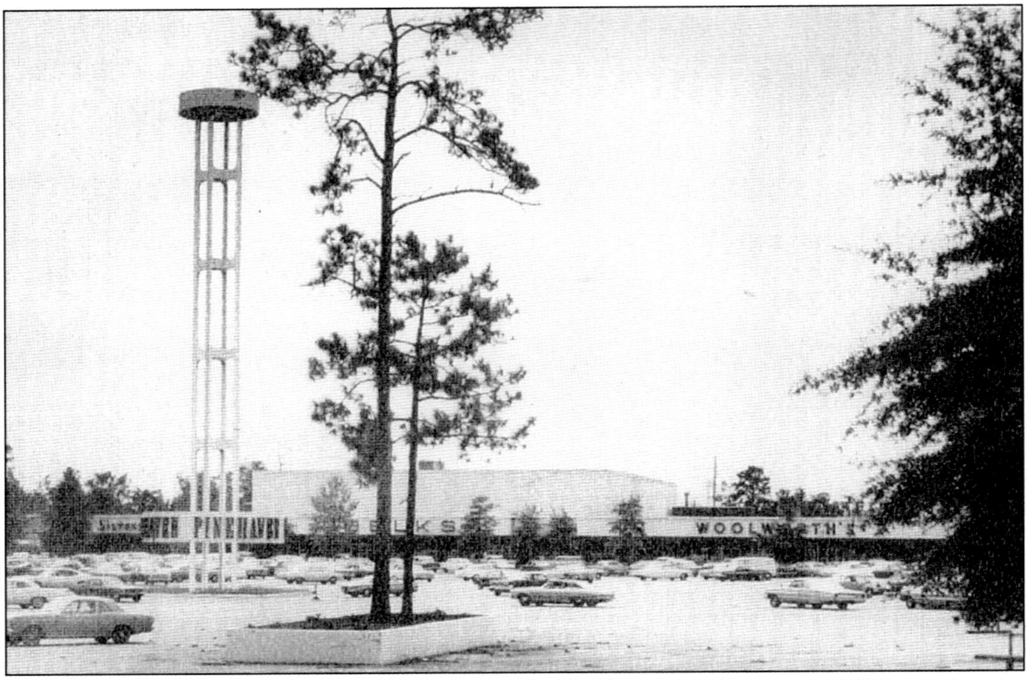

A mammoth shopping center was built in North Charleston on January 2, 1959, on the site where the former Pinehaven Hospital once stood. Destined to be the largest in the state, Pinehaven Shopping Center offered the convenience of all shopping without having to travel downtown. Today it is known as Shipwatch Square, and the Winn Dixie Store is the only original store to remain. (Courtesy of *The Post and Courier*.)

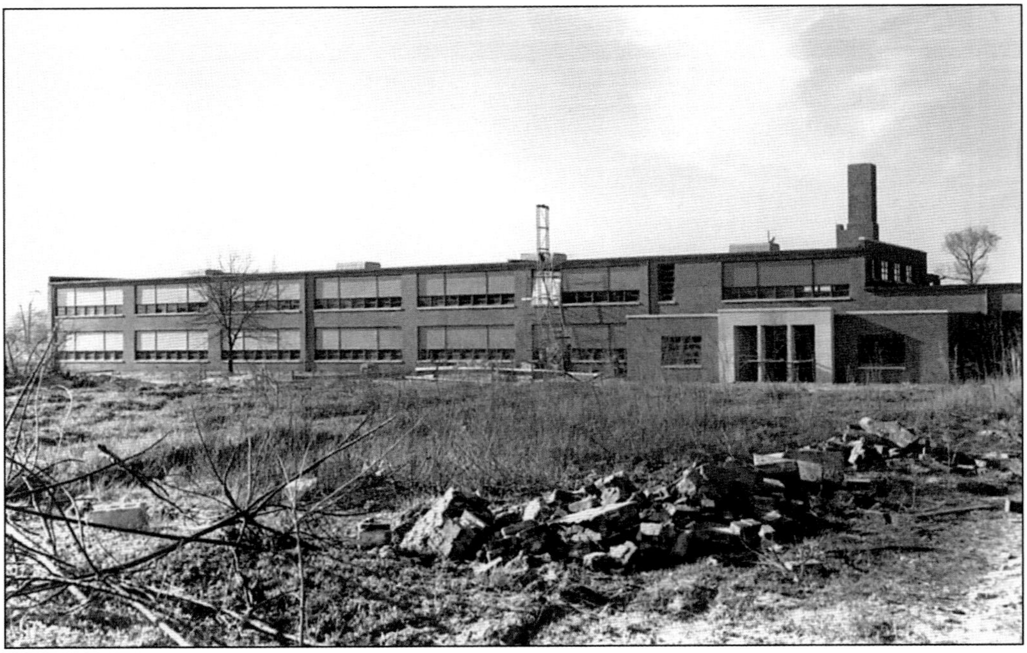

Bonds Wilson High School in Liberty Hill was the all-black high school for many years. The school's band was always rated best in competitions. The building remains today but is not used. (Courtesy of the Avery Research Center for African American History and Culture.)

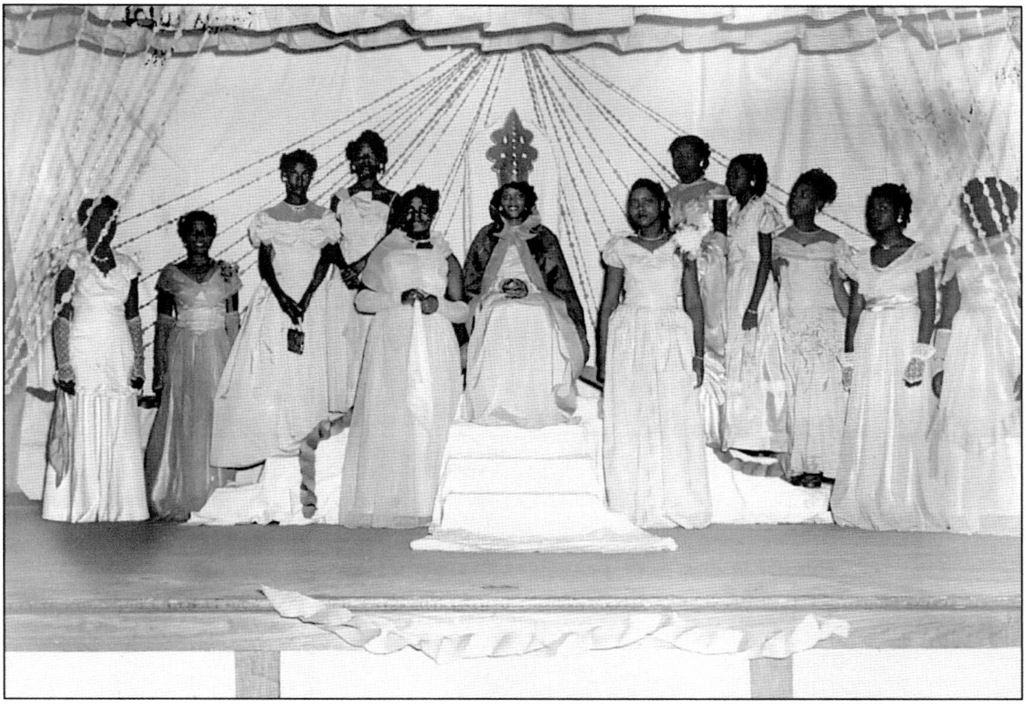

The women above were the contestants for the Miss Bonds Wilson Pageant, *c.* 1960. (Courtesy of the Avery Research Center for African American History and Culture.)

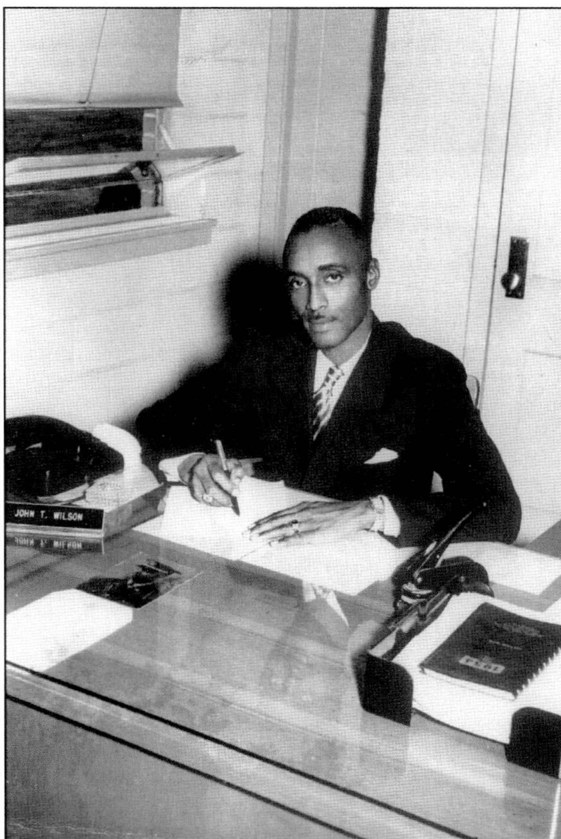

Mr. John T. Wilson served as principal at both Bonds-Wilson High School and at Liberty Hill Elementary School. (courtesy of the Avery Research Center for African American History and Culture.)

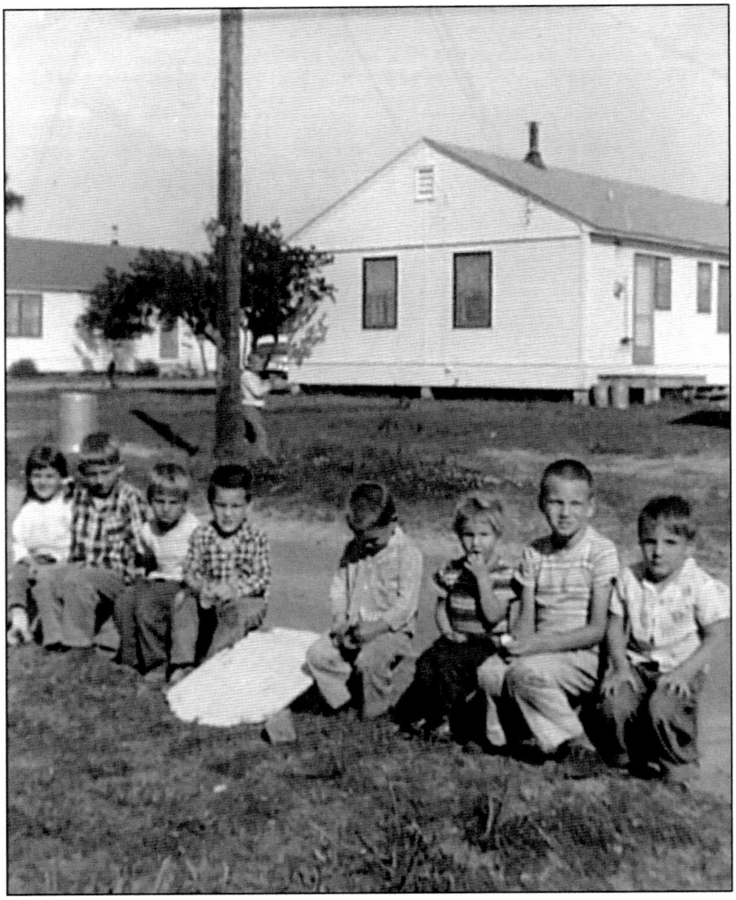

These children take time out from their busy playtime to pose for a photo in 1961 at Liberty Homes. (Courtesy of Glenn Bowdoin.)

These children on the Joan Simmons School of Dancing float in the North Charleston Christmas Parade took home an award for their decorations. (Courtesy of Ruth Cupp.)

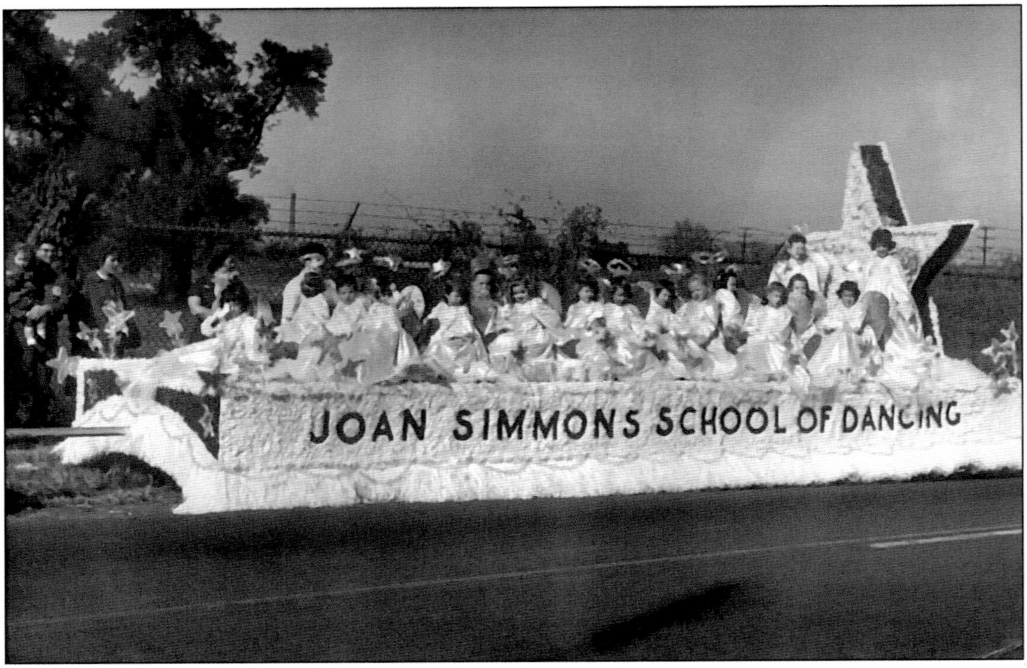

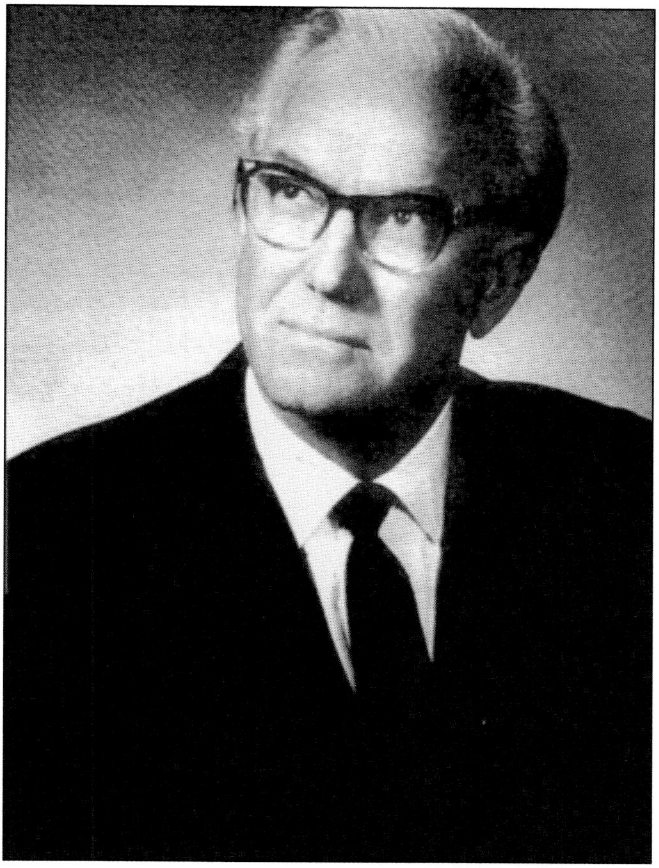

The Cooper River Memorial Library was chosen as the site for the monument dedicated to L. Mendel Rivers, shown here, who had served more than 25 years in the United States House of Representatives. The project was sponsored by the North Charleston Kiwanis Club with full cooperation from the trustees of the Cooper River Memorial Library Association in 1965. (Courtesy of Helen Blanton.)

In the early 1970s construction began on the Golden Dream Motel that is still located on Montague Avenue. (Courtesy of Carolyn Lecque Collins.)

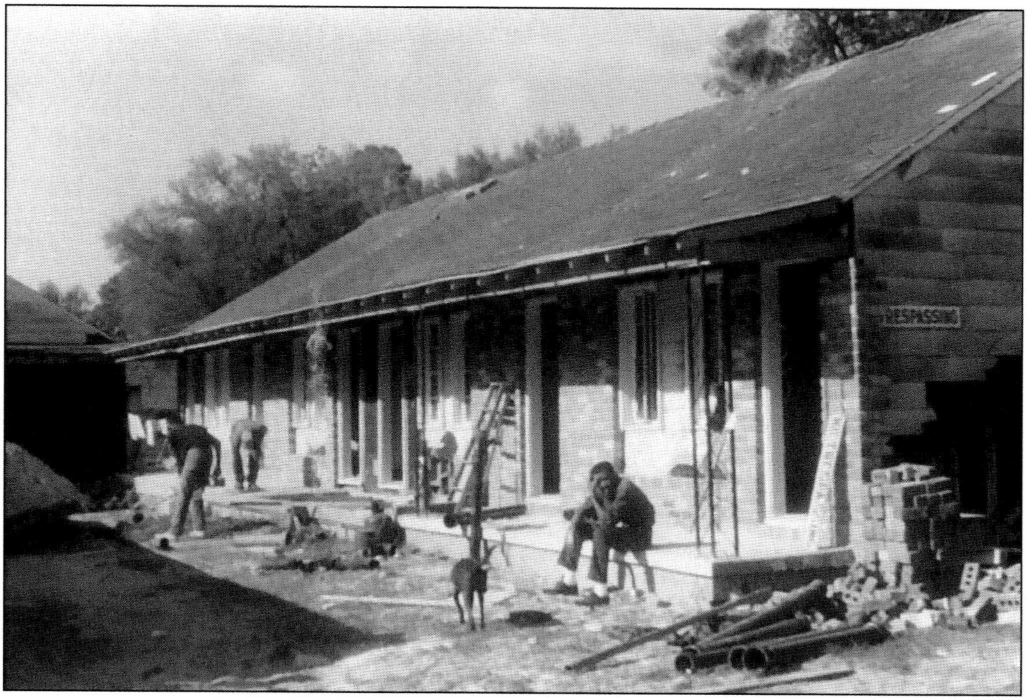

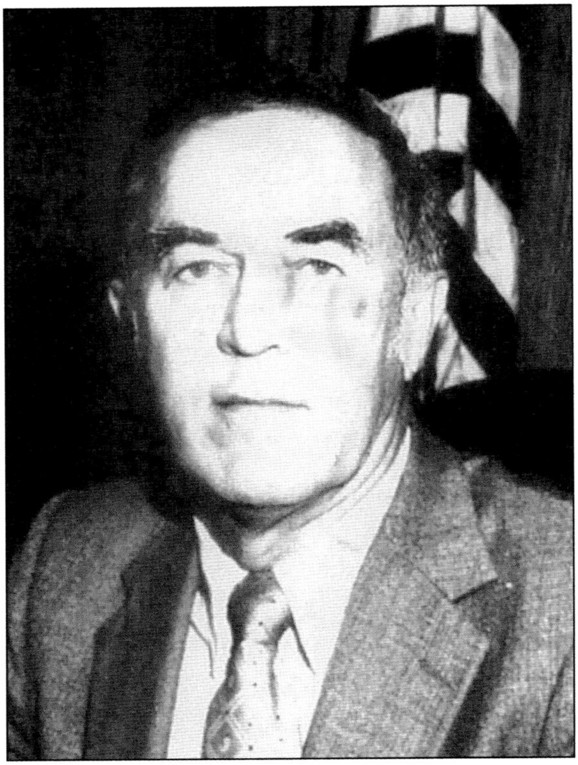

John E. Bourne Jr served as North Charleston's first mayor from 1972 to 1991. He was a former member of Charleston City Council and the South Carolina Senate. (Courtesy of the City of North Charleston.)

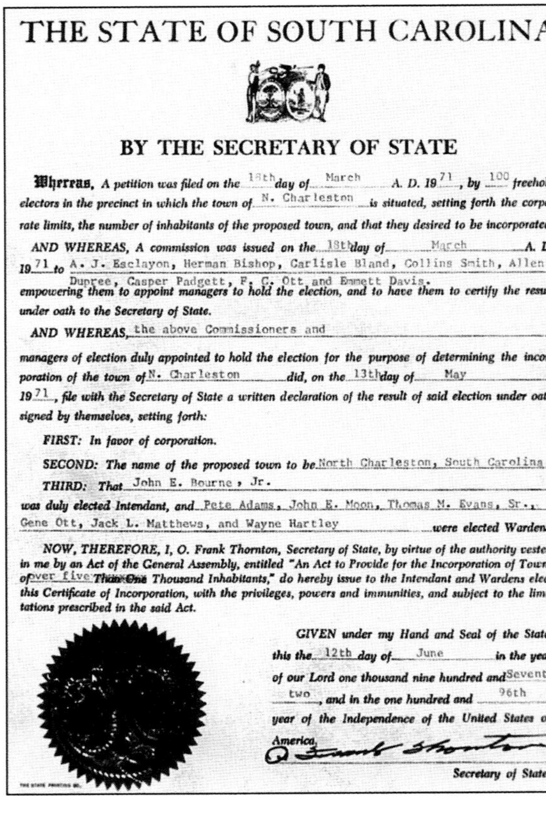

THE STATE OF SOUTH CAROLINA

BY THE SECRETARY OF STATE

Whereas, *A petition was filed on the* 18th *day of* March *A. D. 19*71, *by* 100 *freehold electors in the precinct in which the town of* N. Charleston *is situated, setting forth the corporate limits, the number of inhabitants of the proposed town, and that they desired to be incorporated.*

AND WHEREAS, A commission was issued on the 18th *day of* March *A. D. 19*71 *to* A. J. Esclayon, Herman Bishop, Carlisle Bland, Collins Smith, Allen Dupree, Casper Padgett, F. C. Ott and Emmett Davis. *empowering them to appoint managers to hold the election, and to have them to certify the result under oath to the Secretary of State.*

AND WHEREAS, the above Commissioners and *managers of election duly appointed to hold the election for the purpose of determining the incorporation of the town of* N. Charleston *did, on the* 13th *day of* May *19*71, *file with the Secretary of State a written declaration of the result of said election under oath signed by themselves, setting forth:*

FIRST: In favor of corporation.

SECOND: The name of the proposed town to be North Charleston, South Carolina

THIRD: That John E. Bourne, Jr.

was duly elected Intendant, and Pete Adams, John E. Moon, Thomas M. Evans, Sr., Gene Ott, Jack L. Matthews, and Wayne Hartley *were elected Wardens.*

NOW, THEREFORE, I, O. Frank Thornton, Secretary of State, by virtue of the authority vested in me by an Act of the General Assembly, entitled "An Act to Provide for the Incorporation of Towns of over five ~~*Than One*~~ *Thousand Inhabitants," do hereby issue to the Intendant and Wardens elect this Certificate of Incorporation, with the privileges, powers and immunities, and subject to the limitations prescribed in the said Act.*

GIVEN under my Hand and Seal of the State, this the 12th *day of* June *in the year of our Lord one thousand nine hundred and* Seventy two, *and in the one hundred and* 96th *year of the Independence of the United States of America.*

O. Frank Thornton

Secretary of State.

In 1972, the South Carolina General Assembly presented this Certificate of Incorporation to the city and North Charleston's status as a city was official by June of that year. (Courtesy of the City of North Charleston.)

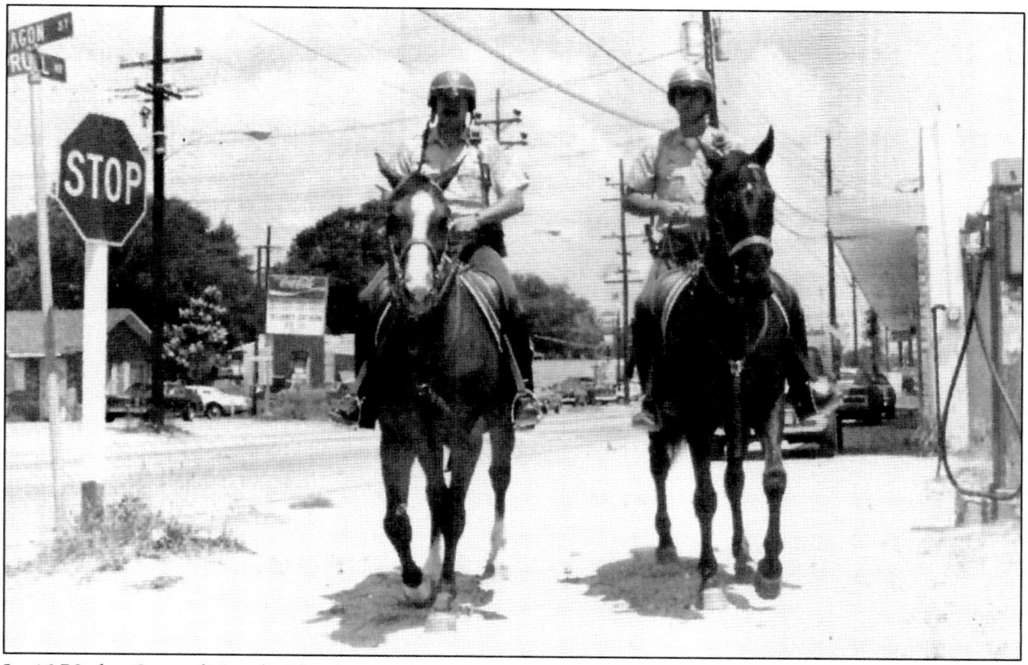

In 1973 the City of North Charleston formed its very own police department under the direction of Chief Roger F. Poston. Eighteen police officers were hired. In the department's early days some officers patrolled the area on horseback.

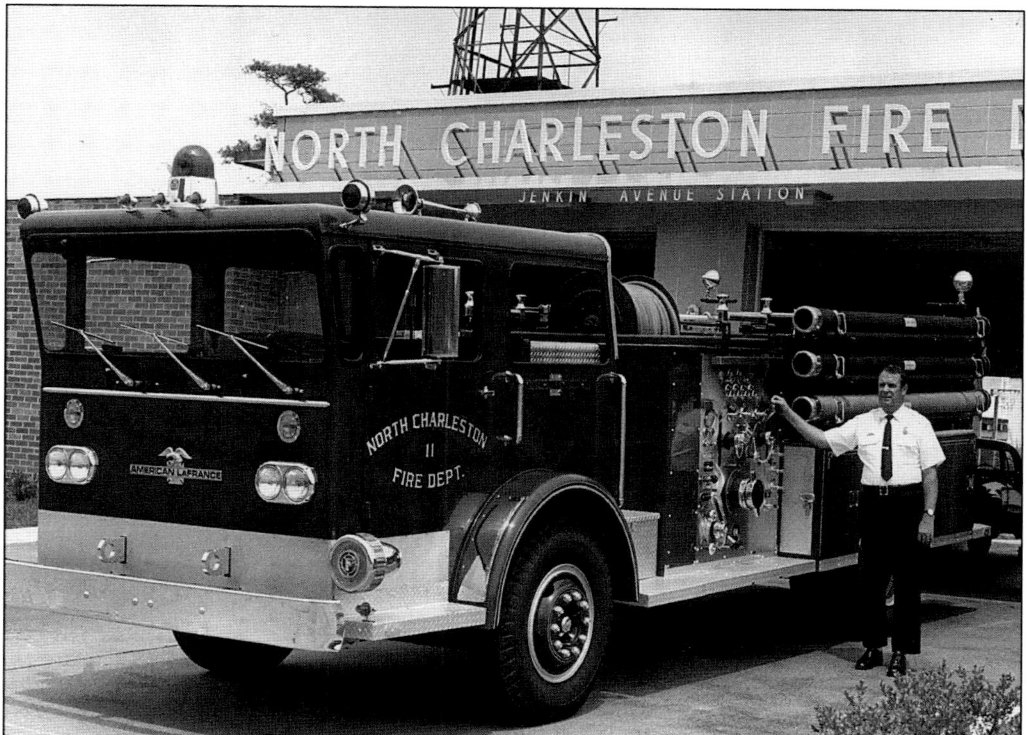

William Frank New Sr. became the first fire chief for the newly formed city of North Charleston in 1973. (Courtesy of Lucy New.)

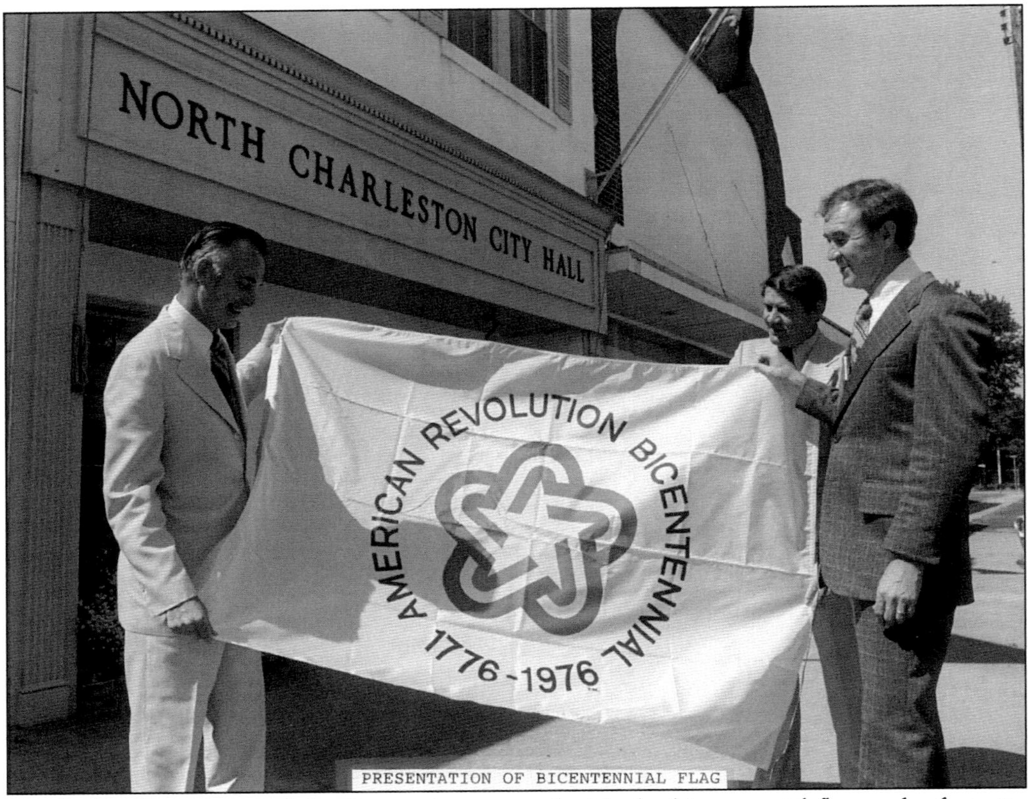

North Charleston mayor John Bourne is presented with the bicentennial flag at the first city hall building located in the Olde Village of North Charleston.

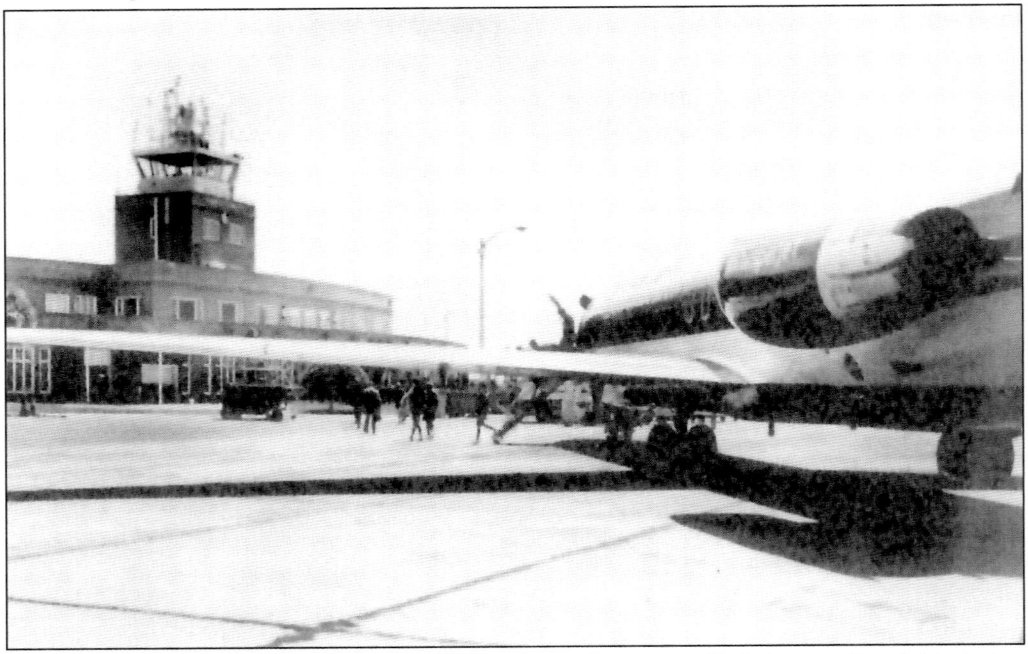

Pictured is the old Charleston Airport located on what was called Airport Road (Aviation Avenue). A more modern facility was later built just a few miles away.

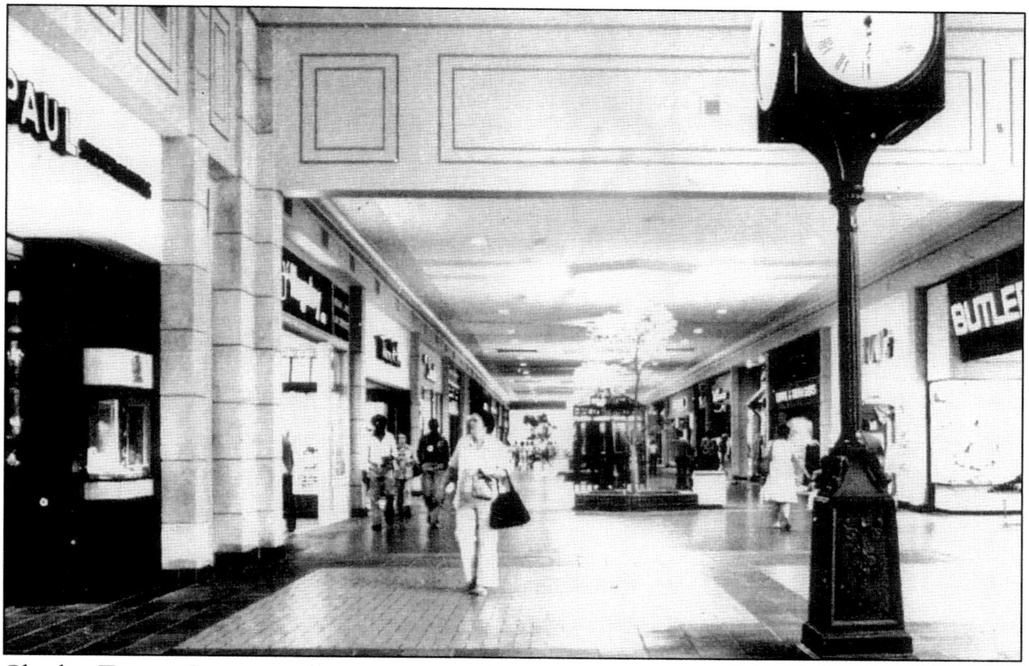

Charles Towne Square Mall was built off Montague Avenue and included such stores as Montgomery Ward, JC Penney, and Service Merchandise. The mall was closed in 1997.

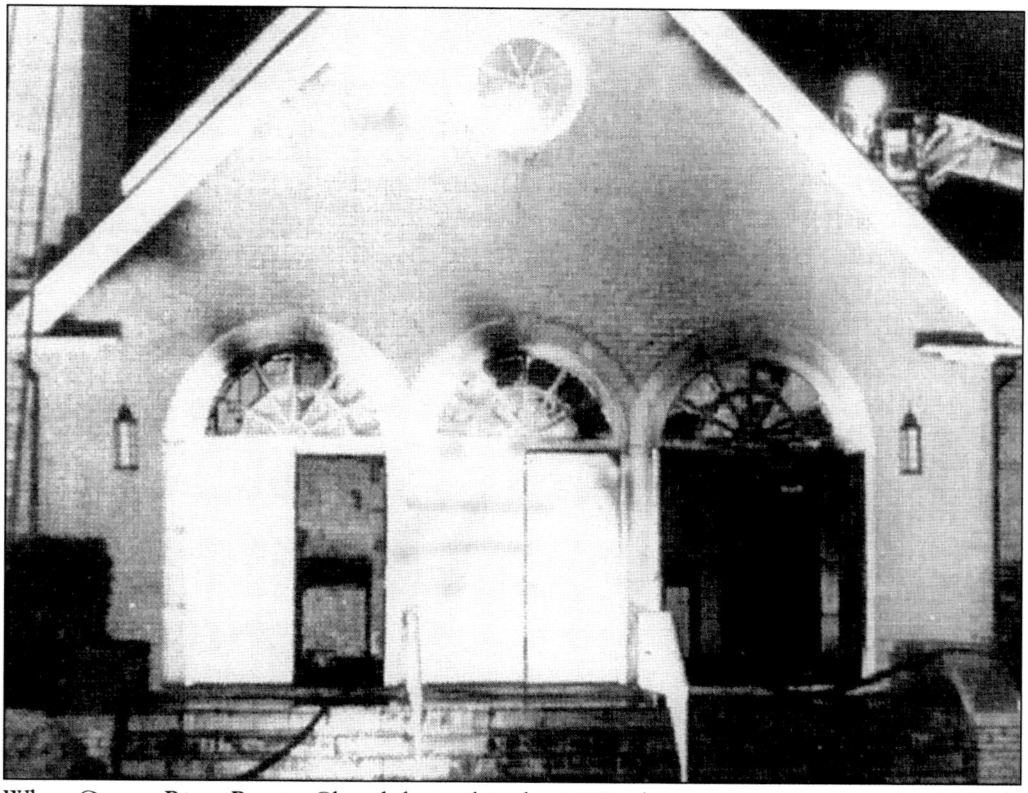

When Cooper River Baptist Church burned in the 1980s, the congregation met at both North Charleston High School and Park Circle Elementary School.

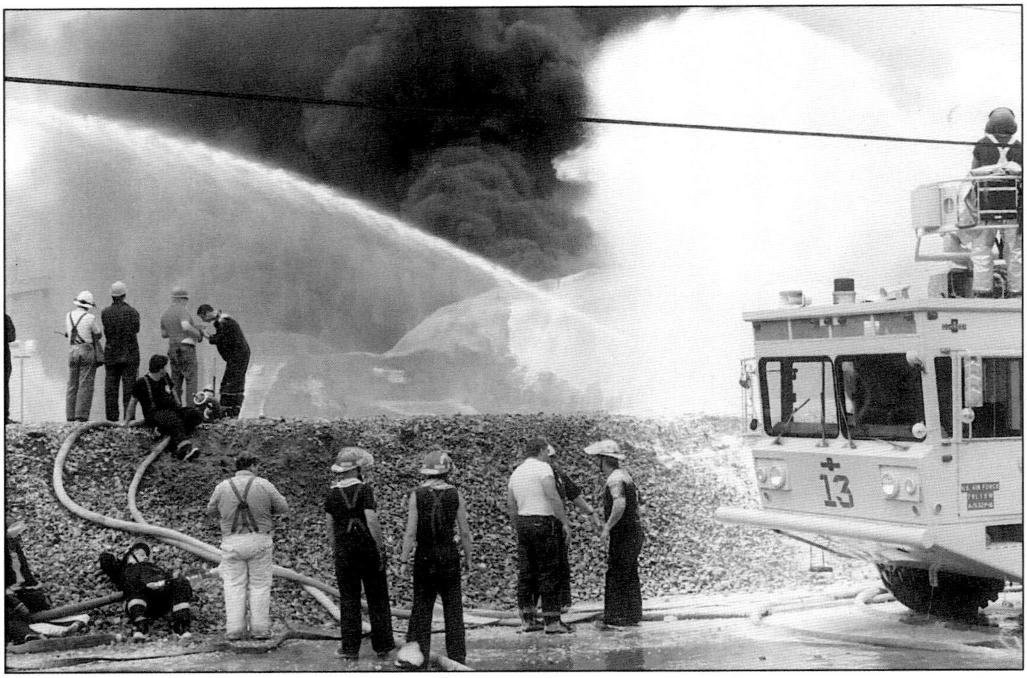

On June 20, 1987, lightning hit a fuel tank at the Hess Refinery and 25 million gallons of fuel burned out of control. Pictured are members of the North Charleston Fire Department who manned the fire for nearly two weeks. (Courtesy of Glenn Bowdoin.)

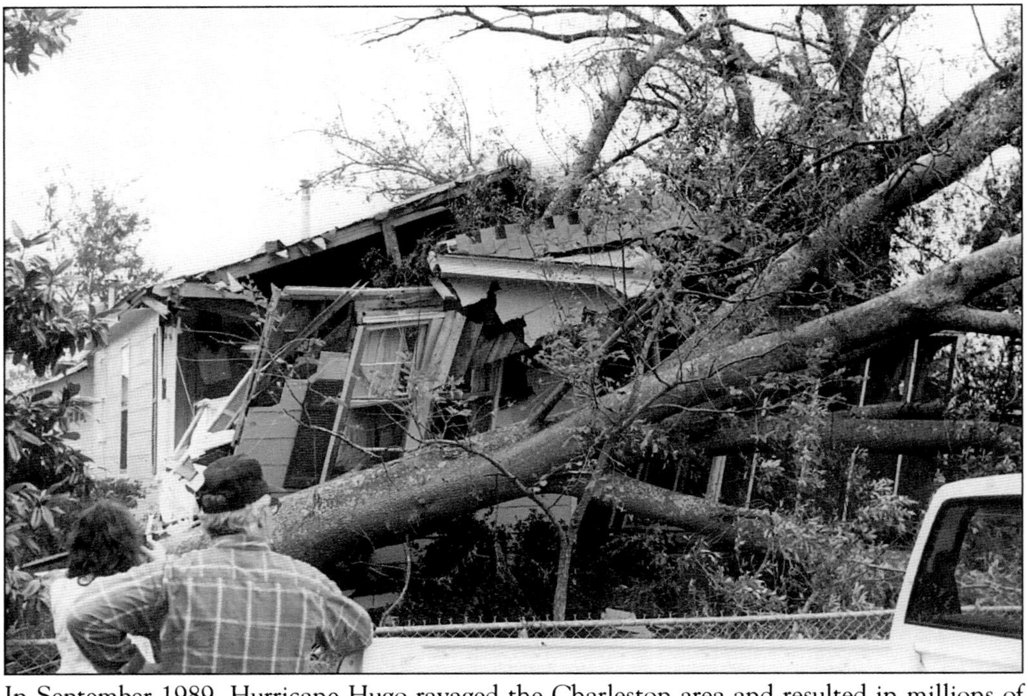

In September 1989, Hurricane Hugo ravaged the Charleston area and resulted in millions of dollars worth of damage to homes and businesses in the North Charleston area. This house on Woodlawn Avenue was completely destroyed when a tree fell through it as a result of the tornadoes associated with the storm. (Courtesy of Edith Painter.)

Five

A City with a Vision

North Charleston has undergone tremendous change as a result of its continued growth, and its future appears brighter than ever before. With improving quality of life for the citizens of the city as its main priority, the vision includes not only greater economic development, but also deeper recreational and cultural development. The North Charleston Performing Arts Center provides a venue for many different types of shows that come to the area, including theater, comedians, and concerts. The annual Arts Festival is one of the best in the state and continues to grow larger each year. More programs are offered through the North Charleston Recreation Department each year, and many relate to everyone from ages six to sixty. Plans for redevelopment of several historic neighborhoods and communities, a planned museum, a marina, and a water-front park to be located on the former Naval Base make up just a small taste of the the city's vision for its residents. The city is growing by leaps and bounds, and much like the great oaks that grow throughout the area, North Charleston is branching out, but its roots are planted firmly and deeply in its rich history.

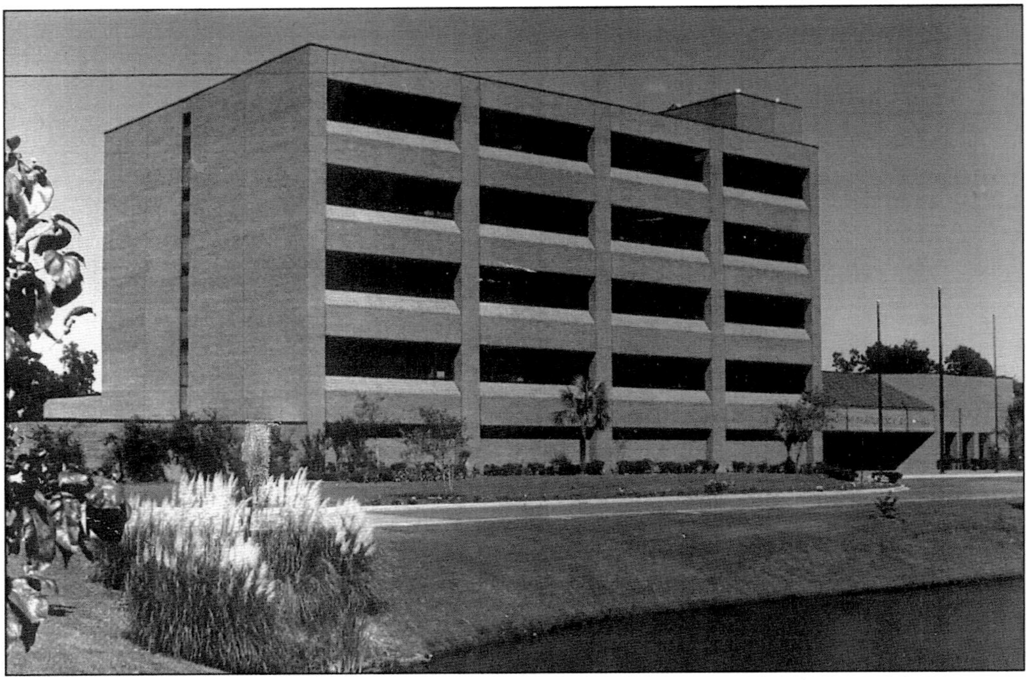

The North Charleston City Hall Building is located at 4900 LaCross Road.

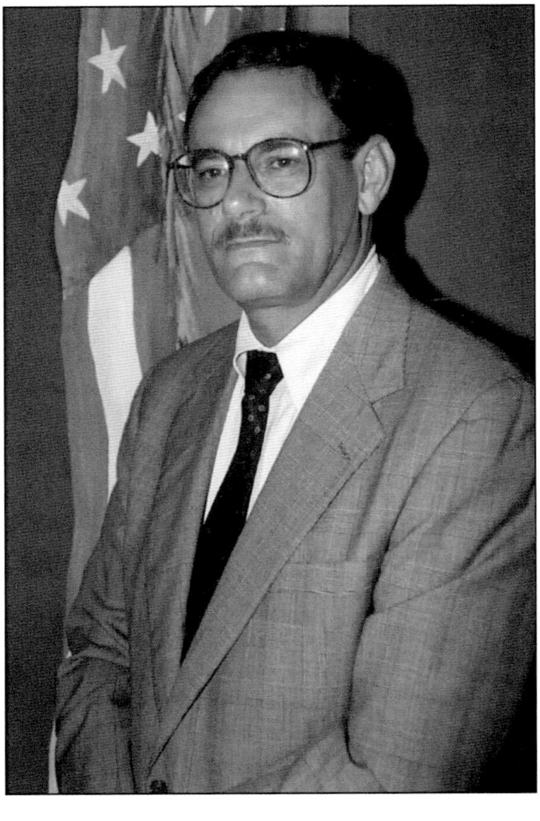

W. Robert Kinard became mayor of North Charleston in June of 1991. A native of North Charleston, Kinard graduated from North Charleston High School and attended the Citadel and the University of South Carolina Law School. He served in the U. S. Air Force from 1966 to 1970 and in the Vietnam War from 1969 to 1970. He served on the South Carolina House of Representatives and is a former city judge. He resigned his office of mayor in April of 1994.

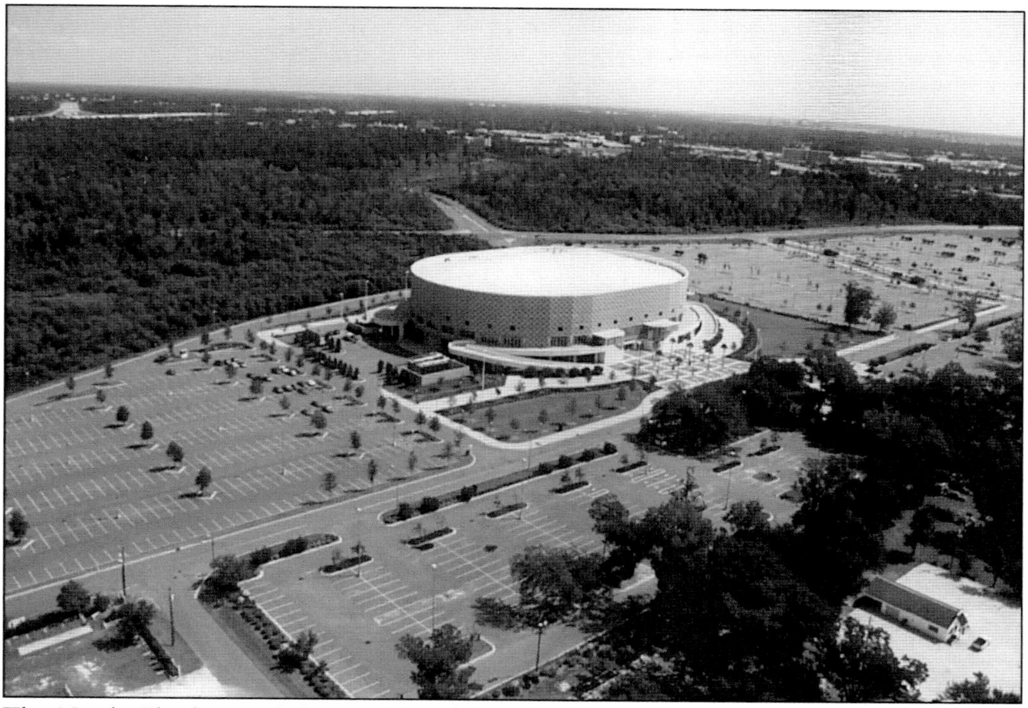

The North Charleston Coliseum opened its doors January 29, 1993. Located on Coliseum Drive, the 14,000-seat sports and entertainment complex serves as the homebase for the ECHL's South Carolina Stingrays. It also hosts various events ranging from college basketball to arena football. Some of the world's biggest entertainers have performed here as well. (Courtesy of the City of North Charleston.

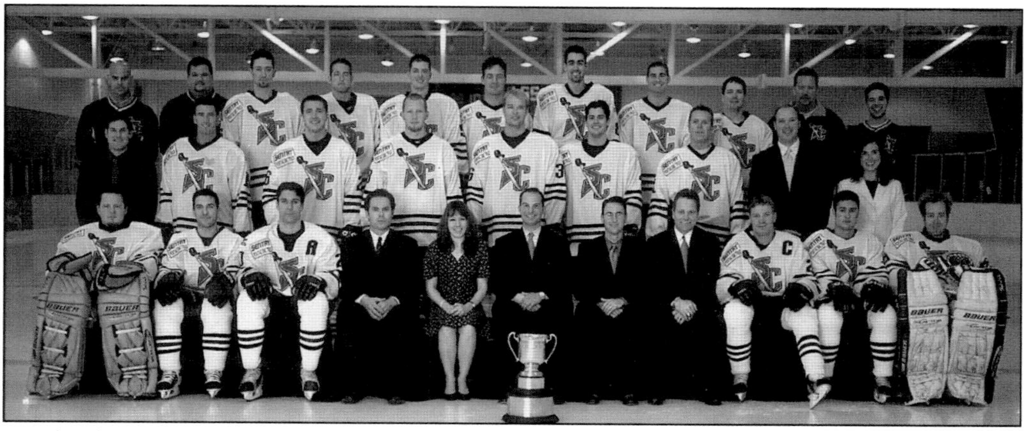

North Charleston residents are big fans of the South Carolina Stingrays. In addition to playing hockey, the team members are considered great ambassadors within the community. The Stingrays are two-time winners of the Kelly Cup. (Courtesy of the South Carolina Stingrays.)

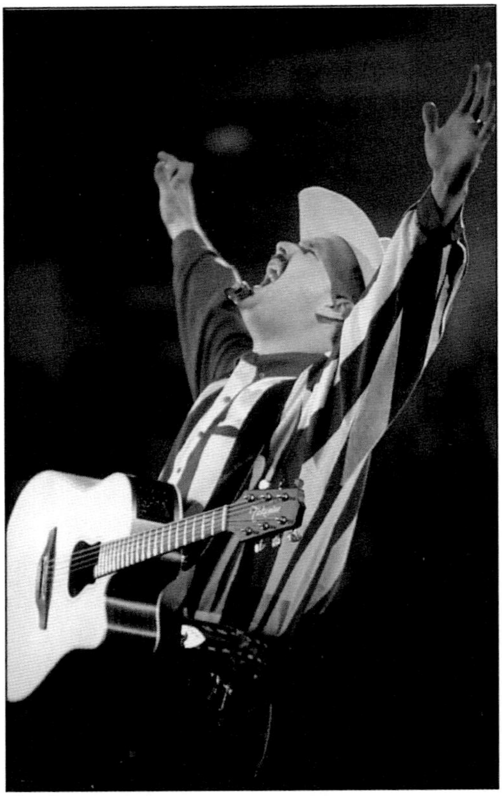

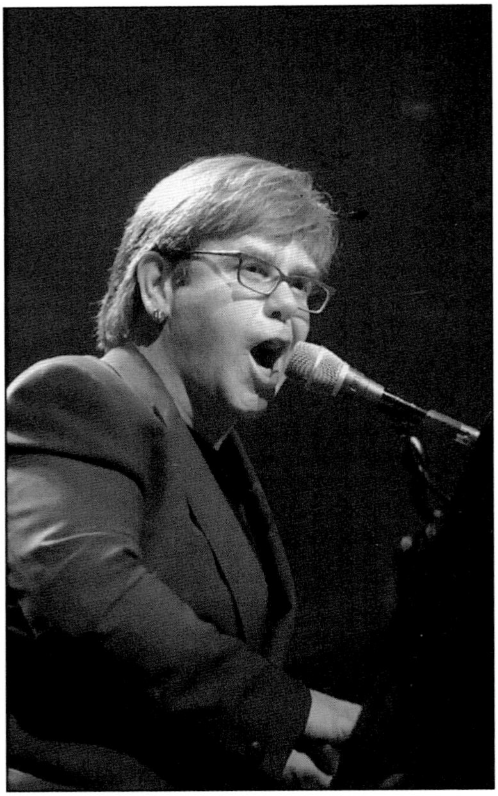

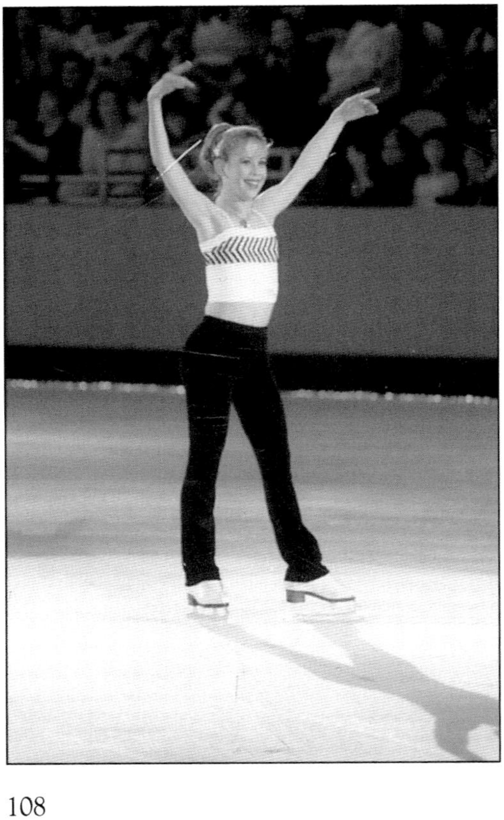

Entertainers such as Garth Brooks (top, left) and Elton John (top, right) have played to sold-out crowds at the North Charleston Coliseum. After the Olympics, gold medalist Tara Lapinsky (below) made one of her first appearances at the North Charleston Coliseum. (Courtesy of the North Charleston Coliseum and Don Wilkinson.)

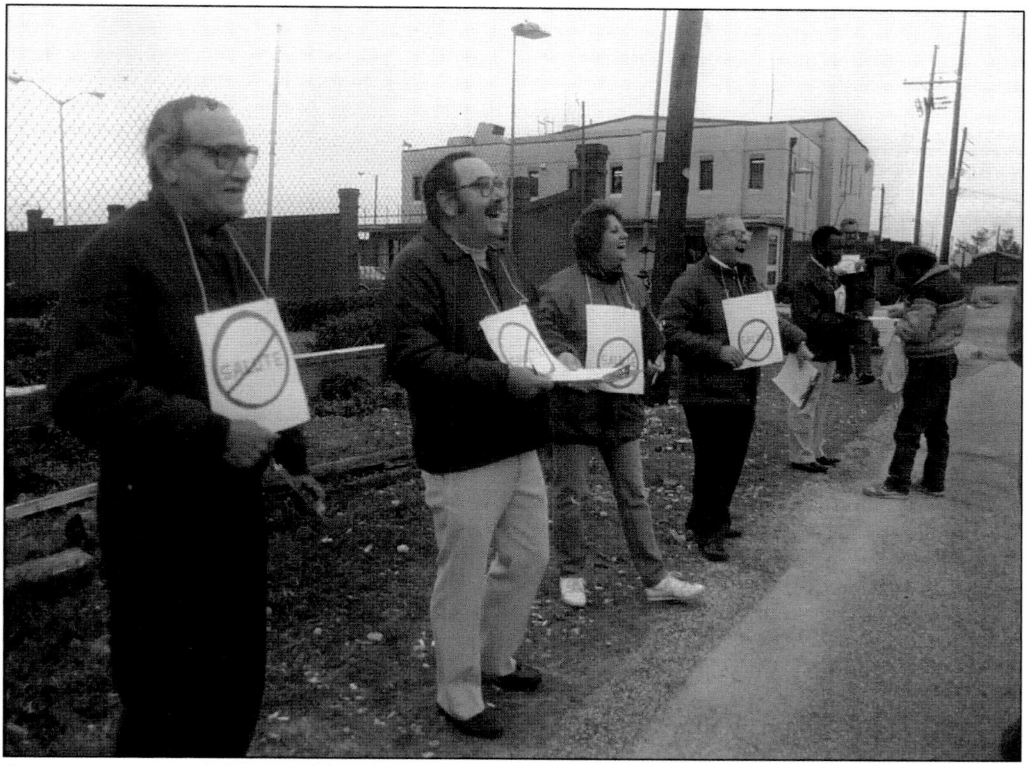

Announcements of the possible closing of the Charleston Naval Shipyard prompted many in North Charleston to protest. Pictured are protesters outside the Navy Yard's gate. (Courtesy of *The Post and Courier*.)

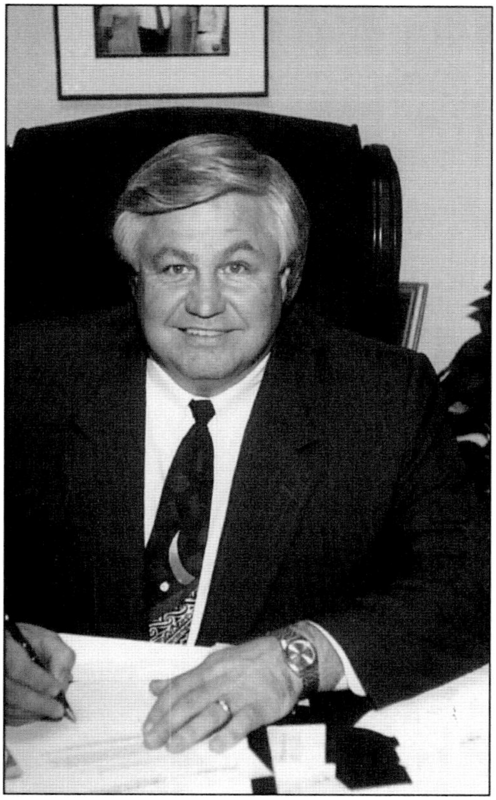

Mayor R. Keith Summey was chosen in a special election to lead North Charleston in October of 1994. A Lowcountry native, Summey graduated from Chicora High School and the Baptist College at Charleston (Charleston Southern University). He was elected to Charleston County Council in 1988 and served as Chairman from 1992 to 1994. He is married to the former Debbie Crosby and is the proud father of two. (Courtesy of the City of North Charleston.)

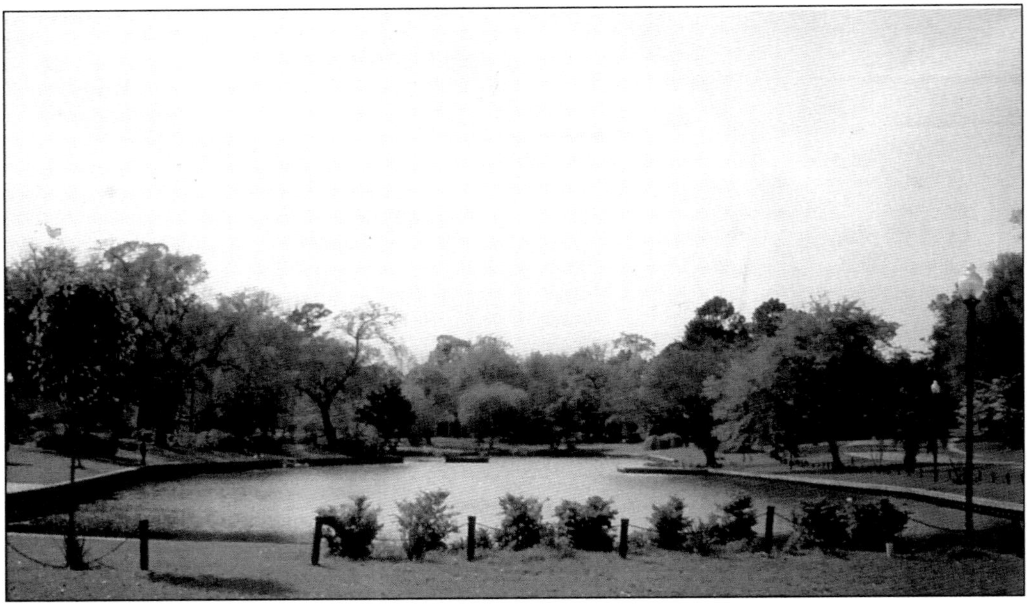

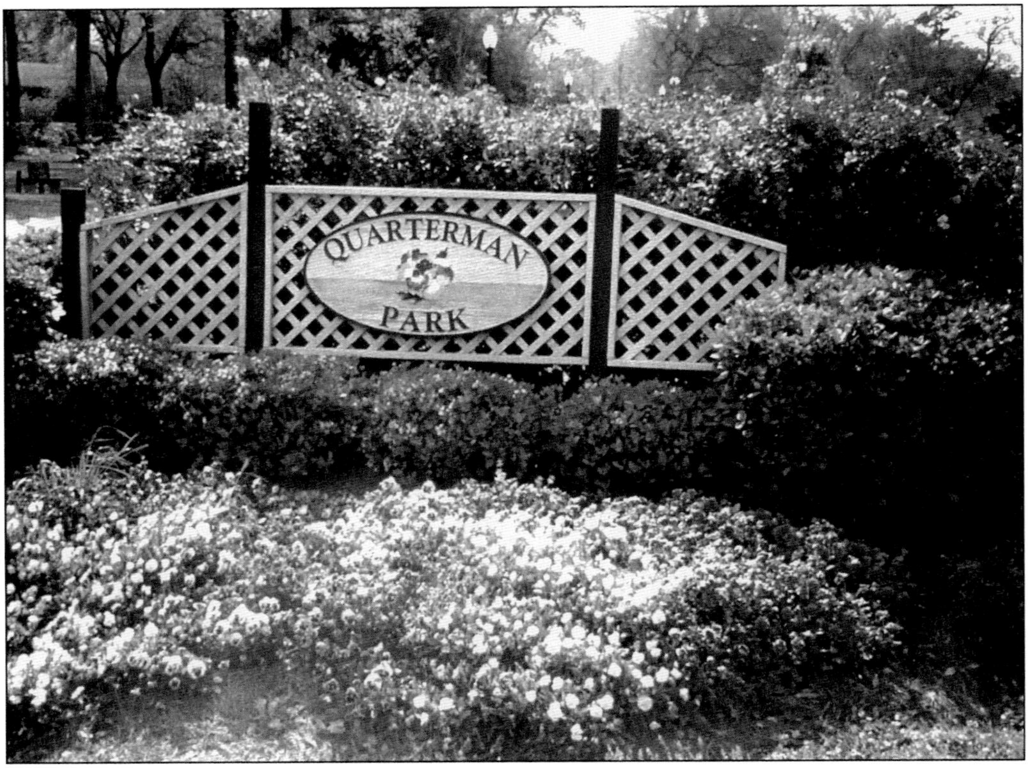

Quarterman Park is one place that people immediately think of whenever North Charleston comes to mind. "The Duck Pond," as it was called for many years, is located on Buist Avenue and is one of the most beautiful places in the city. Generations of children have visited to feed the ducks or to fish. (Courtesy of the City of North Charleston.)

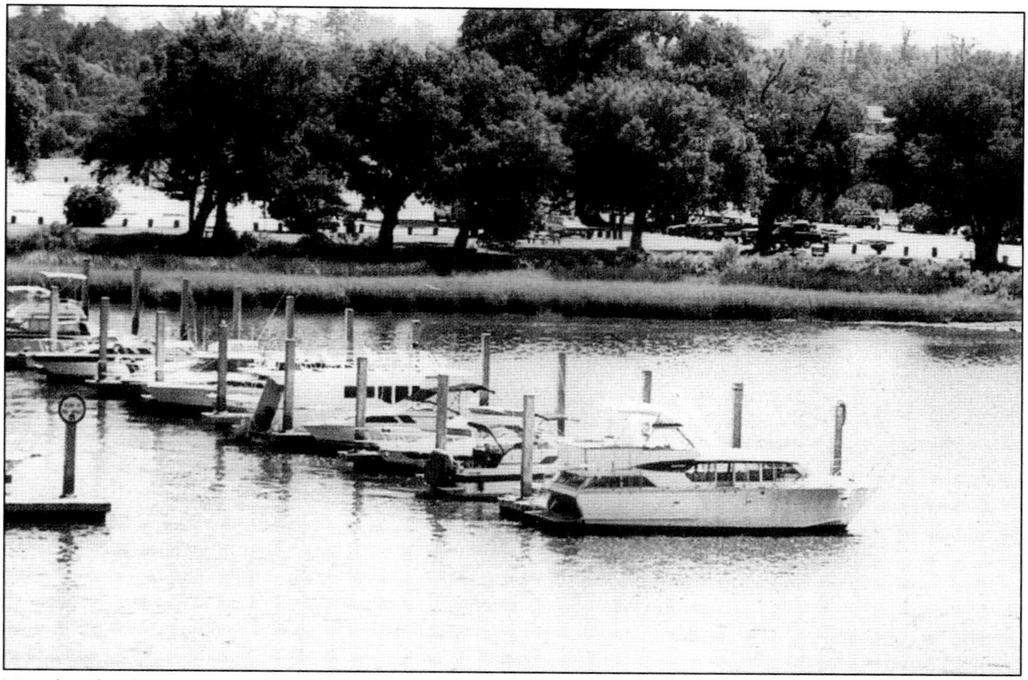

North Charleston is centrally located on the shores of two rivers, which allows for a great deal of aquatic activity. Duncan Boat Harbor maintains this small marina on the Ashley River. (Courtesy of the City of North Charleston.)

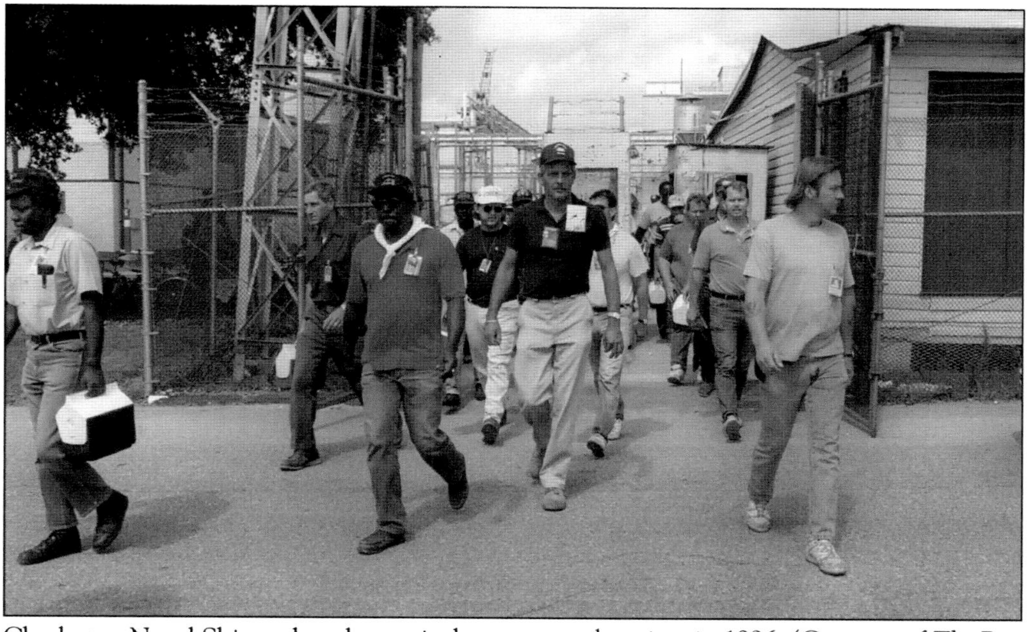

Charleston Naval Shipyard workers exit the gates one last time in 1996. (Courtesy of *The Post and Courier*.)

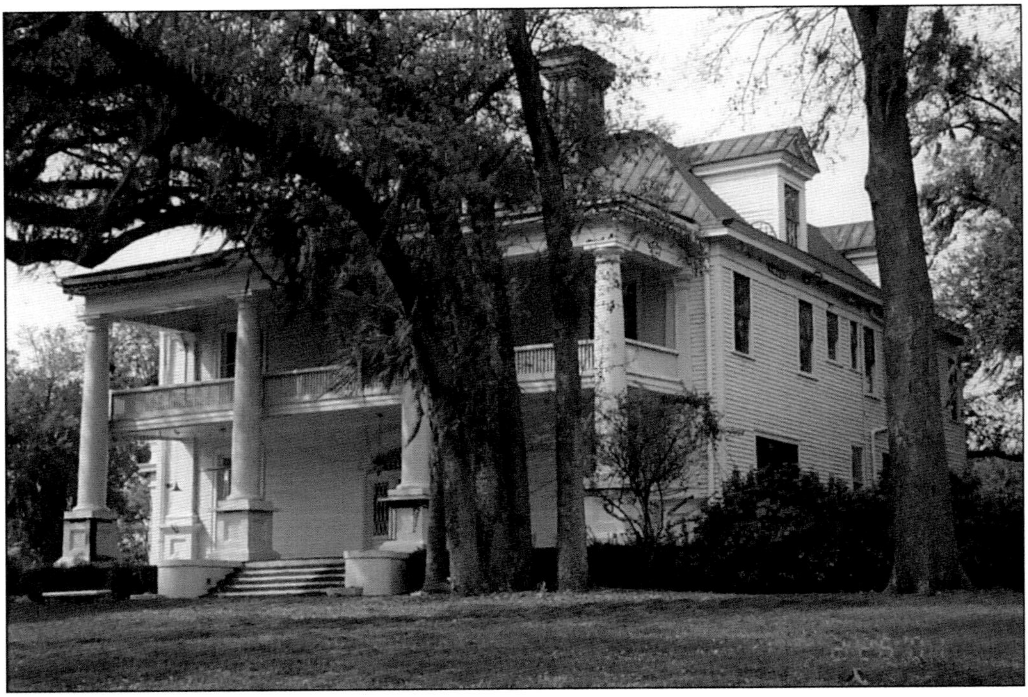

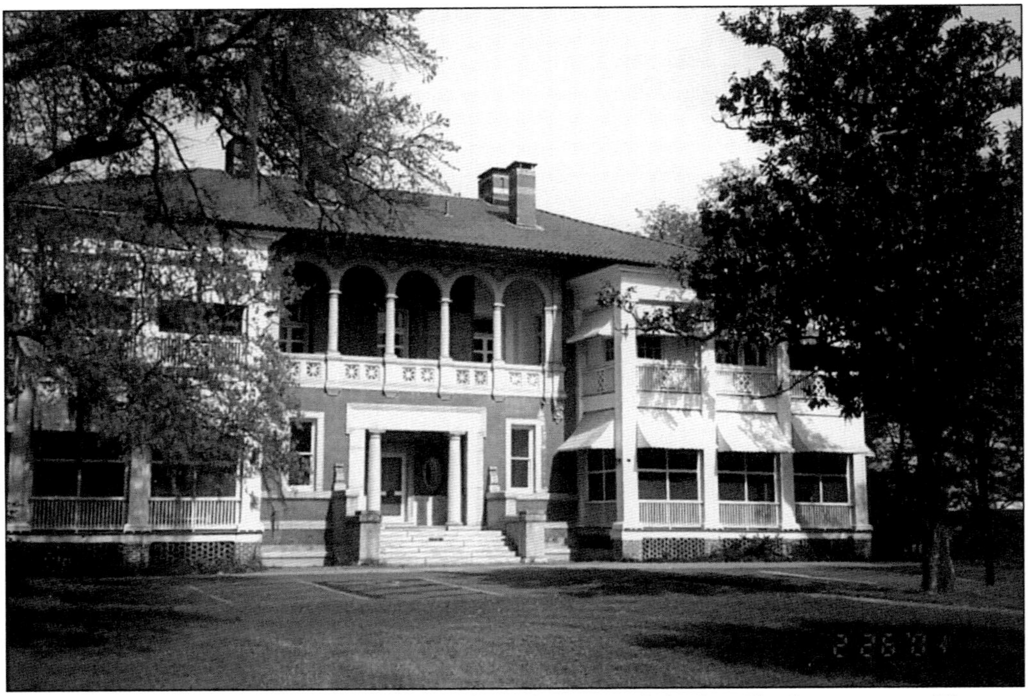

These two historic buildings remained when the Navy left the Charleston area. The top photograph depicts the Admirals Quarters and the bottom depicts the Officers Quarters. North Charleston has plans to use both buildings once they are officially turned over to the city.

Westvaco (West Virginia Pulp and Paper Company) was offered a 300- acre tract of land on the Cooper River in the 1930s. In 1936 construction began on the paper mill. Today, with its many divisions including Kraft and Chemical, Westvaco is the leading supplier of saturating kraft, which is used in manufacturing plastic laminates, and the chemicals that are found in many household products.

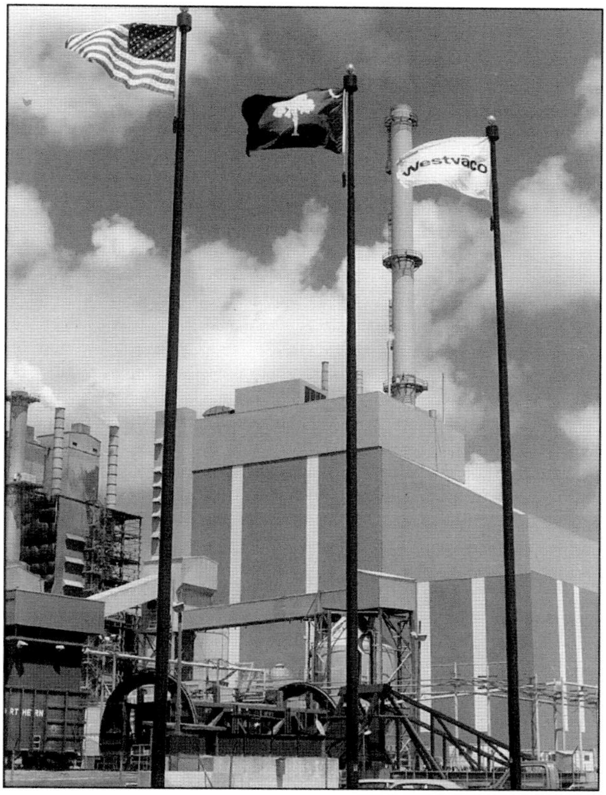

The Charleston Air Force Base employs thousands of personnel as the home for the U.S. Air Force's 437th Airlift Wing.

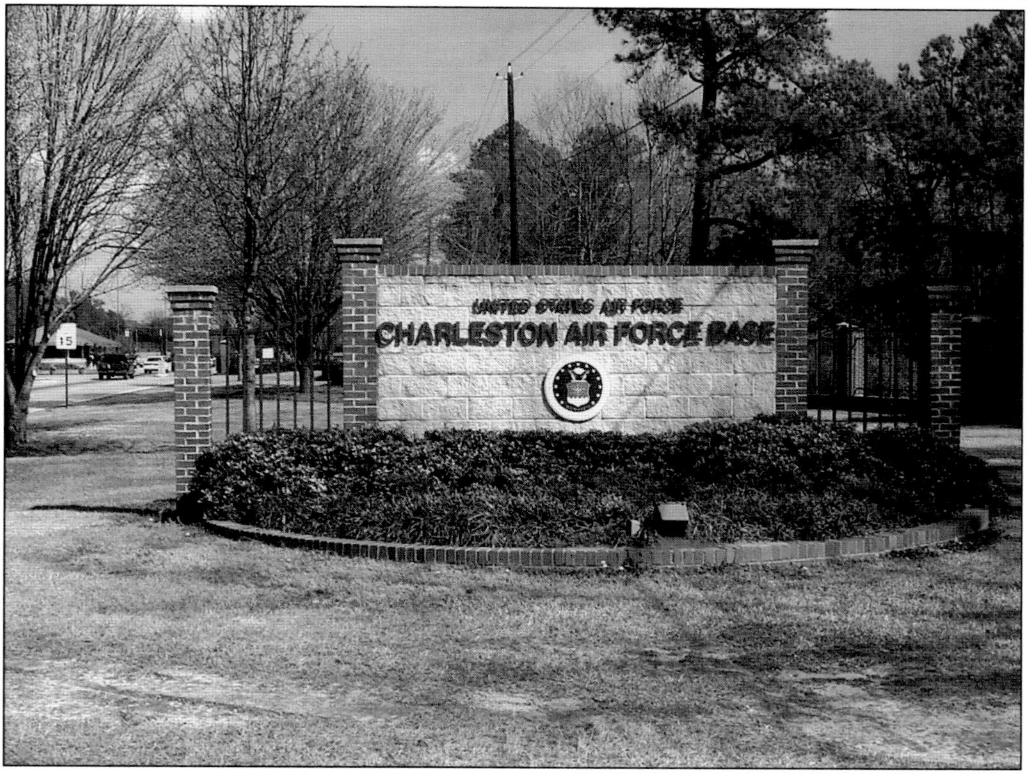

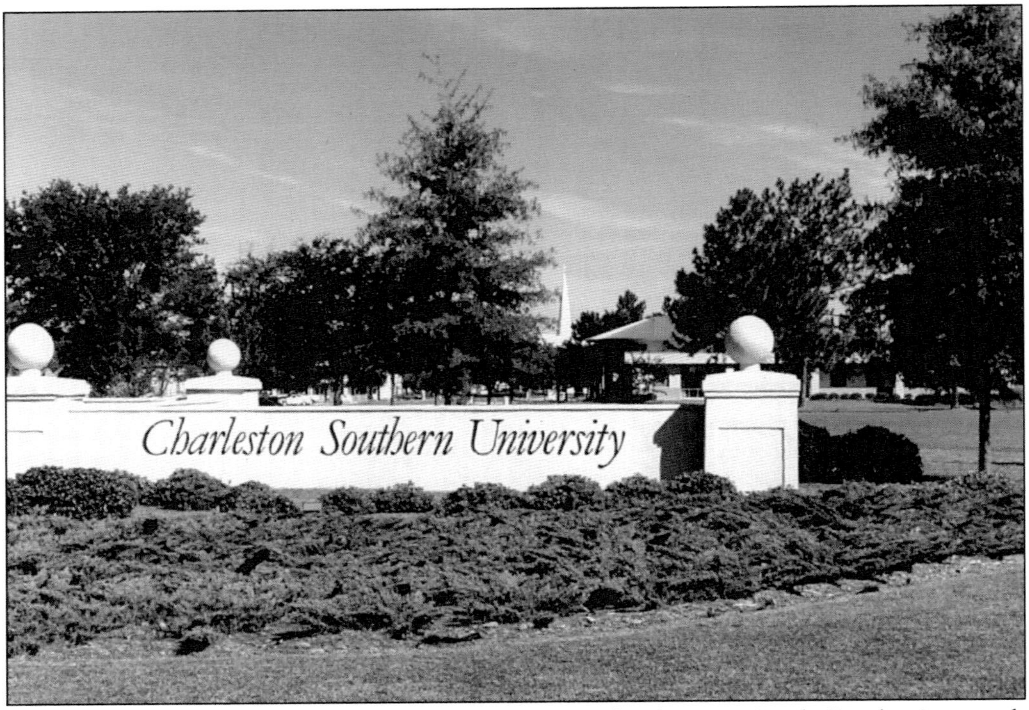

In just three decades, Charleston Southern University has become South Carolina's second-largest private, accredited school with approximately 3,000 students. Situated at the intersection of SC Highway 78 and I-26, CSU promotes academic excellence in a Christian environment and offers more than 30 undergraduate and graduate degrees in daytime and evening classes.

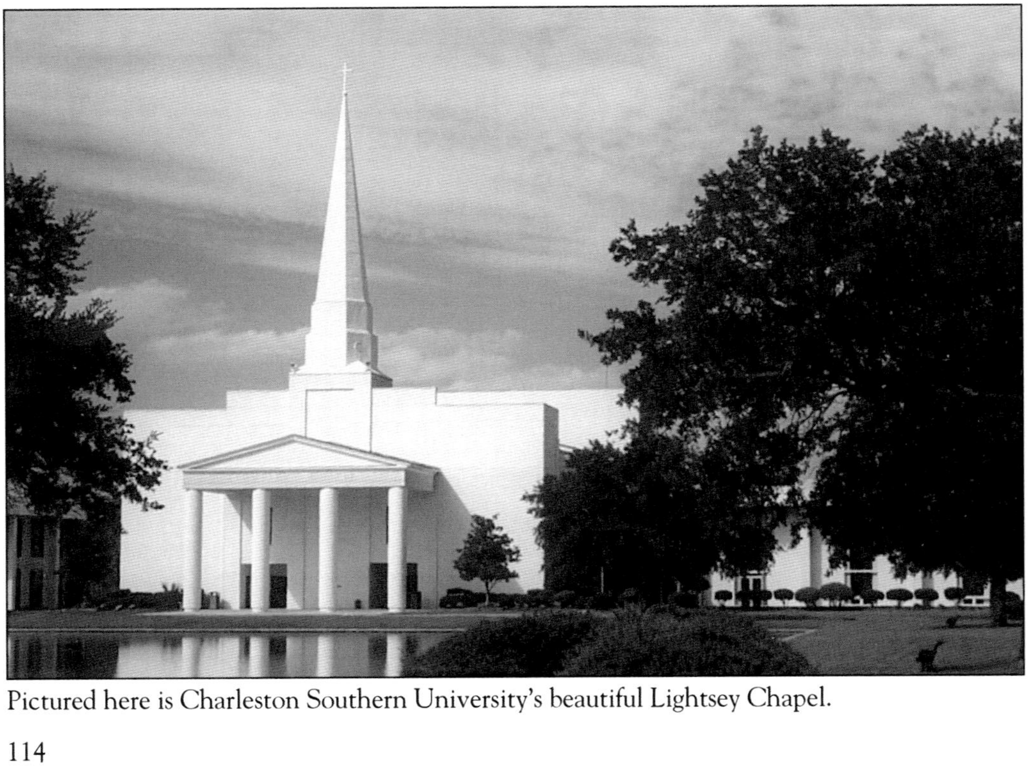

Pictured here is Charleston Southern University's beautiful Lightsey Chapel.

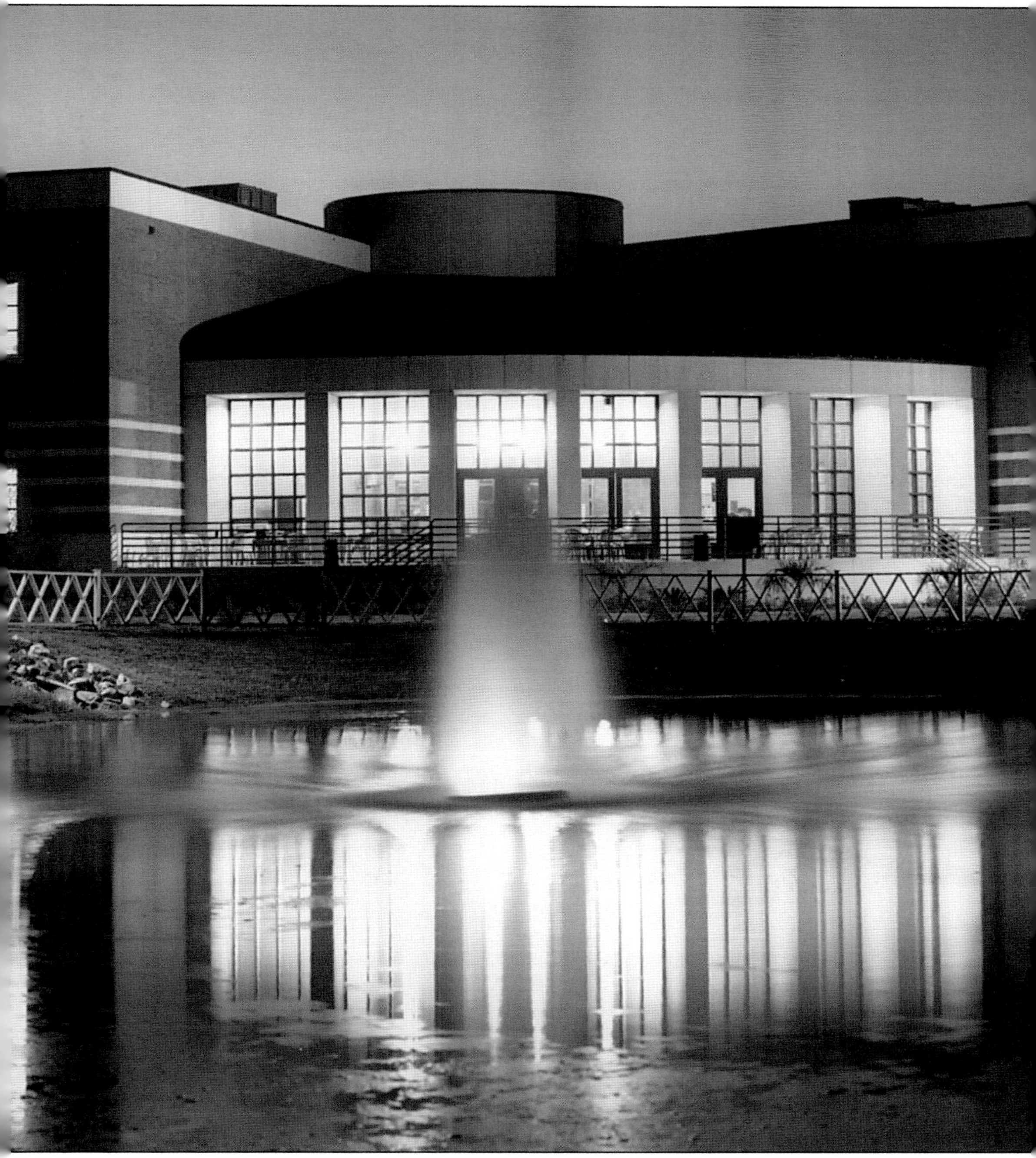

Trident Technical College serves Berkeley, Charleston, and Dorchester County residents. The community college provides quality education and promotes economic development. Nearly 9,000 students attend credit courses and more than 20,000 take continuing education classes each year. TTC's main campus is located in North Charleston and the school has satellite campuses in Moncks Corner and Downtown Charleston.

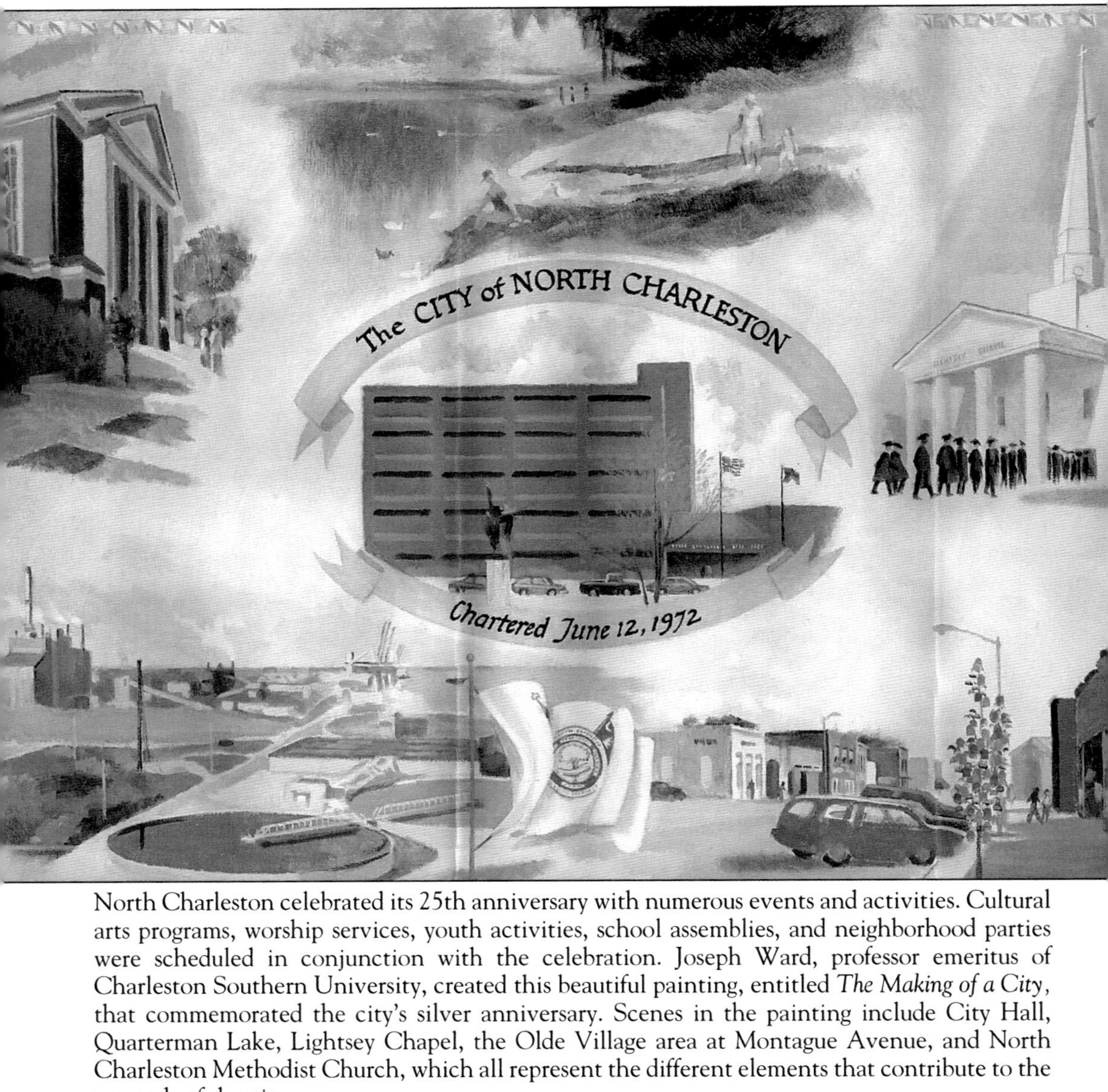

North Charleston celebrated its 25th anniversary with numerous events and activities. Cultural arts programs, worship services, youth activities, school assemblies, and neighborhood parties were scheduled in conjunction with the celebration. Joseph Ward, professor emeritus of Charleston Southern University, created this beautiful painting, entitled *The Making of a City*, that commemorated the city's silver anniversary. Scenes in the painting include City Hall, Quarterman Lake, Lightsey Chapel, the Olde Village area at Montague Avenue, and North Charleston Methodist Church, which all represent the different elements that contribute to the strength of the city.

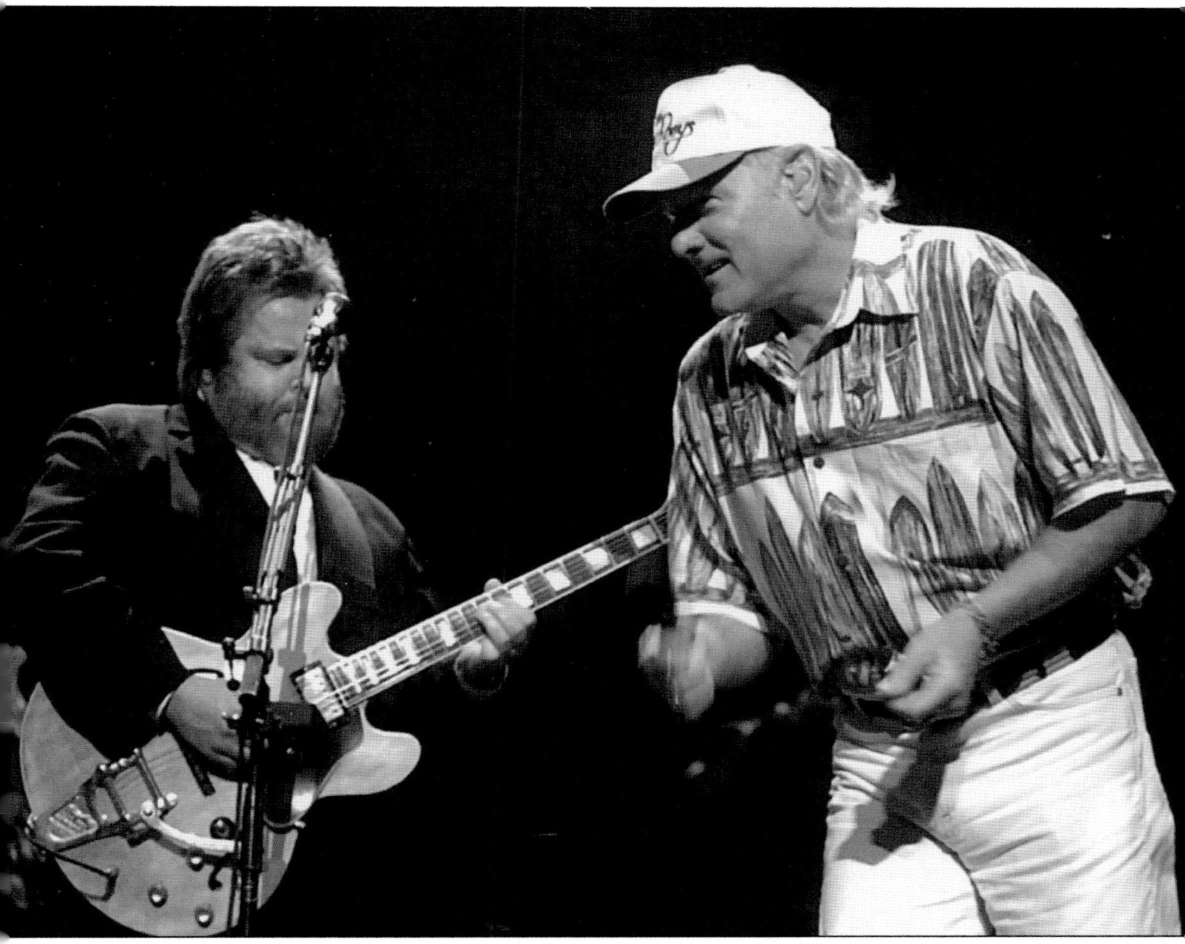

The Beach Boys performed at the North Charleston Coliseum for the city's 25th anniversary. (Courtesy of North Charleston Coliseum.)

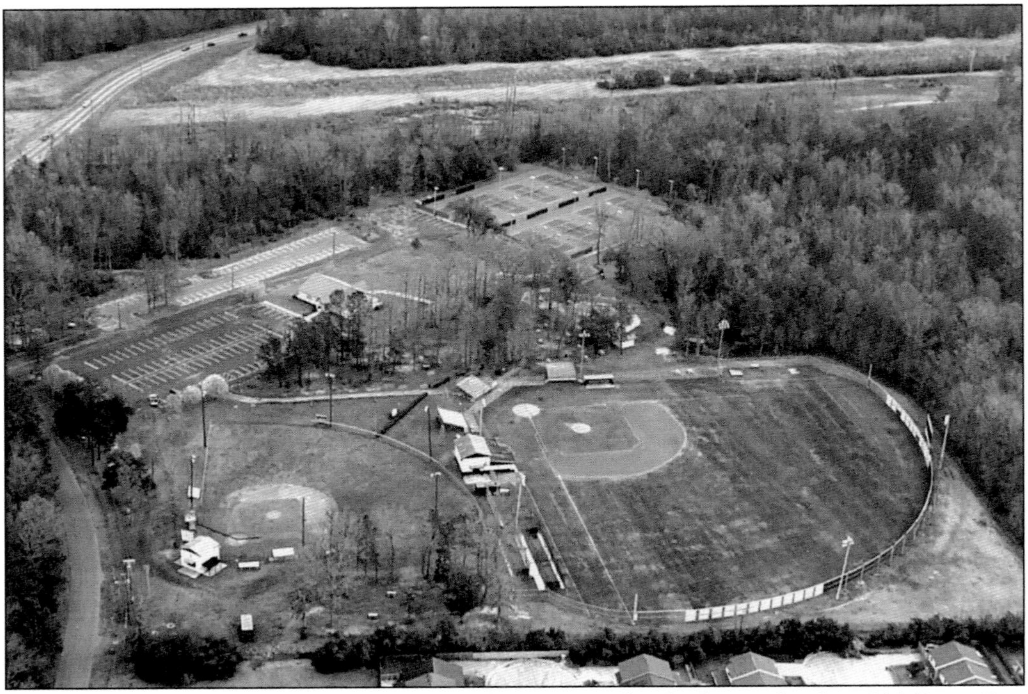

Beautiful Collins Park has been the preferred site in North Charleston for the 1998 Dixie Pre-Majors World Series and the 2001 Dixie Majors World Series for a number of years.

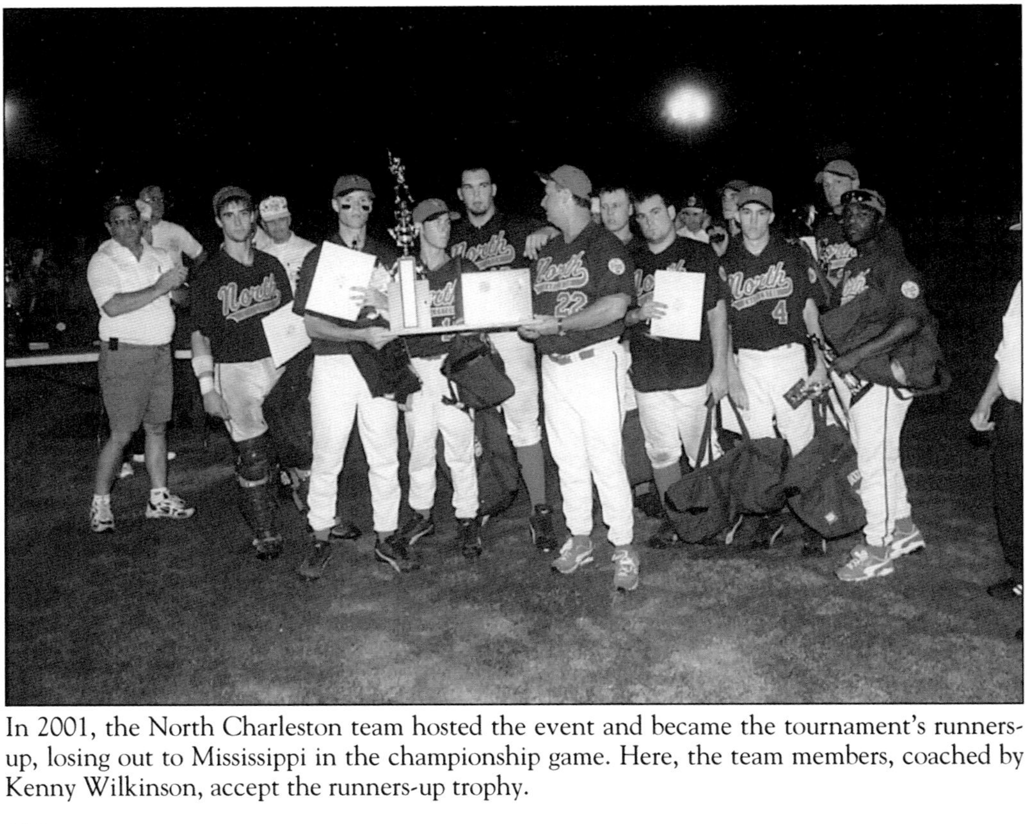

In 2001, the North Charleston team hosted the event and became the tournament's runners-up, losing out to Mississippi in the championship game. Here, the team members, coached by Kenny Wilkinson, accept the runners-up trophy.

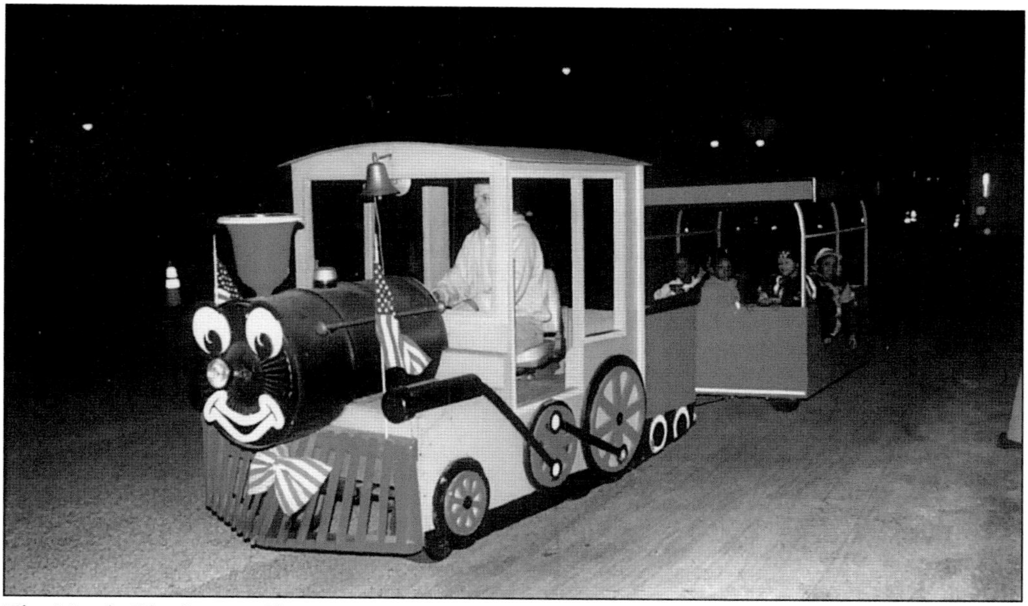

The North Charleston Christmas Tree Lighting Festival is one of the most anticipated events held during the year. Park Circle and the surrounding area is aglow with millions of beautiful lights during the season. Events at the lighting include a parade, craft shows, a carnival, and much more. Kids can even take a ride in a little train.

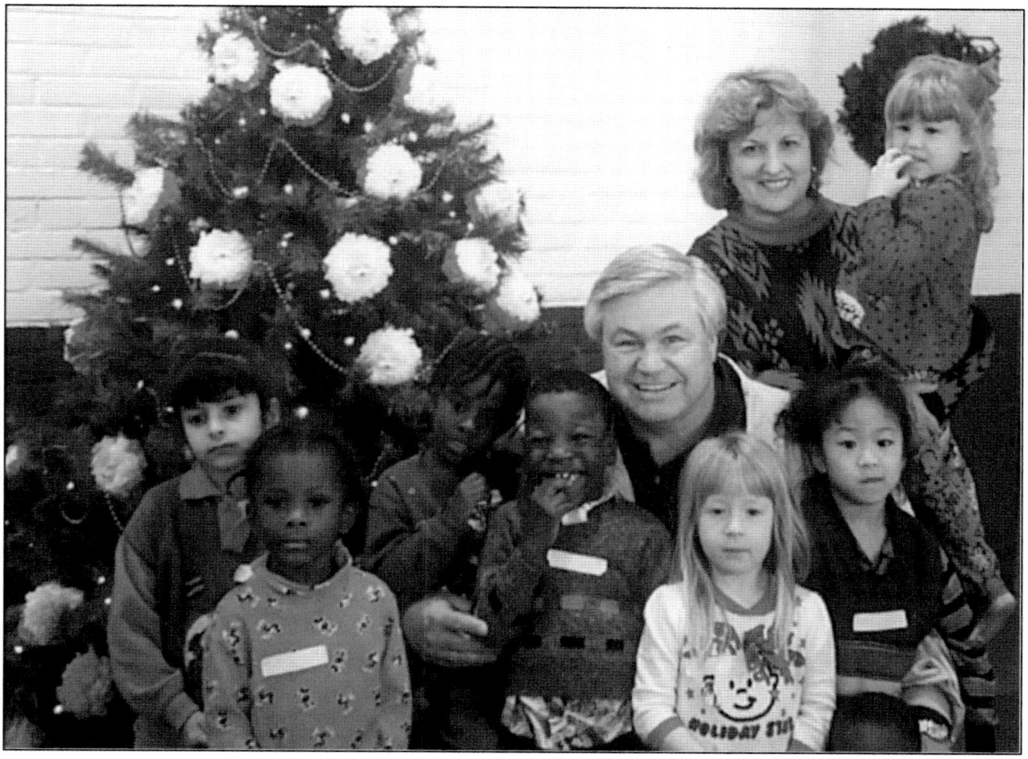

Jingle Bells Fun for Tots is a Christmas program for pre-school children. Activities include a visit to the North Pole, music, games, crafts, and a visit from Santa and Mrs. Clause. Mayor Summey and his wife, Debbie, take part in the 2001 program.

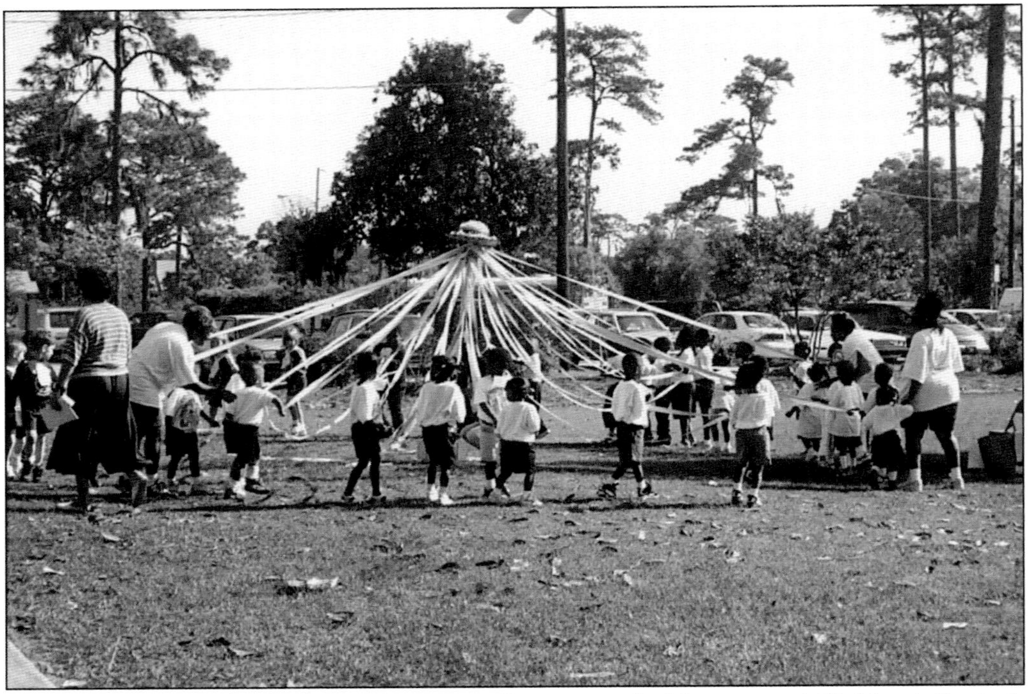

Every year, the North Charleston Recreation Department holds its annual Children's Festival. Geared for children ages 2 to 5 years old, the festival includes riding big wheels, obstacle courses, ball tosses, and even a Maypole.

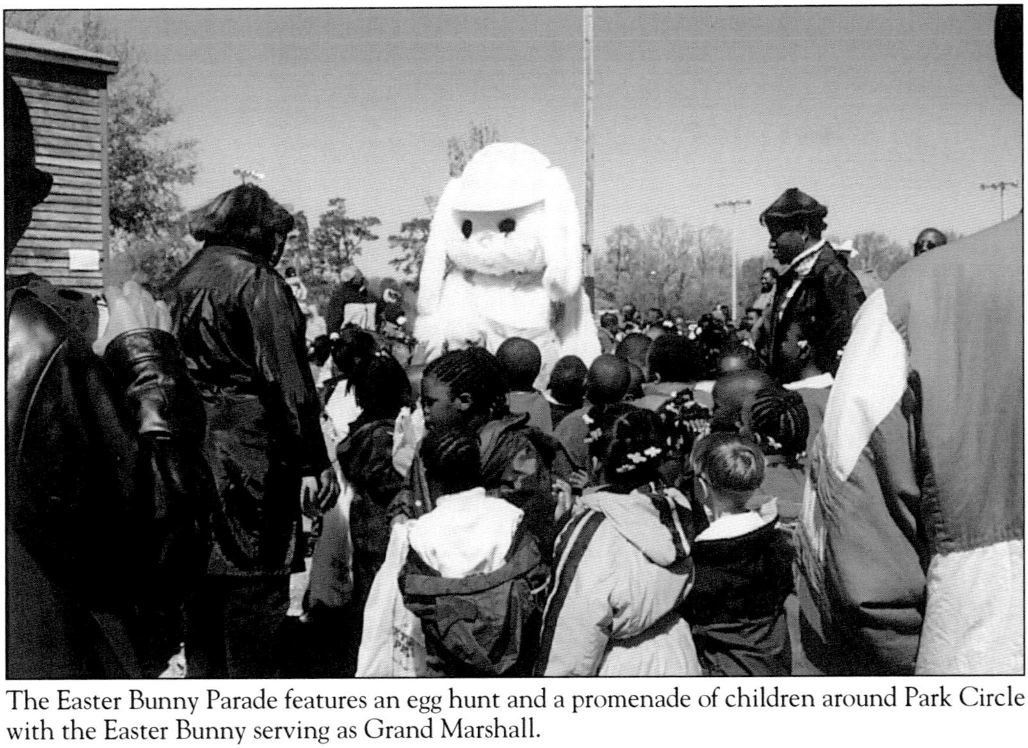

The Easter Bunny Parade features an egg hunt and a promenade of children around Park Circle with the Easter Bunny serving as Grand Marshall.

The Cultural Arts Program was created to plan and support the arts and cultural activities throughout the community. The staff, along with a 25-member advisory committee, work to provide programs and services that enhance the quality of life for the citizens of North Charleston. In 2000, the North Charleston Cultural Arts Program was chosen to be the recipient of the coveted Elizabeth O'Neill Verner Governor's Award for the Arts.

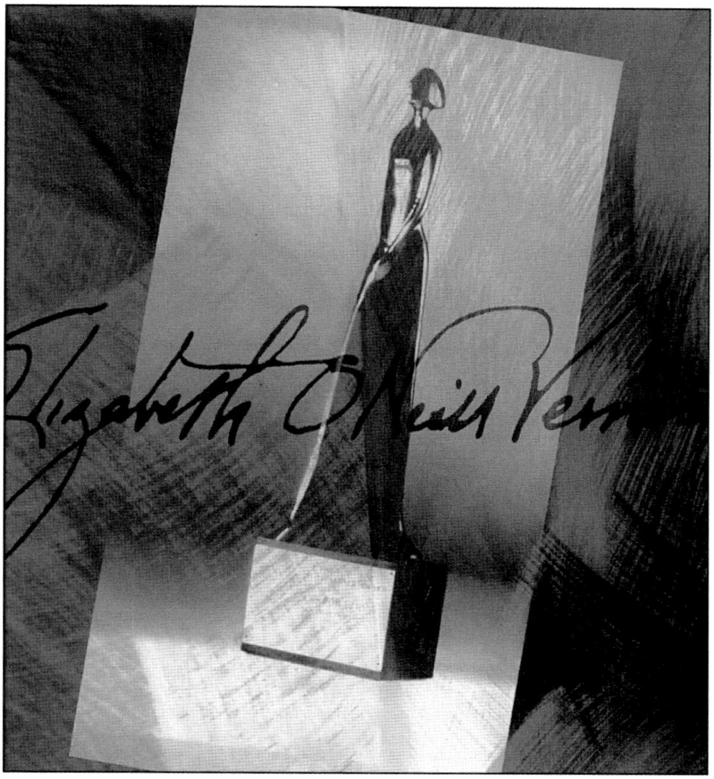

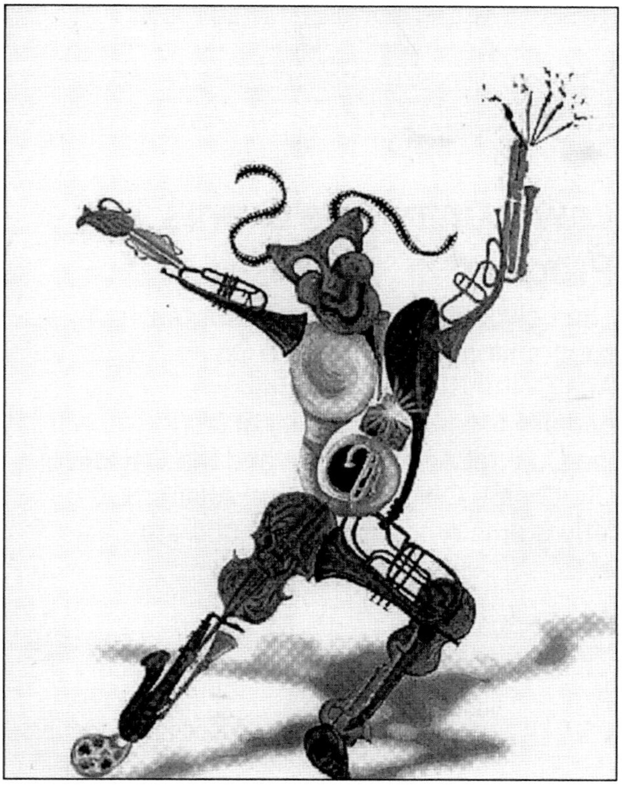

The North Charleston Arts Festival, which started out as a small one-day event held outdoors at Park Circle, has turned into one of the most outstanding festivals in the state. The festival offers everything from performances from some of the area's most outstanding entertainers to hands-on children's activities. They also provide wonderful food and exhibits. Many free and ticketed events take place throughout the week-long event. The festival wraps up with a fabulous gala.

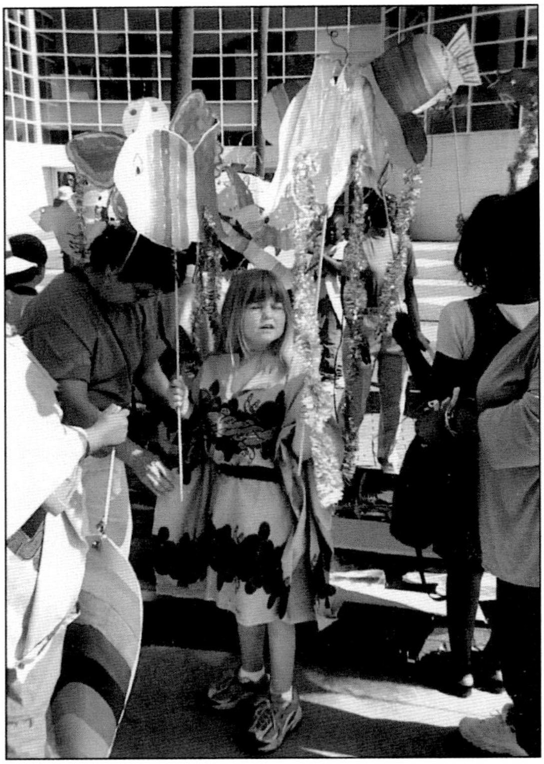

A little girl takes part in the opening processional at the North Charleston Arts Festival.

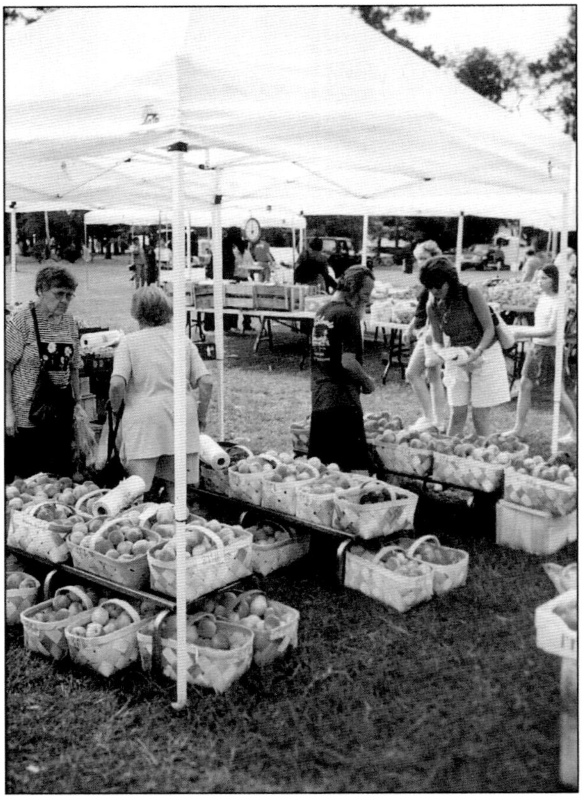

The City of North Charleston holds a farmers market annually that runs from April through November at Cook Field. Venders from all over sell produce and specialty items. It offers convenient hours with plenty of free parking, and includes special events such as cooking demonstrations, nutrition classes, and health screenings. (Courtesy of the North Charleston Cultural Arts Program.)

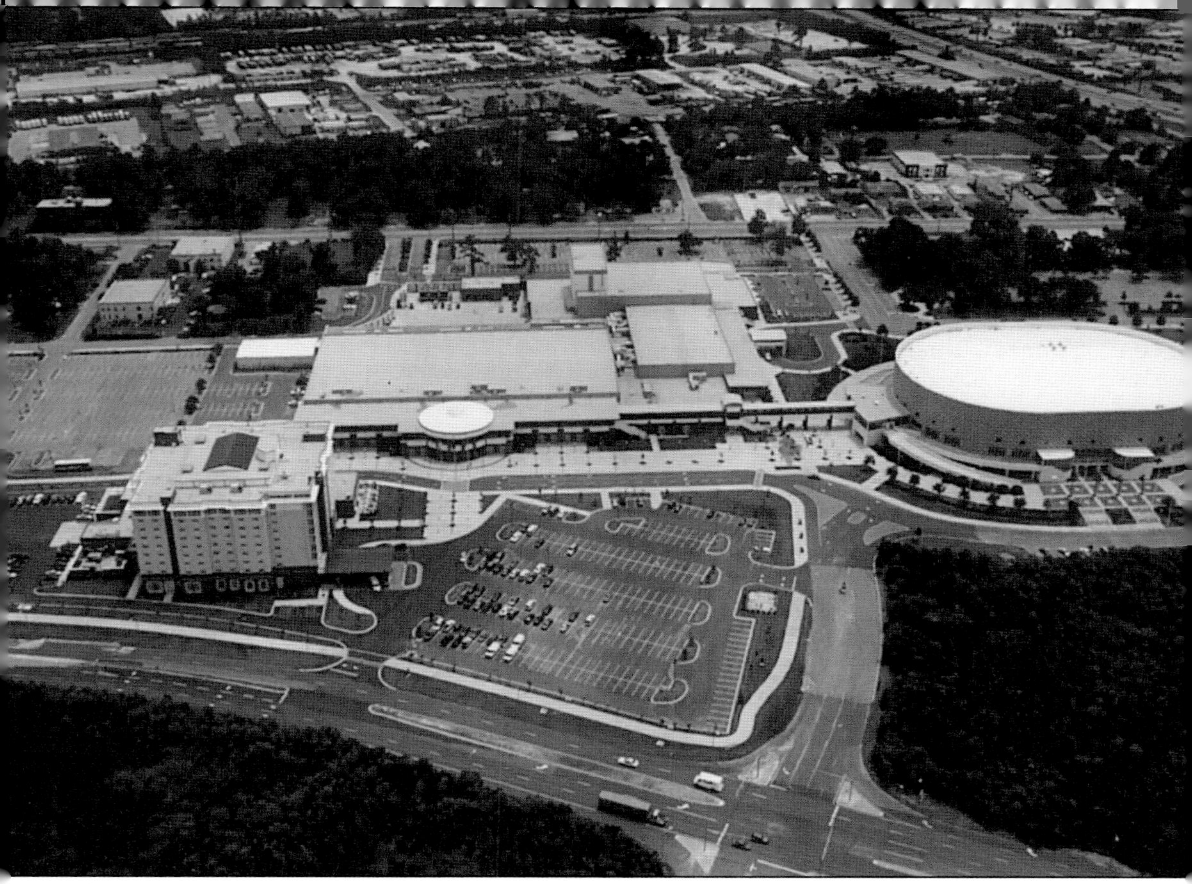

The North Charleston Convention and Performing Arts Centers are interconnected to the coliseum and the Embassy Suites Hotel. The state-of-the-art convention center is the site of a variety of local, national, and international meetings, as well as a number of conventions, and trade shows.

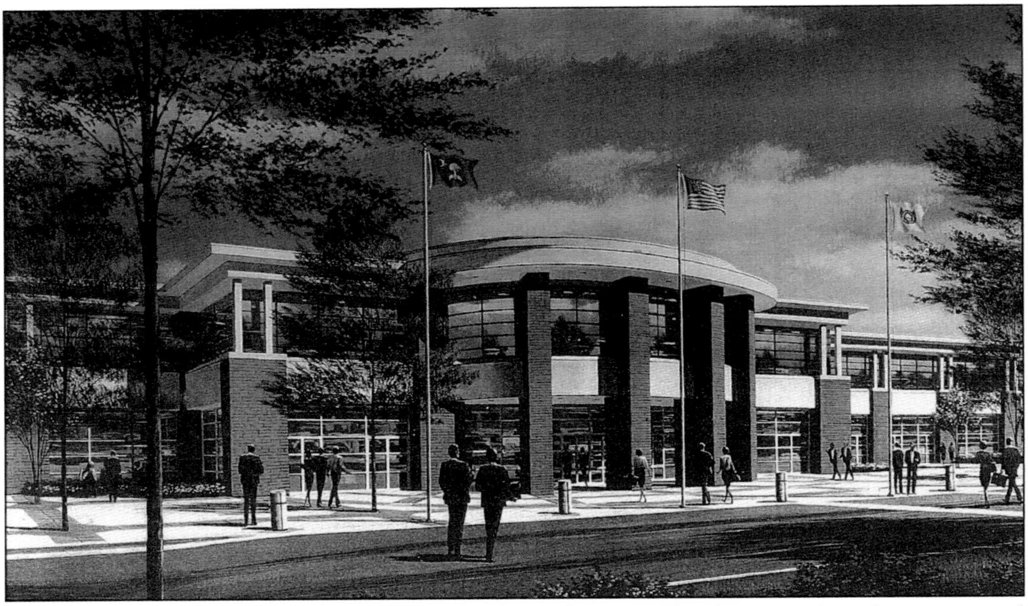

The Charleston Area Convention Center has been the site of local, national, and international meetings and trade shows. Its 80,000 square feet of pre-function (lobby) space provides a perfect setting for such events.

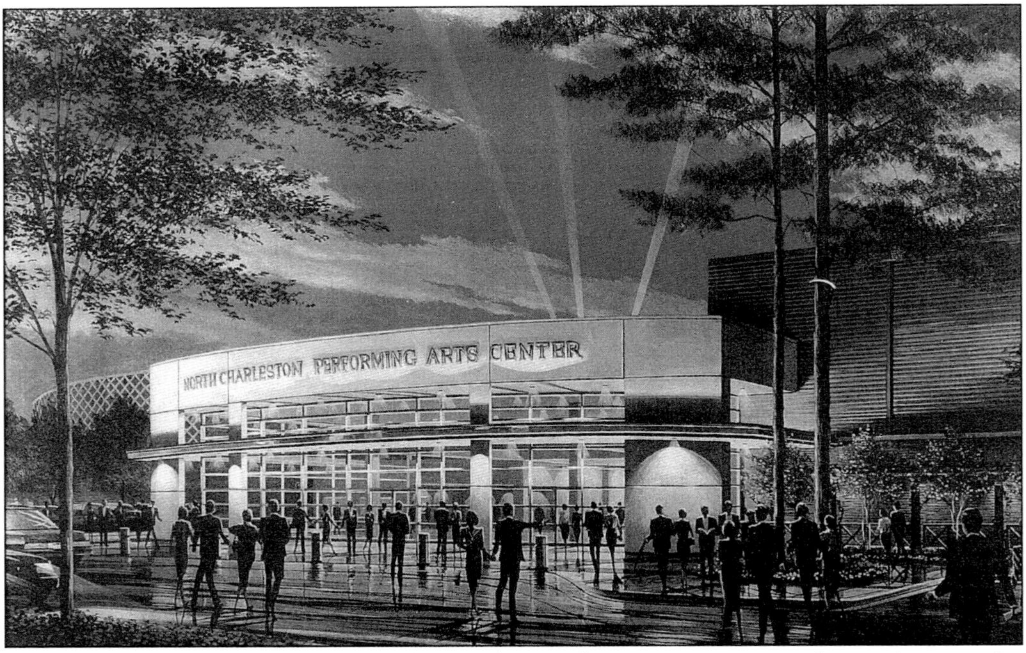

The Performing Arts Center (PAC) provides smaller meeting sites and compliments the coliseum and convention center. With 2,300 seats, the PAC sets the stage for events such as touring Broadway shows, concerts, and comedians.

North Charleston's very own Sarah Medley was crowned Miss South Carolina Teen USA 2001 at the North Charleston Performing Arts Center. Medley is the first North Charlestonian to hold the title. The city is the home of the Miss South Carolina USA and SC Teen USA Pageants each year.

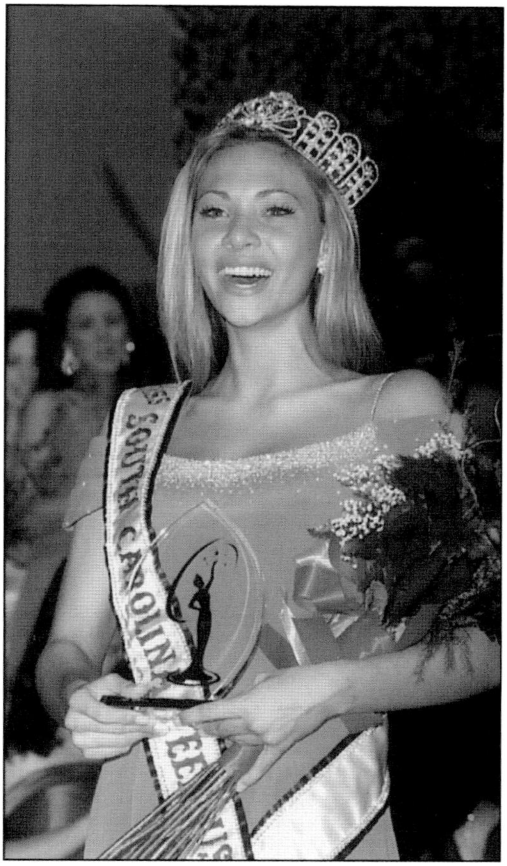

The new Public Service Building for Charleston County is located in North Charleston. Named for long-time public servant and area resident, Lonnie Hamilton III, the facility houses all county offices.

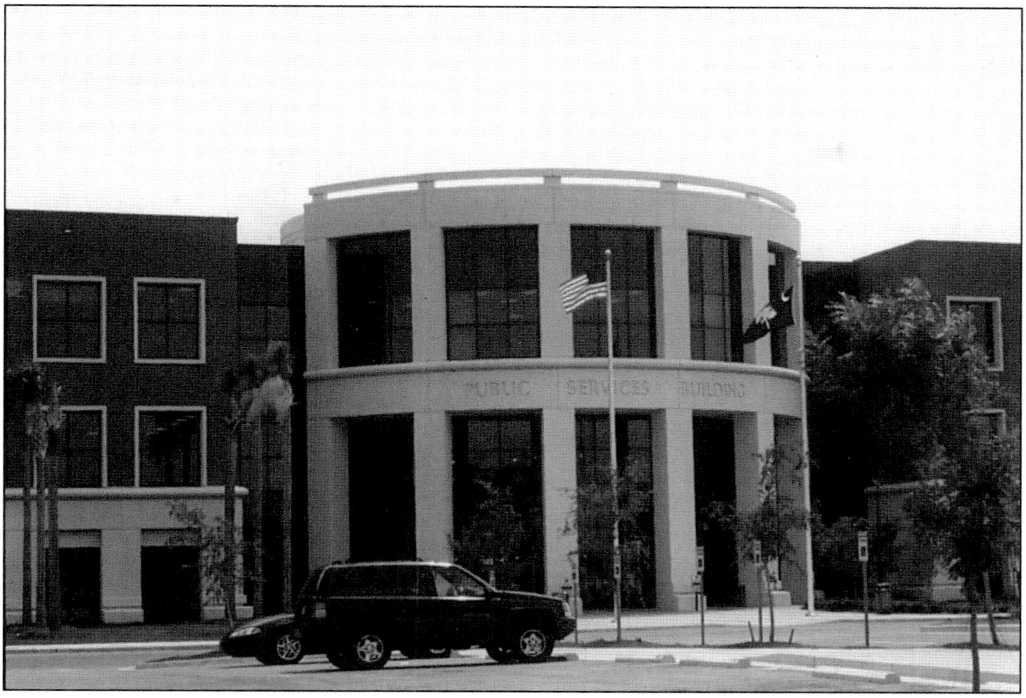

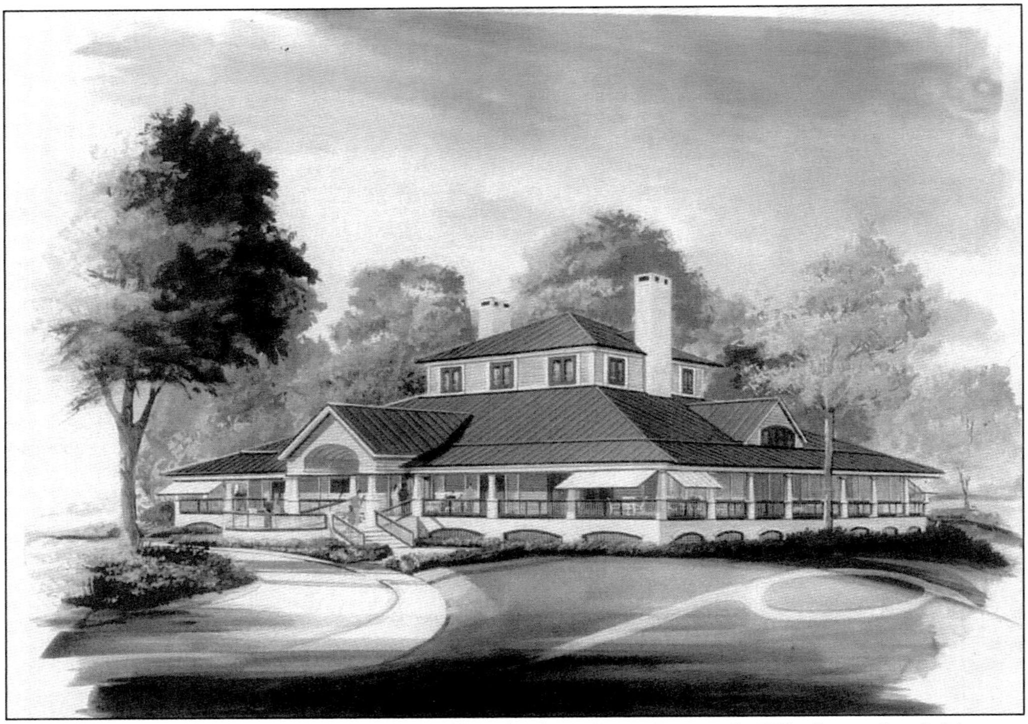

The Golf Club at Westcott is the city's golfing facility. Complete with 27 holes and a clubhouse, which is depicted in the artist's rendering above, Westcott provides recreation and relaxation for many North Charleston residents.

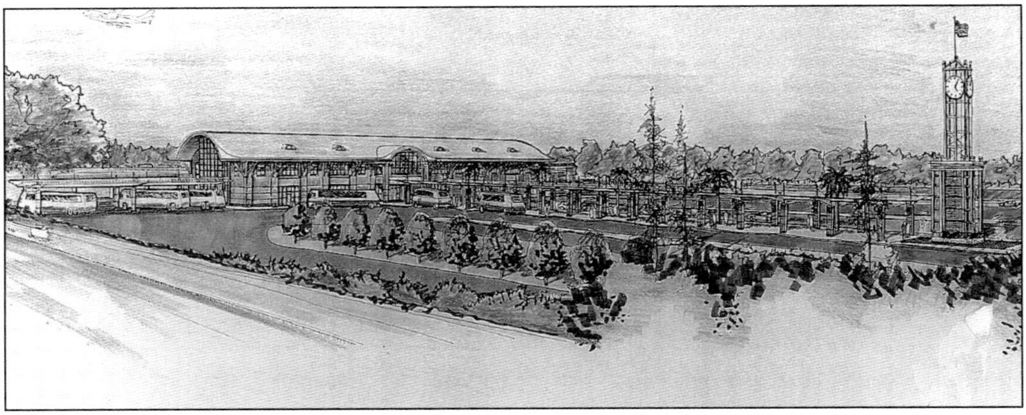

North Charleston will soon be part of the exciting "rail-Volution" efforts to construct an intermodal transportation center that will consolidate Amtrak and Greyhound into one location. The transportation center will include a welcome center with gift shop, a rail museum exhibit area, and office space for private meetings and functions.

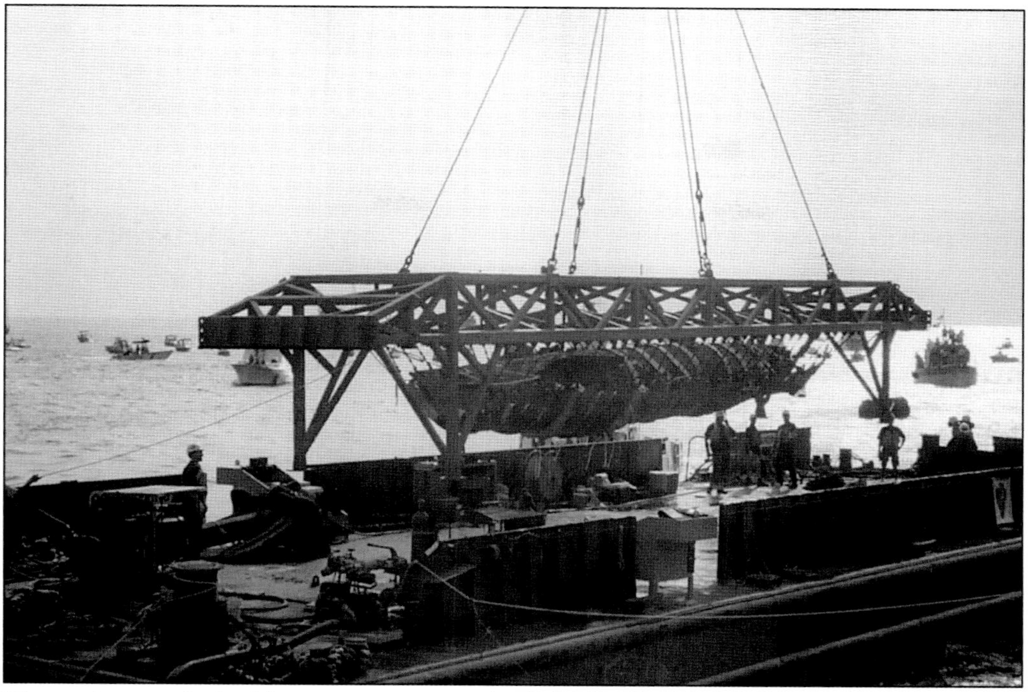

The nation watched with great intensity as the *H.L. Hunley* was brought up from the ocean's depths where it had been resting for more than 100 years. Today the *Hunley* is housed at the former naval base in North Charleston at the Warren Lasch Research Center. Many hope that North Charleston will become the permanent home for the Civil War–era submarine.

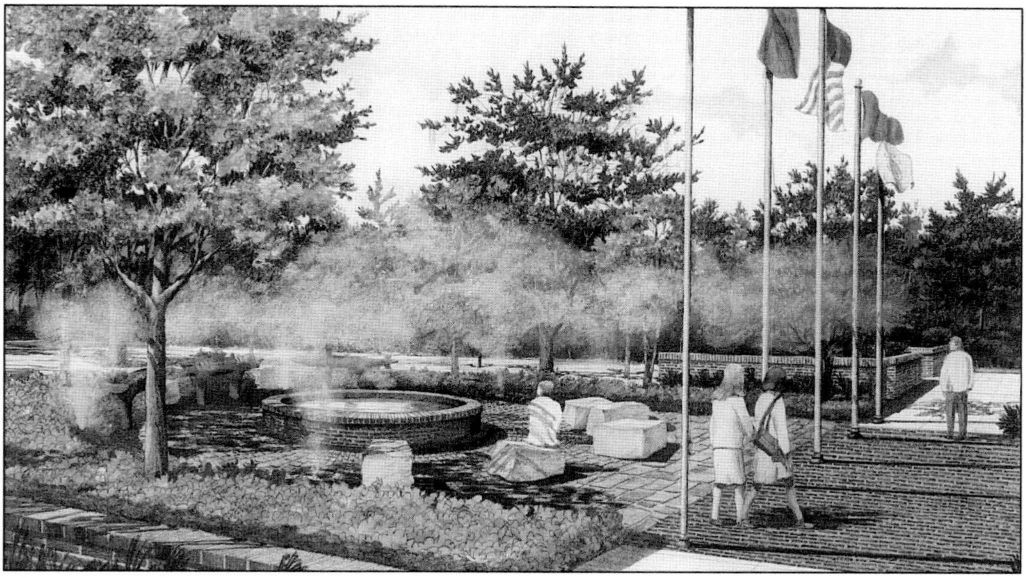

The Greater Charleston Naval Base Memorial, to be located on nearly three acres of the former Naval Base, will be a moving tribute to the tens of thousands of military and civilian personnel who served there during its 95-year existence. It will consist of a garden area, a fountain emitting a fog-like mist, bronze replicas of the types of ships built there, a pavilion for special events, and historical "garden rooms" depicting the base's proud history. (Courtesy of the Greater Charleston Naval Base Memorial.)

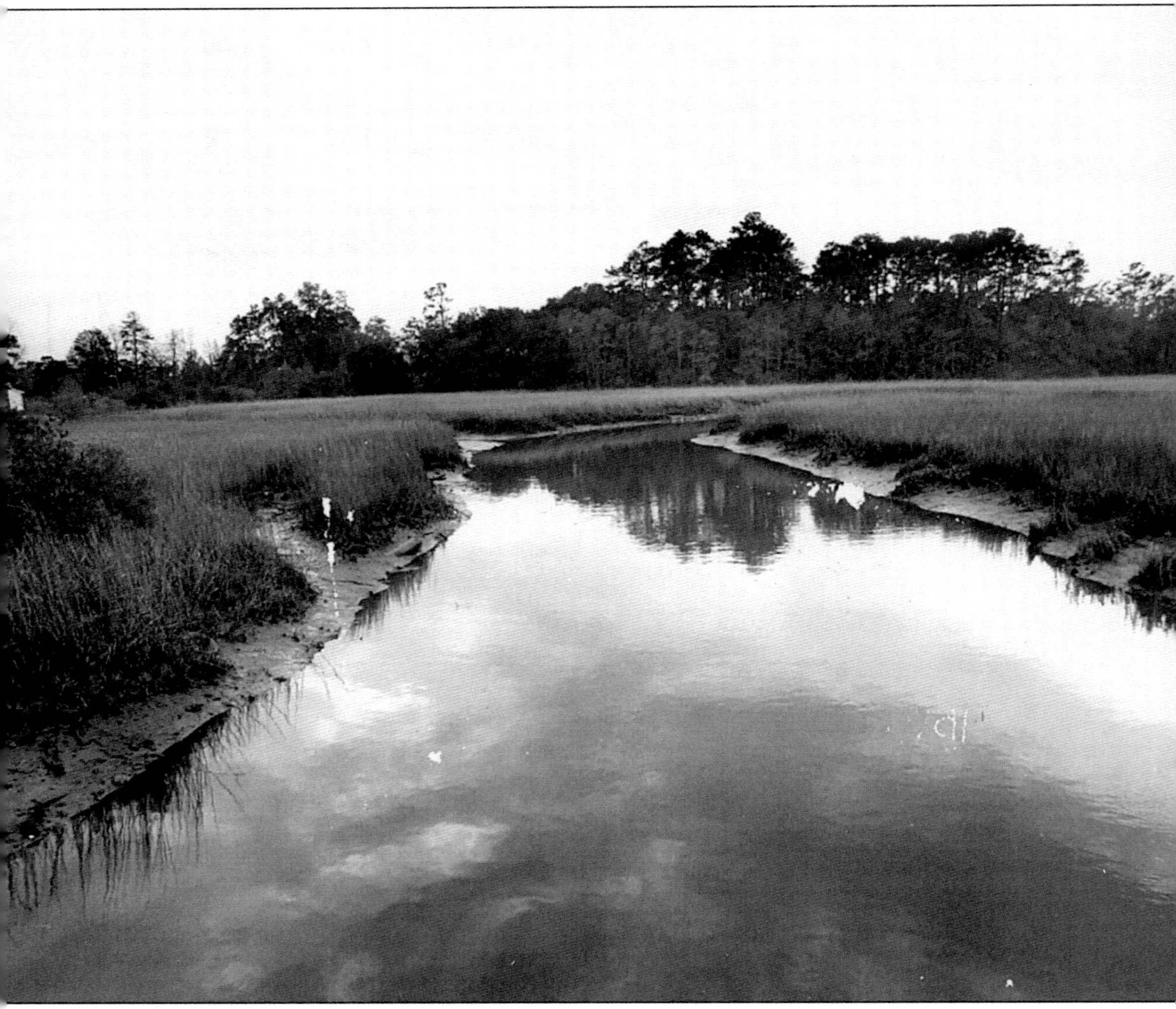

North Charleston's future looks bright. This beautiful picture of Noisette Creek serves to keep residents mindful of the promising ideas, such as the riverfront park, which are just a small part of the city's vision for the future.